BORZOI
BOOKS

FIFTY
YEARS

Also by Richard Hofstadter

Anti-intellectualism in American Life
(1963)

Great Issues in American History: A Documentary Record
TWO VOLUMES (1958)

The Age of Reform
(1955)

The Development of
Academic Freedom in the United States
(*with Walter P. Metzger*)
(1955)

The American Political Tradition
(1948)

Social Darwinism in American Thought
(1944)

The Paranoid Style
in American Politics
and Other Essays

Richard Hofstadter

THE

Paranoid Style
in American Politics
and Other Essays

NEW YORK: Alfred · A · Knopf

1965

L. C. catalog card number: 65-18758

THIS IS A BORZOI BOOK,

PUBLISHED BY ALFRED A. KNOPF, INC.

FIRST EDITION

The essay "What Happened to the Antitrust Movement?" originally appeared in *The Business Establishment*, edited by Earl F. Cheit, published by John Wiley & Sons, Inc., in 1964. Reprinted here by permission of the publisher.

The essay "Free Silver and the Mind of 'Coin' Harvey" originally appeared as the Introduction to the John Harvard Library edition of *Coin's Financial School*, published in 1963. Reprinted here by permission of the President and Fellows of Harvard College.

TO THE MEMORY OF

HARRY J. CARMAN

Introduction

THE most difficult and delicate task that faces the author of a book of essays is that of writing an introduction that makes his various pieces seem considerably more unified, in theme and argument, than they were in fact when they were written. The best case for gathering essays in a book is simply that it makes them more accessible and more permanent. The best case that can be made for the unity of any such collection is a personal and informal one, and perhaps for that reason is rarely resorted to: it is that the several parts, as the product of a single mind, have a certain stamp upon them; they must be, at least in their style of thought and their concerns, unified by some underlying intellectual intent.

The pieces in this book were written over a span of fourteen years, and during that time I have not always been of the same mind about historical and political matters in general or about some of the particulars dealt with here. Some unresolved tensions undoubtedly remain. It is not, then, a single consistent argument but a set of related concerns and methods that unites these essays. They fall into two groups: one deals with conditions that have given rise to the extreme right of the 1950's and the 1960's, the other with the origins of certain characteristic problems of the earlier modern era when the American mind was beginning to respond to the facts of industrialism and world power. All deal with public responses to a critical situation or an enduring dilemma, whether it is the sudden threat posed by giant business to competition, the panic of the 1890's and the long-standing monetary disputes and sectional animosities it brought to a head, the moral shock of our nascent imperialism, the effects of resurgent fundamentalism on secular politics, the impact of the cold war on the public consciousness.

Since these studies have to do with the style of our political culture as a whole, and with certain special styles of thought and rhetoric that have prevailed within it, they tell more about the milieu of our politics than about its structure. They are more centrally concerned with the symbolic aspect of politics than with the formation of institutions and the distribution of power. They focus on the way large segments of the public respond to civic issues, make them their own, put them to work on national problems, and express their response to these problems in distinctive rhetorical styles. Because my concern is in this sense a bit one-sided, it is necessary to be clear—it is here that the intent of these essays is most likely to be misunderstood—that my reasons for emphasizing milieu rather than structure do not stem from the belief that, of the two, milieu is more important. My case is a more moderate one: it rests—quite aside from the pleasure I take in analyzing styles of thought—on two convictions: first, that our political and historical writing, until recently, has tended to emphasize structure at the cost of substantially neglecting milieu; and second, that an understanding of political styles and of the symbolic aspect of politics is a valuable way of locating ourselves and others in relation to public issues.

The older conception of politics was that it deals with the question: Who gets what, when, how? Politics was taken as an arena in which people define their interests as rationally as possible and behave in a way calculated to realize them as fully as possible. But Harold Lasswell, who made this monosyllabic question the title of a well-known book on the substance of politics, was one of the first in this country to be dissatisfied with the rationalistic assumptions which it implied and to turn to the study of the emotional and symbolic side of political life. It became important to add a new conception to the older one: Who perceives what public issues, in what way, and why? To the present generation of historical and political writers it has become increasingly clear that people not only seek their interests but also express and even in a measure define themselves in politics; that political life acts as a sounding board for identities, values, fears, and aspirations. In a study of the political milieu these things are brought to the surface.

No doubt it is, more than anything else, the events of our time, and among these some of the most ominous and appalling, that have launched students of society upon a restless search for new methods of understanding. But the work of other intellectual disciplines has also made the present generation of historians more conscious of important aspects of behavior which our predecessors left largely in the background. An increasing interest of philosophers, anthropologists, and literary critics in the symbolic and myth-making aspects of the human mind has found its way into historical writing, and with it has come a growing sensitivity to the possibilities of textual analysis. The application of depth psychology to politics, chancy though it is, has at least made us acutely aware that politics can be a projective arena for feelings and impulses that are only marginally related to the manifest issues. The findings of public-opinion polls have made us far less confident than we used to be that the public responds to the issues as they are debated, and more aware that it reacts to them chiefly when they become the object of striking symbolic acts or memorable statements, or are taken up by public figures who themselves have a symbolic appeal. Our enhanced feeling for the non-rational side of politics has thrown into question a whole series of once confidently asserted propositions about the behavior of voters in the past.

People respond, in short, to the great drama of the public scene. But this drama, as it is set before them and as they perceive it, is not identical with questions involving material interests and the possession of power. Even those who exercise power are not immune to the content of the drama. In any case, they are forced to deal, as an element in their calculations, with the emotional life of the masses, which is not something that they can altogether create or manipulate, but something that they must cope with. The political contest itself is deeply affected by the way in which it is perceived and felt.

This does not mean that the material interests of politics can be psychologized away or reduced to episodes in intellectual history. It means only that historians and political scientists have always worked, implicitly or explicitly, with psychological assumptions; that these ought to be made as conscious as possible; and that they should be sophisticated enough to take ample account of the complexity of political action. I have no interest in denying the reality, or even the primacy, of the problems of money and power, but only in helping to define their reality by turning attention to the human context in which they arise and in which they have to be settled.

To accept all this is not to abandon whatever was of value in the old conception of political history; it suggests that this conception ought to be supplemented by another which amplifies our sense of political life and does justice to the variety of political activity. The intellectual currents stirred by such minds as Freud and Weber, Cassirer and Mannheim, have begun to move American historical writing in exploratory directions. The work of analyzing the significance of intellectual and rhetorical styles, of symbolic gestures, and of the specialized ethos of various subgroups within the population has already produced some remarkable studies. Henry Nash

Smith has applied such techniques to the role of the frontier as myth and symbol, Oscar Handlin to the clashing ethos of native and immigrant groups, David Potter to the cultural effects of American wealth, Lee Benson, Marvin Meyers, and John William Ward to the issues of Jacksonian democracy, David B. Davis to the social politics of the middle period, David Donald and Stanley Elkins to the slavery question, Eric McKitrick to Reconstruction, C. Vann Woodward and W. J. Cash to the problems of Southern identity, and Irwin Unger to the contrasting mentalities of money reformers and their opponents.

This volume embodies comparable preoccupations of my own. For many years I have been interested in the conspiratorial mind portrayed in the essay on the paranoid style. Today this mentality is of particular interest as it is manifest on the extreme right wing, among those I have called pseudo-conservatives, who believe that we have lived for a generation in the grip of a vast conspiracy. But this is not a style of mind confined to the right wing. With modulations and differences, it exists today, as it has in the past, on the left, and it has recurred at times in democratic movements from anti-Masonry to populism. "Coin" Harvey's interpretation of American history, for example, sets forth a conspiratorial view of events which has much in common with that of the founder of the John Birch Society, though the first of these men spoke in the interests of the oppressed and downtrodden, while the other is enthralled by rugged individualism.

The mind of "Coin" Harvey illustrates another tendency of our politics which runs through these pieces—the tendency to secularize a religiously derived view of the world, to deal with political issues in Christian imagery, and to color them with the dark symbology of a certain side of Christian tradition. "Coin" Harvey's expectations of this profane world were based on a faith, stated quite explicitly in his later years, that social issues could be reduced rather simply to a battle between a Good and an Evil influence. His almost superstitious Manicheanism, his belief that the Evil influence, if not soon curbed, would bring about a terrible social apocalypse, were not unlike the conceptions prevalent on the extreme right today. (Unfortunately, in our time the views of the extreme right have greater capacity for becoming a self-fulfilling prophecy.) Of course, the power of world communism, which has taken the place of the international bankers' syndicate as the central embodiment of evil, is a far more imposing reality. But my point is that the model on which the world is interpreted contains the same exaggerations, the same crusading mentality, the same sense that all our ills can be traced to a single center and hence can be eliminated by some kind of final act of victory over the evil source. If the warnings of those who diagnose the central treachery are not heeded soon enough, it is argued, we are finished: the world confronts an apocalypse of a sort prefigured in the Book of Revelation.

It is not only in its Manichean and apocalyptic carryovers that the evangelical spirit has entered our thinking about politics. Modern "conservatism" is still pervaded by the spirit of ascetic Protestantism—by the old conviction that economic life, quite as much as religious life, ought to provide a machinery for the disciplining of character. As I have tried to show in my studies of the antitrust movement and of pseudo-conservatism and the Goldwater movement, much of our national anxiety can be traced to the fear that the decline of entrepreneurial competition will destroy our national character, or that the same effect will be brought about by our hedonistic mass culture and by the moral laxity that has grown up with and is charged to our liberal and relativistic intellectual climate.

A further concern which underlies several of the essays is the history of our ethnic animosities, which in America have been at times almost a substitute for the class struggle and in any case have always affected its character. Today we are acutely aware once again of the pressing issue of racial justice. But the especially poignant problem of the American Negro is only the largest and most difficult of a number of ethnic problems arising out of our polyglot population. Our ethnic mixture has imposed upon our class structure a peculiar, complex status system, and has made the achievement of a full American identity a recurrent difficulty which has had profound political effects. The curse of what we call "second-class citizenship" is perennial in American politics.

Finally, one of these essays deals with the way in which public preoccupations with feelings of outraged humanity and with aggressive desires have influenced a foreign-policy decision. The public debates over our policy toward Cuba and the Philippines in the 1890's showed in rapid sequence how the American sense of mission had its aggressive as well as its benign content. Again, in discussing the Goldwater campaign, I have tried to show how the contemporary craving for finality in our foreign policy is related to our national experience, especially to our singular transition from a continental power with more or less complete hegemony in the Western Hemisphere to a world power whose aspirations now outrun its reach.

Since so many of these pages deal with the contemporary right wing and its backgrounds, a word of clarification may be necessary. The prominence of the right wing reflects a certain recurrent interest on my part in writing about the historical background of contemporary events. It does not result from any disposition to exaggerate the numbers or the representativeness of our right-wing enthusiasts. As I hope I have made clear in more than one of these studies, the American right wing represents only a small portion of the American public. Anyone whose own observations of our political life still leave him in doubt about this judgment can put it to the test by drawing up a list of typical right-wing attitudes and policies on public questions and comparing them with the responses of the general public to relevant questions in opinion polls. The polls, of course, are not infallible, but their findings here, as in many other situations, can be verified in other ways—for example, by examining the lengthening list of right-wing senators and other politicians of similar persuasion whose recent careers have been cut short by the electorate. Nonetheless, the right wing, from McCarthyism to Goldwaterism, has made itself acutely felt in our time. Its effectiveness rests in part, no doubt, on plenty of enthusiasm, money, and zealous activity and on increasingly adequate organization. But it rests as well, I believe, on certain points of contact with real problems of domestic life and foreign policy and with widespread and deeply rooted American ideas and impulses. It is against this larger background that I have tried to illuminate some of its themes.

R.H.

June 1965

Contents

Part I

Studies in
the American Right

THE
PARANOID STYLE
IN AMERICAN POLITICS

This essay is a revised and expanded version of the Herbert Spencer Lecture, delivered at Oxford in November 1963. An abridged text appeared in *Harper's Magazine*, November 1964.

I

ALTHOUGH American political life has rarely been touched by the most acute varieties of class conflict, it has served again and again as an arena for uncommonly angry minds. Today this fact is most evident on the extreme right wing, which has shown, particularly in the Goldwater movement, how much political leverage can be got out of the animosities and passions of a small minority. Behind such movements there is a style of mind, not always right-wing in its affiliations, that has a long and varied history. I call it the paranoid style simply because no other word adequately evokes the qualities of heated exaggeration, suspiciousness, and conspiratorial fantasy that I have in mind. In using the expression "paranoid style," I am not speaking in a clinical sense, but borrowing a clinical term for other purposes. I have neither the competence nor the desire to classify any figures of the past or present as certifiable lunatics. In fact, the idea of the paranoid style would have little contemporary relevance or historical value if it were applied only to people with profoundly disturbed minds. It is the use of paranoid modes of expression by more or less normal people that makes the phenomenon significant.

When I speak of the paranoid style, I use the term much as a historian of art might speak of the baroque or the mannerist style. It is, above all, a way of seeing the world and of expressing oneself. Webster defines paranoia, the clinical entity, as a chronic mental disorder characterized by systematized delusions of persecution and of one's own greatness. In the paranoid style, as I conceive it, the feeling of persecution is central, and it is indeed systematized in grandiose theories of conspiracy. But there is a vital difference between the paranoid spokesman in politics and the clinical paranoiac: although they both tend to be overheated, oversuspicious, overaggressive, grandiose, and apocalyptic in expression, the clinical paranoid sees the hostile and conspiratorial world in which he feels himself to be living as directed specifically *against him;* whereas the spokesman of the paranoid style finds it directed against a nation, a culture, a way of life whose fate affects not himself alone but millions of others. Insofar as he does not usually see himself singled out as the individual victim of a personal conspiracy,[1] he is somewhat more rational and much more disinterested. His sense that his political passions are unselfish and patriotic, in fact, goes far to intensify his feeling of righteousness and his moral indignation.

---

[1] There are, of course, exceptions to this rule, particularly among the most outré right-wing agitators—see especially Leo Lowenthal and Norbert Guterman: *Prophets of Deceit: A Study of the Techniques of the American Agitator* (New York, 1949), ch. 9—but their significance is arguable. See, however, the interesting suggestions on the relation between styles of thought and patterns of psychosis in N. McConaghy: "Modes of Abstract Thinking and Psychosis," *American Journal of Psychiatry,* CXVII (August 1960), 106–10.

Of course, the term "paranoid style" is pejorative, and it is meant to be; the paranoid style has a greater affinity for bad causes than good. But nothing entirely prevents a sound program or a sound issue from being advocated in the paranoid style, and it is admittedly impossible to settle the merits of an argument because we think we hear in its presentation the characteristic paranoid accents. Style has to do with the way in which ideas are believed and advocated rather than with the truth or falsity of their content.[2]

A few simple and relatively non-controversial examples may make this distinction wholly clear. Shortly after the assassination of President Kennedy, a great deal of publicity was given to a bill, sponsored chiefly by Senator Thomas E. Dodd of Connecticut, to tighten federal controls over the sale of firearms through the mail. When hearings were being held on the measure, three men drove 2,500 miles to Washington from Bagdad, Arizona, to testify against it. Now there are arguments against the Dodd bill which, however unpersuasive one may find them, have the color of conventional political reasoning. But one of the Arizonans opposed it with what might be considered representative paranoid arguments, insisting that it was "a further attempt by a subversive power to make us part of one world socialistic government" and that it threatened to "create chaos" that would help "our enemies" to seize power.[3]

Again, it is common knowledge that the movement against the fluoridation of municipal water supplies has been catnip for cranks of all kinds, especially for those who have obsessive

---

[2] Milton Rokeach, in *The Open and Closed Mind* (New York, 1960), has attempted to distinguish systematically between the content of ideas and the way in which they are espoused. It is important to bear in mind, however, that while any system of beliefs can be espoused in the paranoid style, there are certain beliefs which seem to be espoused almost entirely in this way.

[3] *Interstate Shipment of Firearms*, Hearings before the Committee on Commerce, U.S. Senate, 85th Cong., 1st and 2nd sess. (1964), p. 241; cf. pp. 240–54, passim (January 30, 1964).

fear of poisoning. It is conceivable that at some time scientists may turn up conclusive evidence that this practice is, on balance, harmful; and such a discovery would prove the anti-fluoridationists quite right on the substance of their position. But it could hardly, at the same time, validate the contentions of those among them who, in characteristic paranoid fashion, have charged that fluoridation was an attempt to advance socialism under the guise of public health or to rot out the brains of the community by introducing chemicals in the water supply in order to make people more vulnerable to socialist or communist schemes.

A distorted style is, then, a possible signal that may alert us to a distorted judgment, just as in art an ugly style is a cue to fundamental defects of taste. What interests me here is the possibility of using political rhetoric to get at political pathology. One of the most impressive facts about the paranoid style, in this connection, is that it represents an old and recurrent mode of expression in our public life which has frequently been linked with movements of suspicious discontent and whose content remains much the same even when it is adopted by men of distinctly different purposes. Our experience suggests too that, while it comes in waves of different intensity, it appears to be all but ineradicable.

I choose American history to illustrate the paranoid style only because I happen to be an Americanist, and it is for me a choice of convenience. But the phenomenon is no more limited to American experience than it is to our contemporaries. Notions about an all-embracing conspiracy on the part of Jesuits or Freemasons, international capitalists, international Jews, or Communists are familiar phenomena in many countries throughout modern history.[4] One need only think of the

---

[4] See Franz Neumann's essay "Anxiety and Politics," in *The Democratic and the Authoritarian State* (Glencoe, Ill., 1957), pp. 270–300. For two studies in European paranoid styles in widely different settings, see Fritz Stern: *The Politics of Cultural Despair* (Berkeley, 1961), and Stanley Hoffmann: *Le Mouvement Poujade* (Paris, 1956).

response to President Kennedy's assassination in Europe to be reminded that Americans have no monopoly of the gift for paranoid improvisation.[5] More important, the single case in modern history in which one might say that the paranoid style has had a consummatory triumph occurred not in the United States but in Germany. It is a common ingredient of fascism, and of frustrated nationalisms, though it appeals to many who are hardly fascists and it can frequently be seen in the left-wing press. The famous Stalin purge trials incorporated, in a supposedly juridical form, a wildly imaginative and devastating exercise in the paranoid style. In America it has been the preferred style only of *minority* movements. It can be argued, of course, that certain features of our history have given the paranoid style more scope and force among us than it has had in many other countries of the Western world. My intention here, however, is not to make such comparative judgments but simply to establish the reality of the style and to illustrate its frequent historical recurrence.

We may begin with a few American examples. Here is Senator McCarthy, speaking in June 1951 about the parlous situation of the United States:

> How can we account for our present situation unless we believe that men high in this government are concerting to deliver us to disaster? This must be the product of a great conspiracy, a conspiracy on a scale so immense as to dwarf any previous such venture in the history of man. A conspiracy of infamy so black that, when it is finally exposed, its principals shall be forever deserving of the maledictions of all honest men. . . . What can be made of this unbroken series of decisions and acts contribut-

---

[5] Conspiratorial explanations of Kennedy's assassination have a far wider currency in Europe than they do in the United States, but no European, to my knowledge, has matched the ingenuity of Professor Revilo P. Oliver of the University of Illinois, who suggests that while Kennedy had performed many services for the Communist conspiracy, he was falling behind in a schedule for the "effective capture of the United States in 1963" and was "rapidly becoming a political liability." He therefore had to be shot. *The New York Times*, February 11, 1964.

ing to the strategy of defeat? They cannot be attributed to incompetence. . . . The laws of probability would dictate that part of . . . [the] decisions would serve this country's interest.[6]

Now let us turn back fifty years to a manifesto signed in 1895 by a number of leaders of the Populist party:

> As early as 1865–66 a conspiracy was entered into between the gold gamblers of Europe and America. . . . For nearly thirty years these conspirators have kept the people quarreling over less important matters, while they have pursued with unrelenting zeal their one central purpose. . . . Every device of treachery, every resource of statecraft, and every artifice known to the secret cabals of the international gold ring are being made use of to deal a blow to the prosperity of the people and the financial and commercial independence of the country.[7]

Next, a Texas newspaper article of 1855:

> . . . It is a notorious fact that the Monarchs of Europe and the Pope of Rome are at this very moment plotting our destruction and threatening the extinction of our political, civil, and religious institutions. We have the best reasons for believing that corruption has found its way into our Executive Chamber, and that our Executive head is tainted with the infectious venom of Catholicism. . . . The Pope has recently sent his ambassador of state to this country on a secret commission, the effect of which is an extraordinary boldness of the Catholic Church throughout the United States. . . . These minions of the Pope are boldly insulting our Senators; reprimanding our Statesmen; propagating the adulterous union of Church and state; abusing with foul calumny all governments but Catholic; and spewing out the bitterest

---

[6] *Congressional Record*, 82nd Cong., 1st sess. (June 14, 1951), p. 6602; for a similar passage, see McCarthy's book *McCarthyism: The Fight for America* (New York, 1952), p. 2.

[7] The manifesto is reprinted in Frank McVey: "The Populist Movement," *Economic Studies*, I (August 1896), 201–2; the platform of the Populist party for 1892 asserts: "A vast conspiracy against mankind has been organized on two continents, and it is rapidly taking possession of the world. If not met and overthrown at once, it forbodes terrible social convulsions, the destruction of civilization, or the establishment of an absolute despotism."

8

execrations on all Protestantism. The Catholics in the United States receive from abroad more than $200,000 annually for the propagation of their creed. Add to this the vast revenue collected here. . . .[8]

Finally, this from a sermon preached in Massachusetts in 1798:

> Secret and systematic means have been adopted and pursued, with zeal and activity, by wicked and artful men, in foreign countries, to undermine the foundations of this Religion [Christianity], and to overthrow its Altars, and thus to deprive the world of its benign influence on society. . . . These impious conspirators and philosophists have completely effected their purposes in a large portion of Europe, and boast of their means of accomplishing their plans in all parts of Christendom, glory in the certainty of their success, and set opposition at defiance. . . .[9]

These quotations, taken from intervals of half a century, give the keynote of the style of thought. In the history of the United States one finds it, for example, in the anti-Masonic movement, the nativist and anti-Catholic movement, in certain spokesmen for abolitionism who regarded the United States as being in the grip of a slaveholders' conspiracy, in many writers alarmed by Mormonism, in some Greenback and Populist writers who constructed a great conspiracy of international bankers, in the exposure of a munitions makers' conspiracy of the First World War, in the popular left-wing press, in the contemporary American right wing, and on both sides of the race controversy today, among White Citizens Councils and Black Muslims. I do not propose to try to trace the variations of the paranoid style that can be found in all

---

[8] Quoted by Sister Paul of the Cross McGrath: *Political Nativism in Texas, 1825–1860* (Washington, 1930), pp. 114–15, from *Texas State Times*, September 15, 1855.

[9] Jedidiah Morse: *A Sermon Preached at Charlestown, November 29, 1798* . . . (Worcester, Mass., 1799), pp. 20–1.

these movements, but will confine myself to a few leading episodes in our past history in which the style emerged in full and archetypal splendor.

I I

A SUITABLE POINT of departure is the panic that broke out in some quarters at the end of the eighteenth century over the allegedly subversive activities of the Bavarian Illuminati. This panic, which came with the general Western reaction to the French Revolution, was heightened here by the response of certain reactionaries, mostly in New England and among the established clergy, to the rise of Jeffersonian democracy. Illuminism had been founded in 1776 by Adam Weishaupt, a professor of law at the University of Ingolstadt. Its teachings today seem to be no more than another version of Enlightenment rationalism, spiced with an anticlerical animus that seems an inevitable response to the reactionary-clerical atmosphere of eighteenth-century Bavaria. A somewhat naïve and utopian movement which aspired ultimately to bring the human race under the rules of reason, it made many converts after 1780 among outstanding dukes and princes of the German states, and is reported to have had the allegiance of such men as Herder, Goethe, and Pestalozzi. Although the order of the Illuminati was shattered by persecution in its native principality, its humanitarian rationalism appears to have acquired a fairly wide influence in Masonic lodges. It is very easy to believe that it was attractive to some radicals with a conspiratorial cast of mind.

Americans first learned of Illuminism in 1797, from a volume published in Edinburgh (later reprinted in New York) under the title *Proofs of a Conspiracy Against All the Religions and Governments of Europe, carried on in the Secret*

Meetings of Free Masons, Illuminati, and Reading Societies.
Its author was a well-known Scottish scientist, John Robison,
who had himself been a somewhat casual adherent of Masonry in Britain, but whose imagination had been inflamed by
what he considered to be the far less innocent Masonic movement on the Continent. Robison's book was a conscientious
account, laboriously pieced together out of the German
sources, of the origins and development of Weishaupt's movement. For the most part, Robison seems to have made his
work as factual as he could, but when he came to estimating
the moral character and the political influence of Illuminism,
he made the characteristic paranoid leap into fantasy. The
association, he thought, was formed, "for the express purpose
of ROOTING OUT ALL THE RELIGIOUS ESTABLISHMENTS, AND
OVERTURNING ALL THE EXISTING GOVERNMENTS OF EUROPE."
The most active leaders of the French Revolution, he claimed,
were members; it had become "one great and wicked project
fermenting and working all over Europe," and to it he attributed a central role in bringing about the French Revolution. He saw it as a libertine, anti-Christian movement, given
to the corruption of women, the cultivation of sensual pleas-
ures, and the violation of property rights. Its members had
plans for making a tea that caused abortion, a secret substance
that "blinds or kills when spurted in the face," and a device
that sounds like a stench bomb—a "method for filling a bed-
chamber with pestilential vapours."[1] Robison's credulity was
exercised not only on these matters but also on a conviction
that the Illuminati, while resolutely anti-Christian, were also
heavily infiltrated by the Jesuits.
Almost simultaneously with Robison's book there appeared

[1] Robison: *Proofs of a Conspiracy* (New York, 1798), pp. 14, 376,
311. For a detailed study of the American response to Illuminism, see
Vernon Stauffer: *New England and the Bavarian Illuminati* (New
York, 1918).

in London a formidable four-volume work by the Abbé Barruel, a Jesuit who had been expelled from France when that order was suppressed in 1773, under the title *Mémoires pour servir à l'histoire du Jacobinisme*. This work, which was translated into English and published both in England and in the United States, elaborated views similar to Robison's, and traced a "triple conspiracy" of anti-Christians, Freemasons, and Illuminati to destroy religion and order. "We shall demonstrate," wrote Barruel,

> what it is imperative for the nations and their leaders to know. We shall say to them: everything in the French Revolution, even the most dreadful of crimes, was foreseen, contemplated, contrived, resolved upon, decreed; that everything was the consequence of the most profound villainy, and was prepared and produced by those men who alone held the leading threads of conspiracies long before woven in the secret societies, and who knew how to choose and to hasten the favorable moments for their schemes. Although among the day-by-day events there were some circumstances which hardly seemed the effects of conspiracies, there existed nonetheless one cause with its secret agents, who called forth these events, who knew how to profit by circumstances or even how to bring them about, and who directed everything towards their main end. The circumstances may have served as pretext and opportunity, but the grand cause of the Revolution, of its great crimes, its huge atrocities, was always independent and self-contained, and it consisted in plots long hatched and deeply premeditated.[2]

These notions were quick to make themselves felt in America, even though it is uncertain whether any member of the

---

[2] *Mémoires pour servir à l'histoire du Jacobinisme* (Hamburg, 1803), I, ix–x. In *The Age of the Democratic Revolution: The Struggle* (Princeton, 1964) Robert R. Palmer puts the writings of men like Robison and Barruel in the context of the general reaction to the French Revolution and does justice to the modest element of reality behind their fantasies. See esp. pp. 51–4, 141–5, 163–4, 249–55, 343–6, 429–30, 451–6, 540–3; cf. J. Droz: *L'Allemagne et la Révolution française* (Paris, 1949). On the role of the idea of conspiracy in the background of the American Revolution, see Bernard Bailyn's observations in the Introduction to *Pamphlets of the American Revolution* (Cambridge, Mass., 1965), I, 60–89.

Illuminati ever came here. In May 1798, a prominent minister of the Massachusetts Congregational establishment in Boston, Jedidiah Morse, delivered a timely sermon of great import to the young country, which was then sharply divided between Jeffersonians and Federalists, Francophiles and Anglophiles. After reading Robison, Morse was convinced that the United States too was the victim of a Jacobinical plot touched off by Illuminism, and that the country should be rallied to defend itself against the machinations of the international conspiracy. His warnings were heeded throughout New England wherever Federalists brooded about the rising tide of religious infidelity or Jeffersonian democracy. Timothy Dwight, the president of Yale, followed Morse's sermon with a Fourth of July discourse, *The Duty of Americans in the Present Crisis*, in which he held forth against the Antichrist in his own glowing rhetoric.

> The sins of these enemies of Christ, and Christians, are of numbers and degrees which mock account and description. All that the malice and atheism of the Dragon, the cruelty and rapacity of the Beast, and the fraud and deceit of the false Prophet, can generate, or accomplish, swell the list. No personal or national interest of man has been uninvaded; no impious sentiment, or action, against God has been spared. . . . Shall we, my brethren, become partakers of these sins? Shall we introduce them into our government, our schools, our families? Shall our sons become the disciples of Voltaire, and the dragoons of Marat; or our daughters the concubines of the Illuminati?[3]

This note was taken up by others, and soon the pulpits of New England were ringing with denunciations of the Illuminati, as though the country were swarming with them. The prevalence of these denunciations is more intelligible if one remembers that the United States did have, if not any Illuminati, a few Democratic-Republican societies which were widely believed to be Jacobinical and to have instigated the

---

[3] New Haven, 1798, pp. 20–1.

Whiskey Rebellion. It was now "generally believed," as one preacher put it,

> that the present day is unfolding a design the most extensive, flagitious, and diabolical, that human art and malice have ever invented. Its object is the total destruction of all religion and civil order. If accomplished, the earth can be nothing better than a sink of impurities, a theatre of violence and murder, and a hell of miseries.[4]

These writers illustrate the central preconception of the paranoid style—the existence of a vast, insidious, preternaturally effective international conspiratorial network designed to perpetrate acts of the most fiendish character. There are, of course, certain ancillary themes which appear less frequently. But before going on to characterize the other motifs in the paranoid style, let us look at a few more historical manifestations.

The anti-Masonic movement of the late 1820's and 1830's took up and extended the obsession with conspiracy. At first blush, this movement may seem to be no more than an extension or repetition of the anti-Masonic theme sounded in the earlier outcry against the Bavarian Illuminati—and, indeed, the works of writers like Robison and Barruel were often cited again as evidence of the sinister character of Masonry.

But whereas the panic of the 1790's was confined mainly to New England and linked to an ultra-conservative argument, the later anti-Masonic movement affected many parts of the northern United States and was altogether congenial to popular democracy and rural egalitarianism.[5] Although anti-

---

[4] Abiel Abbot: *A Memorial of Divine Benefits* (Haverhill, Mass., 1798), p. 18.

[5] The status of those who were opposed by these anti movements of the nineteenth century varied widely. Freemasonry was largely an affair of the upper crust of society. Catholics were preponderantly poor immigrants. Mormons drew their strength from the native rural middle class. Ironically, the victims themselves were associated with

Masonry happened to be anti-Jacksonian (Jackson was a Mason), it showed the same fear that opportunities for the common man would be closed, the same passionate dislike of aristocratic institutions that one finds in the Jacksonian crusade against the Bank of the United States.

The anti-Masonic movement, though a product of spontaneous enthusiasm, soon fell victim to the changing fortunes of party politics. It was joined and used by a great many men who did not share its original anti-Masonic feelings. It attracted, for example, the support of several reputable statesmen who had only mild sympathy with its fundamental bias, but who as politicians could not afford to ignore it. Still, it was a folk movement of considerable power, and the rural enthusiasts who provided its real impetus believed in it wholeheartedly.

There must have been some considerable suspicion of the Masonic order to begin with, perhaps a residue of the feeling against Illuminism. At any rate, the movement was precipitated by the mysterious disappearance of one William Morgan in 1826. Morgan was an ex-Mason living in western New York State who was at work on a book exposing the order. There can be no doubt that he was abducted by a small group of Masons, and it was widely and quite understandably believed that he had been murdered, though no certainly identifiable body was ever found. The details of the case need not detain us. Morgan's disappearance was followed by an outbreak of similar charges against Masons, invariably un-

---

similar anti sentiments. Freemasonry had strong anti-Catholic associations. Mormons were anti-Catholic, and, to a degree, anti-Masonic. Yet their detractors did not hesitate to couple staunch foes. It was sometimes said, for example, that the Jesuits had infiltrated Freemasonry, and the menace of the Catholicism was frequently compared with the menace of Mormonism. All these movements had an interest for minds obsessed with secrecy and concerned with an all-or-nothing world struggle over ultimate values. The ecumenicism of hatred is a great breaker-down of precise intellectual discriminations.

founded, of other conspiracies to kidnap or to hold in false imprisonment. Within very short order an anti-Masonic party was making itself felt in the politics of New York State, and the party soon became national. But it is its ideology not its political history that concerns us here.

As a secret society, Masonry was considered to be a standing conspiracy against republican government. It was held to be particularly liable to treason—for example, Aaron Burr's famous conspiracy was alleged to have been conducted by Masons.[6] Masonry was also accused of constituting a separate system of loyalty, a separate imperium within the framework of American and state governments, inconsistent with loyalty to them. Quite plausibly it was argued that the Masons had set up a jurisdiction of their own, with their own obligations and punishments, liable to enforcement even by the penalty of death. Anti-Masons were fascinated by the horrid oaths that Masons were said to take, invoking terrible reprisals upon themselves if they should fail in their Masonic obligations. The conflict between secrecy and democracy was felt to be so basic that other, more innocent societies, such as Phi Beta Kappa, also came under attack.

Since Masons were pledged to come to each other's aid under circumstances of distress, and to extend fraternal indulgence at all times, it was held that the order nullified the enforcement of regular law. Masonic constables, sheriffs, juries, judges, and the like would all be in league with Masonic

---

[6] In his *Anti-Masonic Review* Henry Dana Ward charged in September 1829 that "the private correspondence of that conspiracy was carried on in the *Royal Arch cypher,* which is a proof that the agents were exalted Freemasons. This accounts also for their escaping the vengeance of the law: the evidence of their guilt was chiefly in the mystic characters of Freemasonry, and in Royal Arch breasts, and thus closed against the search of human tribunals by the profane oath, and impious penalty of a Royal Arch Mason's obligations." Leland M. Griffin: *The Anti-Masonic Persuasion,* unpublished doctoral dissertation, Cornell University (1950), pp. 627–8.

criminals and fugitives. The press too was held to have been so "muzzled" by Masonic editors and proprietors that news of Masonic malfeasance could be suppressed—which was the main reason why so shocking a scandal as the Morgan case had received relatively little publicity. Finally, at a moment when practically every alleged citadel of privilege in America was under democratic assault, Masonry was held to be a fraternity of the privileged classes, closing business opportunities and nearly monopolizing political offices, thus shutting out hardy common citizens of the type the anti-Masonic movement liked to claim for its own.

There may have been certain elements of truth and reality in these views of Masonry, and many distinguished and responsible leaders accepted them, at least in part. Not all of these charges and fears need be dismissed as entirely without foundation. What must be emphasized here, however, is the apocalyptic and absolutist framework in which this hostility to Masonry was usually expressed. Anti-Masons were not content simply to say that secret societies were rather a bad idea. David Bernard, in the standard handbook of anti-Masonic materials, *Light on Masonry*, declared that Freemasonry was the most dangerous institution that ever was imposed on man, "an engine of Satan . . . dark, unfruitful, selfish, demoralizing, blasphemous, murderous, anti-republican and anti-Christian."[7] One of the many anti-Masonic pulpit orators called the order "a work of darkness because IT BEARS DECIDED MARKS OF BEING ONE OF THE CONFEDERATE

---

[7] *Light on Masonry* (Utica, 1829), pp. iii, x. *The Address of the United States Anti-Masonic Convention* (Philadelphia, 1830) asserted (p. 17): "The abuses of which we complain involve the highest crimes of which man can be guilty, because they indicate the deepest malice, and the most fatal aim. They bespeak the most imminent danger, because they have proceeded from a conspiracy more numerous and better organized for mischief, than any other detailed in the records of man, and yet, though exposed, maintaining itself, in all its monstrous power."

POWERS OF INIQUITY PREDICTED BY THE APOSTLE JOHN . . .
WHICH WOULD COMBINE THE WORLD IN ARMS AGAINST GOD,
AND BE OVERCOME AT THE BATTLE OF THE GREAT DAY JUST
BEFORE THE MILLENNIUM."[8]

A further aspect of anti-Masonry that is at once arresting
and puzzling to the modern mind is its obsession with the
character of Masonic oaths. Oaths were considered to be
blasphemous, since they were profanations of a transaction
with God, and contrary to civil order, since they set up a
secret pattern of loyalties inconsistent with normal civil obligations. At the first national anti-Masonic convention a committee spent a great deal of time solemnly demonstrating that
such oaths were subversive and could not be regarded as binding commitments. Many anti-Masons were particularly fascinated by the penalties invoked if Masons failed to live up to
their obligations, and these penalties were ingeniously and
bloodily imagined. The mark master mason was alleged to call
down upon himself having "my right ear smote off and my
right hand chopped off as an imposter," in the event of such a
failure. My own favorite is the oath attributed to a royal
arch mason who invited "having my skull smote off, and my
brains exposed to the scorching rays of the sun."[9] The san-
guinary character of Masonry was also thought to be shown
by the ritual of the lodges, which supposedly required drinking wine from human skulls—this in temperance communities
where drinking wine from any kind of container was considered a sin.

[8] Griffin: op. cit., pp. 27–8.
[9] *Proceedings of the United States Anti-Masonic Convention* . . .
(Philadelphia, 1830), pp. 57, 58.

III

FEAR of a Masonic plot had hardly been quieted when rumors arose of a Catholic plot against American values. One finds here again the same frame of mind, the same conviction of a conspiracy against a way of life, but now a different villain. Of course, the anti-Catholic movement converged with a growing nativism, and while they were not identical, together they cut such a wide swath in American life that they were bound to embrace many moderates to whom the paranoid style, in its full glory, did not appeal. Moreover, we need not dismiss out of hand as wholly parochial or mean-spirited the desire of Yankee Americans to maintain an ethnically and religiously homogeneous society, nor the particular Protestant commitments to individualism and freedom that were brought into play. But the movement had a large paranoid infusion, and the most influential anti-Catholic militants certainly had a strong affinity for the paranoid style.

Two books which appeared in 1835 described the new danger to the American way of life, and may be taken as expressions of the anti-Catholic mentality. One, *Foreign Conspiracy against the Liberties of the United States,* was from the hand of the celebrated painter and inventor of the telegraph, S. F. B. Morse, who was the son of Jedidiah Morse, the anti-Illuminist. "A conspiracy exists," Morse proclaimed, and "its plans are already in operation . . . we are attacked in a vulnerable quarter which cannot be defended by our ships, our forts, or our armies." In the great war going on in the Western world between political reaction and ultramontanism on one side and political and religious liberties on the other, America was a bastion of freedom, and hence an inevitable target for popes and despots. The main source of the conspiracy Morse found in Metternich's government: *"Aus-*

tria is now acting in this country. She has devised a grand scheme. She has organized a great plan for doing something here. . . . She has her Jesuit missionaries travelling through the land; she has supplied them with money, and has furnished a fountain for a regular supply."[1]

"It is an ascertained fact," wrote another Protestant militant,

> that Jesuits are prowling about all parts of the United States in every possible disguise, expressly to ascertain the advantageous situations and modes to disseminate Popery. A minister of the Gospel from Ohio has informed us that he discovered one carrying on his devices in his congregation; and he says that the western country swarms with them under the names of puppet show men, dancing masters, music teachers, peddlers of images and ornaments, barrel organ players, and similar practitioners.[2]

Were the plot successful, Morse said, it would not be long before some scion of the House of Habsburg would be installed as Emperor of the United States. Catholics, working "with the minds and the funds of all despotic Europe," were the only possible channel of this influence. Ignorant, ill-educated immigrants, incapable of understanding the institutions of the United States, would supplement the efforts of wily Jesuit agents. The danger was imminent and must be met at once. "The serpent has already commenced his coil about our limbs, and the lethargy of his poison is creeping over us. . . . Is not the enemy already organized in the land? Can we not perceive all around us the evidence of his presence? . . . We must awake, or we are lost."[3]

Lyman Beecher, the elder of a famous family and the father of Harriet Beecher Stowe, wrote in the same year his *Plea for*

---

[1] Morse: *Foreign Conspiracy* . . . (New York, 1835), pp. 14, 21.
[2] Quoted in Ray Allen Billington: *The Protestant Crusade* (New York, 1938), p. 120.
[3] Morse: op. cit., pp. 95–6.

the West, in which he considered the possibility that the Christian millennium might come in the American states. Everything depended, in his judgment, upon what influences dominated the great West, where the future of the country lay. There Protestantism was engaged in a life-or-death struggle with Catholicism. Time was already running out. "Whatever we do, it must be done quickly. . . ." A great tide of immigration, hostile to free institutions, was sweeping in upon the country, subsidized and sent by "the potentates of Europe," multiplying tumult and violence, filling jails, crowding poorhouses, quadrupling taxation, and sending increasing thousands of voters to "lay their inexperienced hand upon the helm of our power." Well might we believe, said Beecher, that Metternich knew that there would be a party in the United States willing to hasten the naturalization and enfranchisement of these multitudes and demagogues, a party that would "sell their country into an everlasting bondage." Even so much as a tenth of the voting population, "condensed and wielded by the Catholic powers of Europe, might decide our elections, perplex our policy, inflame and divide the nation, break the bond of our union, and throw down our free institutions."[4] Beecher did not approve violations of the civil rights of Catholics or the burning of convents, but he urged Protestants to a greater militancy and solidarity to fend off a fate that might be waiting for them in a not very distant future.

Anti-Catholicism has always been the pornography of the Puritan. Whereas the anti-Masons had imagined wild drinking bouts and had entertained themselves with fantasies about the actual enforcement of grisly Masonic oaths, the anti-Catholics developed an immense lore about libertine priests, the confessional as an opportunity for seduction, licentious convents

---

[4] Lyman Beecher: *Plea for the West* (Cincinnati, 1835), pp. 47, 62–3.

and monasteries, and the like. Probably the most widely read contemporary book in the United States before *Uncle Tom's Cabin* was a work supposedly written by one Maria Monk, entitled *Awful Disclosures*, which appeared in 1836. The author, who purported to have escaped from the Hôtel Dieu nunnery in Montreal after a residence of five years as novice and nun, reported her convent life there in elaborate and circumstantial detail. She recalled having been told by the Mother Superior that she must "obey the priests in all things"; to her "utter astonishment and horror," she soon found what the nature of such obedience was. Infants born of convent liaisons were baptized and then killed, she said, so that they might ascend at once to heaven. A high point in the *Awful Disclosures* was Maria Monk's eyewitness account of the strangling of two babies. Her book, hotly attacked and as hotly defended, continued to be read and believed even after her mother, a Protestant living near Montreal, gave testimony that Maria had been somewhat addled ever since childhood when she had rammed a pencil into her head. It was, indeed, read and believed by a dwindling audience even when poor Maria produced a fatherless child two years after the appearance of her book. She died in prison in 1849, after having been arrested in a brothel as a pickpocket.[5]

Anti-Catholicism, like anti-Masonry, mixed its fortunes with American party politics. To trace its political career would take us too far afield, but it did become an enduring factor in American politics. The American Protective Association of the 1890's revived it with ideological variations more suitable to the times—the depression of 1893, for example, was alleged to be an intentional creation of the Catholics, who began it by starting a run on the banks. Some

---

[5] Maria Monk: *Awful Disclosures* (New York, 1836; facsimile ed., Hamden, Conn., 1962); see R. A. Billington's introduction to the 1962 edition and his account in *The Protestant Crusade*, pp. 99–108.

spokesmen of the movement circulated a bogus encyclical attributed to Leo XIII instructing American Catholics on a certain date in 1893 to exterminate all heretics, and a great many anti-Catholics daily expected a nation-wide uprising. The myth of an impending Catholic war of mutilation and extermination of heretics persisted into the twentieth century.[6]

I V

IF WE NOW TAKE the long jump to the contemporary right wing, we find some rather important differences from the nineteenth-century movements. The spokesman of those earlier movements felt that they stood for causes and personal types that were still in possession of their country—that they were fending off threats to a still well-established way of life in which they played an important part. But the modern right wing, as Daniel Bell has put it,[7] feels dispossessed: America has been largely taken away from them and their kind, though they are determined to try to repossess it and to prevent the final destructive act of subversion. The old American virtues have already been eaten away by cosmopolitans and intellectuals; the old competitive capitalism has been gradually undermined by socialist and communist schemers;

---

[6] John Higham: *Strangers in the Land* (New Brunswick, N.J., 1955), pp. 81, 85, 180. Higham, studying Henry F. Bowers, a leader of this later phase of anti-Catholicism, finds "a mind charged with constant excitement and given to rigid categorical judgments," moving "in a world of suspicion and imagined danger. Here a single hostile force explained the trivial events of daily experience, while a sense of grandeur and destiny sustained the struggle against it. Everywhere Bowers saw evidence of the machinations of a foreign ecclesiastical conspiracy endowed with immense power." "The Mind of a Nativist: Henry F. Bowers and the A.P.A.," *American Quarterly*, IV (Spring 1953), 21.

[7] "The Dispossessed," in Daniel Bell (ed.): *The Radical Right* (New York, 1963), pp. 1–38.

the old national security and independence have been destroyed by treasonous plots, having as their most powerful agents not merely outsiders and foreigners but major statesmen seated at the very centers of American power. Their predecessors discovered foreign conspiracies; the modern radical right finds that conspiracy also embraces betrayal at home.

Important changes may be traced to the effects of the mass media. The villains of the modern right are much more vivid than those of their paranoid predecessors, much better known to the public; the contemporary literature of the paranoid style is by the same token richer and more circumstantial in personal description and personal invective. For the vaguely delineated villains of the anti-Masons, for the obscure and disguised Jesuit agents, the little-known papal delegates of the anti-Catholics, for the shadowy international bankers of the monetary conspiracies, we may now substitute eminent public figures like Presidents Roosevelt, Truman, and Eisenhower, Secretaries of State like Marshall, Acheson, and Dulles, justices of the Supreme Court like Frankfurter and Warren, and the whole battery of lesser but still famous and vivid conspirators headed by Alger Hiss.[8]

Events since 1939 have given the contemporary right-wing paranoid a vast theater for his imagination, full of rich and proliferating detail, replete with realistic clues and undeniable proofs of the validity of his views. The theater of action is now the entire world, and he can draw on not only the events of the Second World War but those of the Korean War and the cold war. Any historian of warfare knows that it is in good part a comedy of errors and a museum of incompetence; but if for every error and every act of incompetence one can

---

[8] The appeal of the conspiratorial conception of power is brilliantly and economically set against its historical background by Edward Shils: *The Torment of Secrecy* (Glencoe, Ill., 1956), esp. Ch. 1.

substitute an act of treason, we can see how many points of fascinating interpretation are open to the paranoid imagination: treason in high places can be found at almost every turning—and in the end the real mystery, for one who reads the primary works of paranoid scholarship, is not how the United States has been brought to its present dangerous position, but how it has managed to survive at all.

The basic elements of contemporary right-wing thought can be reduced to three: First, there has been the now familiar sustained conspiracy, running over more than a generation, and reaching its climax in Roosevelt's New Deal, to undermine free capitalism, to bring the economy under the direction of the federal government, and to pave the way for socialism or communism. Details might be open to argument among right-wingers, but many would agree with Frank Chodorov, the author of *The Income Tax: The Root of All Evil*,[9] that this campaign began with the passage of the income tax amendment to the Constitution in 1913.

The second contention is that top government officialdom has been so infiltrated by Communists that American policy,

---

[9] New York, 1954, esp. Ch. 5. For a good brief summary of the history of this alleged conspiracy, see Chesly Manly: *The Twenty-Year Revolution: From Roosevelt to Eisenhower* (Chicago, 1954), which traces all aspects of the "revolution" and finds in the United Nations (p. 179) "the principal instrument of a gigantic conspiracy to control the foreign and domestic policies of the United States, subvert the Constitution, and establish a totalitarian society." A more recent and much more widely read work, particularly popular in the Goldwater movement, is Phyllis Schlafly's *A Choice Not an Echo.* (Alton, Ill., 1964), which traces the work of a small group of "secret kingmakers" in New York who have controlled the affairs of the Republican party from 1936 to 1960. The author believes that Republicans have so many issues on their side that (pp. 23, 25–6) "there is no way Republicans can possibly lose *so long as we have a presidential candidate who campaigns on the issues.*" However, they have lost four major presidential campaigns because "a small group of secret kingmakers, using hidden persuaders and psychological warfare techniques, manipulated the Republican National Convention to nominate candidates who would sidestep or suppress the key issues." A more substantial con-

at least since the days leading up to Pearl Harbor, has been dominated by sinister men who were shrewdly and consistently selling out American national interests.

The final contention is that the country is infused with a network of Communist agents, just as in the old days it was infiltrated by Jesuit agents, so that the whole apparatus of education, religion, the press, and the mass media are engaged in a common effort to paralyze the resistance of loyal Americans.

The details of the modern right-wing case are beyond the scope of any brief discussion. Perhaps the most representative document of its McCarthyist phase was a long indictment of Secretary of State George C. Marshall, delivered in the Senate on June 14, 1951, by Senator McCarthy, and later published in a somewhat different form as *America's Retreat from Victory: The Story of George Catlett Marshall.* McCarthy pictured Marshall as the focal figure in a betrayal of American interests stretching in time from the strategic plans for the Second World War to the formulation of the Marshall Plan. Marshall was associated with practically every American failure or defeat, McCarthy insisted, and none of this was due to either accident or incompetence. There was a "baffling pattern" of Marshall's interventions in the war: "His decisions, maintained with great stubbornness and skill, always and invariably serv[ed] the world policy of the Kremlin." Under

---

temporary manual of conspiratorial views, which traces ramifications in many areas of American life, is John A. Stormer: *None Dare Call It Treason* (Florissant, Mo., 1964). The writer asks (p. 226): "Is there a conspiratorial plan to destroy the United States into which foreign aid, planned inflation, distortion of treaty-making powers and disarmament all fit?" He answers subtly that it makes no difference whether this is all planned or is merely the work of "misguided idealists. The fact is that the pieces exist. They fit the pattern whether they were planned by the communists or some other secret and mysterious revolutionary group or not. . . . Those who constructed the 'pieces' are few in number, but they exert fantastic control in government, financial circles, the press, unions, schools, etc."

his guidance there was conducted at the end of the war "what appeared to be a planned loss of the peace." Marshall's report on his mission to China cannot be understood as the product of incompetence, but appears persuasive and brilliant when it is read as "a propaganda document in behalf of other interests, another country and civilization." Marshall and Acheson were intent on delivering China to Russia. The Marshall Plan was "an evil hoax on the generosity, good will and careless-ness of the American people." And, above all, the sharp de-cline in America's relative strength from 1945 to 1951 did not "just happen," it was "brought about, step by step, by will and intention," the consequence not of mistakes but of a trea-sonous conspiracy, "a conspiracy on a scale so immense as to dwarf any previous such venture in the history of man." The ultimate aim of this conspiracy was "that we shall be con-tained and frustrated and finally fall victim to Soviet intrigue from within and Russian military might from without."[1]

Today the mantle of McCarthy has fallen on the retired candy manufacturer Robert H. Welch, Jr., who is less stra-tegically placed but whose well-organized following in the John Birch Society has had a strong influence. A few years ago Welch proclaimed that "Communist influences are now in almost complete control of our Federal Government"—note the care and scrupulousness of that "almost." He has offered a full-scale interpretation of our recent history in which Communists figure at every turn: They started a run on American banks in 1933 that forced their closure; they contrived the recognition of the Soviet Union by the United States in the same year, just in time to save the Soviets from economic collapse; they have stirred up the fuss over segrega-tion; they have taken over the Supreme Court and made it "one of the most important agencies of Communism." They

---

[1] Joseph R. McCarthy: *America's Retreat from Victory* (New York, 1951), pp. 54, 66, 130, 141, 156, 168, 169, 171.

are winning the struggle for control in "the press, the pulpit, the radio and television media, the labor unions, the schools, the courts, and the legislative halls of America."

Close attention to history wins for Mr. Welch an insight into affairs that is given to few of us. "For many reasons and after a lot of study," he wrote some years ago, "I personally believe [John Foster] Dulles to be a Communist agent." Other apparently innocent figures are similarly unmasked. The job of Professor Arthur F. Burns as the head of Eisenhower's Council of Economic Advisers quite probably was "merely a coverup for Burns' liaison work between Eisenhower and some of his bosses in the Establishment." Eisenhower's brother Milton was "actually [his] superior and boss within the whole Leftwing Establishment." As for Eisenhower himself, Welch characterized him, in words that have made the candy manufacturer famous, as "a dedicated, conscious agent of the Communist conspiracy"—a conclusion, he added, "based on an accumulation of detailed evidence so extensive and so palpable that it seems to put this conviction beyond any reasonable doubt."[2]

The views for which Mr. Welch carefully gathers "detailed evidence" are expressed with less scholarly responsibility by a small but vocal segment of the public. Recently Republican Senator Thomas R. Kuchel, the minority whip of the Senate, revealed that of the 60,000 letters he receives each month, about 10 per cent may be classified as what he calls "fright mail"—indignant or anguished letters about "the latest *PLOT!!* to OVERTHROW America!!!" The imagination of his correspondents is feverishly at work:

---

[2] *The Politician* (Belmont, Mass., 1963), pp. 222, 223, 229. Quotations from Welch vary slightly because his incredible diatribe against Eisenhower was modified in later editions of this book—for example, Eisenhower was later described as (p. 291) "either a willing agent, or an integral and important part of a conspiracy of gangsters determined to rule the world at any cost." Welch's views are ably summarized by Alan Westin, from a different version of the text, in "The John Birch Society," in Daniel Bell (ed): op. cit., pp. 204–6.

Some of the more memorable "plots" that come to mind include these: 35,000 Communist Chinese troops bearing arms and wearing deceptively dyed powder-blue uniforms, are poised on the Mexican border, about to invade San Diego; the United States has turned over—or will at any moment—its Army, Navy and Air Force to the command of a Russian colonel in the United Nations; almost every well-known American or free-world leader is, in reality, a top Communist agent; a United States Army guerilla-warfare exercise in Georgia, called Water Moccasin III, is in actuality a United Nations operation preparatory to taking over our country.[3]

V

LET US NOW ABSTRACT the basic elements in the paranoid style. The central image is that of a vast and sinister conspiracy, a gigantic and yet subtle machinery of influence set in motion to undermine and destroy a way of life. One may object that there *are* conspiratorial acts in history, and there is nothing paranoid about taking note of them. This is true. All political behavior requires strategy, many strategic acts depend for their effect upon a period of secrecy, and anything that is secret may be described, often with but little exaggeration, as conspiratorial. The distinguishing thing about the paranoid style is not that its exponents see conspiracies or plots here and there in history, but that they regard a "vast" or "gigantic" conspiracy as *the motive force* in historical events. History *is* a conspiracy, set in motion by demonic forces of almost transcendent power, and what is felt to be needed to defeat it is not the usual methods of political give-and-take, but an all-out crusade. The paranoid spokesman sees the fate of this conspiracy in apocalyptic terms—he traffics in the birth and death of whole worlds, whole political orders, whole systems of human values. He is always manning the

---

[3] *The New York Times*, July 21, 1963, VI, p. 6.

barricades of civilization. He constantly lives at a turning point: it is now or never in organizing resistance to conspiracy. Time is forever just running out. Like religious millenarians, he expresses the anxiety of those who are living through the last days and he is sometimes disposed to set a date for the apocalypse. "Time is running out," said Welch in 1951. "Evidence is piling up on many sides and from many sources that October 1952 is the fatal month when Stalin will attack."[4] The apocalypticism of the paranoid style runs dangerously near to hopeless pessimism, but usually stops short of it. Apocalyptic warnings arouse passion and militancy, and strike at susceptibility to similar themes in Christianity. Properly expressed, such warnings serve somewhat the same function as a description of the horrible consequences of sin in a revivalist sermon: they portray that which impends but which may still be avoided. They are a secular and demonic version of adventism.

As a member of the avant-garde who is capable of perceiv-

---

[4] *May God Forgive Us* (Chicago, 1952), p. 73. Dr. Fred C. Schwarz of the Christian Anti-Communism Crusade is more circumspect. In his lectures he sets the year 1973 as the date for the Communists to achieve control of the world, if they are not stopped. Most contemporary paranoid spokesmen speak of a "Communist timetable," of whose focal dates they often seem to have intimate knowledge.

Probably the most spectacular American instance of such adventism is the case of William Miller, who flourished in New York in the 1830's. The offspring of a line of Baptist preachers, Miller became preoccupied with millenarian prophecies, and made calculations which indicated that Christ would come at first in 1843, and then on October 22, 1844, and became the leader of an adventist sect with a considerable following. On the appointed day, Millerites gathered to pray, many abandoned their worldly occupations, and some disposed of their property. The Miller movement waned after the fatal day, but other adventists, more cautious about their use of dates, carried on.

A notable quality in Miller's work was the rigorously logical and systematic character of his demonstrations, as was his militant opposition to Masonry, Catholicism, and other seductions. His lieutenants and followers, A. Whitney Cross has remarked, "found the world beyond rescue, legislatures corrupt, and infidelity, idolatry, Romanism, sectarianism, seduction, fraud, murder, and duels all waxing stronger."

ing the conspiracy before it is fully obvious to an as yet un-aroused public, the paranoid is a militant leader. He does not see social conflict as something to be mediated and compro-mised, in the manner of the working politician. Since what is at stake is always a conflict between absolute good and abso-lute evil, the quality needed is not a willingness to compromise but the will to fight things out to a finish. Nothing but com-plete victory will do. Since the enemy is thought of as being totally evil and totally unappeasable, he must be totally elimi-nated—if not from the world, at least from the theater of operations to which the paranoid directs his attention.[5] This demand for unqualified victories leads to the formulation of hopelessly demanding and unrealistic goals, and since these goals are not even remotely attainable, failure constantly heightens the paranoid's frustration. Even partial success leaves him with the same sense of powerlessness with which he began, and this in turn only strengthens his awareness of the vast and terrifying quality of the enemy he opposes.

This enemy is clearly delineated: he is a perfect model of malice, a kind of amoral superman: sinister, ubiquitous, pow-

---

Cross argues that the Millerite movement was not so far from the mainstream of American Protestantism as some might think: "The Millerites cannot be dismissed as ignorant farmers, libertarian fron-tiersmen, impoverished victims of economic change, or hypnotized followers of a maniac thrown into prominence by freak coincidences, when the whole of American Protestantism came so very close to the same beliefs. Their doctrine was the logical absolute of fundamentalist orthodoxy, as perfectionism was the extreme of revivalism. . . . All Protestants expected some grand event about 1843, and no critic from the orthodox side took any serious issue on basic principles with Miller's calculations." *The Burned-Over District* (Ithaca, N.Y., 1950), pp. 320–1; see Ch. 17 for a good account of the Millerite movement.

For the story of an interesting contemporary prophetic cult and some sober reflections on the powerful resistance of true believers to overwhelming disconfirmation, see L. Festinger, H. W. Riecken, and S. Schachter: *When Prophecy Fails* (Minneapolis, 1956).

[5] "The systems are diametrically opposed: one must and will ex-terminate the other." Edward Beecher: *The Papal Conspiracy Ex-posed and Protestantism Defended* (Boston, 1855), p. 29.

erful, cruel, sensual, luxury-loving. Unlike the rest of us, the enemy is not caught in the toils of the vast mechanism of history, himself a victim of his past, his desires, his limitations. He is a free, active, demonic agent. He wills, indeed he manufactures, the mechanism of history himself, or deflects the normal course of history in an evil way. He makes crises, starts runs on banks, causes depressions, manufactures disasters, and then enjoys and profits from the misery he has produced. The paranoid's interpretation of history is in this sense distinctly personal: decisive events are not taken as part of the stream of history, but as the consequences of someone's will. Very often the enemy is held to possess some especially effective source of power: he controls the press; he directs the public mind through "managed news"; he has unlimited funds; he has a new secret for influencing the mind (brainwashing); he has a special technique for seduction (the Catholic confessional); he is gaining a stranglehold on the educational system.

This enemy seems to be on many counts a projection of the self: both the ideal and the unacceptable aspects of the self are attributed to him. A fundamental paradox of the paranoid style is the imitation of the enemy. The enemy, for example, may be the cosmopolitan intellectual, but the paranoid will outdo him in the apparatus of scholarship, even of pedantry. Senator McCarthy, with his heavily documented tracts and his show of information, Mr. Welch with his accumulations of irresistible evidence, John Robison with his laborious study of documents in a language he but poorly used, the anti-Masons with their endlessly painstaking discussions of Masonic ritual—all these offer a kind of implicit compliment to their opponents. Secret organizations set up to combat secret organizations give the same flattery. The Ku Klux Klan imitated Catholicism to the point of donning priestly vestments, developing an elaborate ritual and an equally elaborate hierarchy. The John Birch Society emulates Communist cells and quasi-secret operation through "front" groups, and preaches a ruthless prosecution of the ideological war along lines very similar to those it finds in the Communist enemy. Spokesmen of the various Christian anti-Communist "crusades" openly express their admiration for the dedication, discipline, and strategic ingenuity the Communist cause calls forth.[6]

David Brion Davis, in a remarkable essay on pre-Civil War "counter-subversive" movements, has commented on the manner in which the nineteenth-century nativist unwittingly fashioned himself after his enemy:

> As the nativist searched for participation in a noble cause, for unity in a group sanctioned by tradition and authority, he professed a belief in democracy and equal rights. Yet in his very zeal for freedom he curiously assumed many of the characteristics of the imagined enemy. By condemning the subversive's fanatical allegiance to an ideology, he affirmed a similarly un-critical acceptance of a different ideology; by attacking the subversive's intolerance of dissent, he worked to eliminate dissent and diversity of opinion; by censuring the subversive for alleged licentiousness, he engaged in sensual fantasies; by criticizing the subversive's loyalty to an organization, he sought to prove his unconditional loyalty to the established order. The nativist moved even farther in the direction of his enemies when he formed tightly-knit societies and parties which were often secret and which subordinated the individual to the single purpose of the group. Though the nativists generally agreed that the worst

---

[6] This has now become a fashionable trend in more respectable quarters. Stephen Shadegg, known for his success in Senator Goldwater's senatorial campaigns, writes: "Mao Tse-tung . . . has written a valuable book on the tactics of infiltration. In it he says: 'Give me just two or three men in a village and I will take the village.' In the Goldwater campaigns of 1952 and 1958 and in all other campaigns where I have served as a consultant I have followed the advice of Mao Tse-tung." *How to Win an Election* (New York, 1964), p. 106. Writing about cold-war strategy, Goldwater himself declares: "I would suggest that we analyze and copy the strategy of the enemy; theirs has worked and ours has not." *Why Not Victory?* (New York, 1962), p. 24.

33

evil of subversives was their subordination of means to ends, they themselves recommended the most radical means to purge the nation of troublesome groups and to enforce unquestioned loyalty to the state.[7]

Much of the function of the enemy lies not in what can be imitated but in what can be wholly condemned. The sexual freedom often attributed to him, his lack of moral inhibition, his possession of especially effective techniques for fulfilling his desires, give exponents of the paranoid style an opportunity to project and freely express unacceptable aspects of their own minds. Priests and Mormon patriarchs were commonly thought to have especial attraction for women, and hence licentious privilege. Thus Catholics and Mormons—later Negroes and Jews—lent themselves to a preoccupation with illicit sex. Very often the fantasies of true believers serve as strong sado-masochistic outlets, vividly expressed, for example, in the concern of anti-Masons with the alleged cruelty of Masonic punishments. Concerning this phenomenon, Davis remarks:

> Masons disemboweled or slit the throats of their victims; Catholics cut unborn infants from their mothers' wombs and threw them to the dogs before their parents' eyes; Mormons raped and lashed recalcitrant women, or seared their mouths with red-hot irons. This obsession with details of sadism, which reached pathological proportions in much of the literature, showed a furious determination to purge the enemy of every admirable quality.[8]

Another recurring aspect of the paranoid style is the special significance that attaches to the figure of the renegade from the enemy cause. The anti-Masonic movement seemed at

---

[7] David Brion Davis: "Some Themes of Counter-Subversion: An Analysis of Anti-Masonic, Anti-Catholic, and Anti-Mormon Literature," *Mississippi Valley Historical Review*, XLVII (September 1960), 223.

[8] Ibid., p. 221.

times to be the creation of ex-Masons; it certainly attached the highest significance and gave the most unqualified credulity to their revelations. Similarly anti-Catholicism used the runaway nun and the apostate priest, anti-Mormonism the ex-wife from the harem of polygamy; the avant-garde anti-Communist movements of our time use the ex-Communist. In some part the special authority accorded the renegade derives from the obsession with secrecy so characteristic of such movements: the renegade is the man or woman who has been in the secret world of the enemy, and brings forth with him or her the final verification of suspicions which might otherwise have been doubted by a skeptical world. But I think there is a deeper eschatological significance attached to the person of the renegade: in the spiritual wrestling match between good and evil which is the paranoid's archetypal model of the world struggle, the renegade is living proof that all the conversions are not made by the wrong side. He brings with him the promise of redemption and victory.

In contemporary right-wing movements a particularly important part has been played by ex-Communists who have moved rapidly, though not without anguish, from the paranoid left to the paranoid right, clinging all the while to the fundamentally Manichean psychology that underlies both. Such authorities on communism remind one of those ancient converts from paganism to Christianity of whom it is told that upon their conversion they did not entirely cease to believe in their old gods but converted them into demons.

A final aspect of the paranoid style is related to that quality of pedantry to which I have already referred. One of the impressive things about paranoid literature is precisely the elaborate concern with demonstration it almost invariably shows. One should not be misled by the fantastic conclusions that are so characteristic of this political style into imagining that it is not, so to speak, argued out along factual lines. The

35

very fantastic character of its conclusions leads to heroic strivings for "evidence" to prove that the unbelievable is the only thing that can be believed. Of course, there are highbrow, lowbrow, and middlebrow paranoids, as there are likely to be in any political tendency, and paranoid movements from the Middle Ages onward have had a magnetic attraction for demi-intellectuals. But respectable paranoid literature not only starts from certain moral commitments that can be justified to many non-paranoids but also carefully and all but obsessively accumulates "evidence." Paranoid writing begins with certain defensible judgments. There *was* something to be said for the anti-Masons. After all, a secret society composed of influential men bound by special obligations could conceivably pose some kind of threat to the civil order in which they were suspended. There was also something to be said for the Protestant principles of individuality and freedom, as well as for the nativist desire to develop in North America a homogeneous civilization. Again, in our time innumerable decisions of the Second World War and the cold war can be faulted, and it is easy for the suspicious to believe that such decisions are not simply the mistakes of well-meaning men but the plans of traitors.

The typical procedure of the higher paranoid scholarship is to start with such defensible assumptions and with a careful accumulation of facts, or at least of what appear to be facts, and to marshal these facts toward an overwhelming "proof" of the particular conspiracy that is to be established. It is nothing if not coherent—in fact, the paranoid mentality is far more coherent than the real world, since it leaves no room for mistakes, failures, or ambiguities. It is, if not wholly rational, at least intensely rationalistic; it believes that it is up against an enemy who is as infallibly rational as he is totally evil, and it seeks to match his imputed total competence with its own, leaving nothing unexplained and comprehending all of reality in one overreaching, consistent theory. It is nothing if not "scholarly" in technique. McCarthy's 96-page pamphlet *Mc-Carthyism* contains no less than 313 footnote references, and Mr. Welch's fantastic assault on Eisenhower, *The Politician*, is weighed down by a hundred pages of bibliography and notes. The entire right-wing movement of our time is a parade of experts, study groups, monographs, footnotes, and bibliographies. Sometimes the right-wing striving for scholarly depth and an inclusive world view has startling consequences: Mr. Welch, for example, has charged that the popularity of Arnold Toynbee's historical work is the consequence of a plot on the part of Fabians, "Labour Party bosses in England," and various members of the Anglo-American "liberal establishment" to overshadow the much more truthful and illuminating work of Oswald Spengler.[9]

What distinguishes the paranoid style is not, then, the absence of verifiable facts (though it is occasionally true that in his extravagant passion for facts the paranoid occasionally manufactures them), but rather the curious leap in imagination that is always made at some critical point in the recital of events. John Robison's tract on the Illuminati followed a pattern that has been repeated for over a century and a half. For page after page he patiently records the details he has been able to accumulate about the history of the Illuminati. Then, suddenly, the French Revolution has taken place, and the Illuminati have brought it about. What is missing is not veracious information about the organization, but sensible judgment about what can cause a revolution. The plausibility the paranoid style has for those who find it plausible lies, in good measure, in this appearance of the most careful, conscientious, and seemingly coherent application to detail, the laborious accumulation of what can be taken as convincing evidence for the most fantastic conclusions, the careful preparation for the

---

[9] *The Blue Book of the John Birch Society* (n.p., 1961), pp. 42–3.

big leap from the undeniable to the unbelievable. The singular thing about all this laborious work is that the passion for factual evidence does not, as in most intellectual exchanges, have the effect of putting the paranoid spokesman into effective two-way communication with the world outside his group—least of all with those who doubt his views. He has little real hope that his evidence will convince a hostile world. His effort to amass it has rather the quality of a defensive act which shuts off his receptive apparatus and protects him from having to attend to disturbing considerations that do not fortify his ideas. He has all the evidence he needs; he is not a receiver, he is a transmitter.

Since I have drawn so heavily on American examples, I would like to emphasize again that the paranoid style is an international phenomenon. Nor is it confined to modern times. Studying the millennial sects of Europe from the eleventh to the sixteenth century, Norman Cohn finds, in his brilliant book *The Pursuit of the Millennium*, a persistent psychological complex that closely resembles what I have been considering—a style made up of certain marked preoccupations and fantasies: "the megalomanic view of oneself as the Elect, wholly good, abominably persecuted yet assured of ultimate triumph; the attribution of gigantic and demonic powers to the adversary; the refusal to accept the ineluctable limitations and imperfections of human existence, such as transience, dissention, conflict, fallibility whether intellectual or moral; the obsession with inerrable prophecies . . . systematized misinterpretations, always gross and often grotesque . . . ruthlessness directed towards an end which by its very nature cannot be realised—towards a total and final solution such as cannot be attained at any actual time or in any concrete situation, but only in the timeless and autistic realm of phantasy."[1]

---

[1] *The Pursuit of the Millennium* (London, 1957), pp. 309–10; see also pp. 58–74. In the Middle Ages millenarianism flourished among

The recurrence of the paranoid style over a long span of time and in different places suggests that a mentality disposed to see the world in the paranoid's way may always be present in some considerable minority of the population. But the fact that movements employing the paranoid style are not constant but come in successive episodic waves suggests that the paranoid disposition is mobilized into action chiefly by social conflicts that involve ultimate schemes of values and that bring fundamental fears and hatreds, rather than negotiable interests, into political action. Catastrophe or the fear of catastrophe is most likely to elicit the syndrome of paranoid rhetoric.

In American experience, ethnic and religious conflicts, with their threat of the submergence of whole systems of values, have plainly been the major focus for militant and suspicious minds of this sort, but elsewhere class conflicts have also mobilized such energies. The paranoid tendency is aroused by a confrontation of opposed interests which are (or are felt to be) totally irreconcilable, and thus by nature not susceptible to the normal political processes of bargain and compromise. The situation becomes worse when the representatives of a particular political interest—perhaps because of the very unrealistic and unrealizable nature of their demands—cannot make themselves felt in the political process. Feeling that they have no access to political bargaining or the making of decisions, they find their original conception of the world of power as omnipotent, sinister, and malicious fully confirmed. They see only the consequences of power—and this through distorting lenses—and have little chance to observe its actual

---

the poor, the oppressed, and the hopeless. In Anglo-American experience, as Samuel Shepperson has observed, such movements have never been confined to these classes, but have had a more solid middle-class foundation. "The Comparative Study of Millenarian Movements," in Sylvia Thrupp (ed.): *Millennial Dreams in Action* (The Hague, 1962), pp. 49–52.

39

machinery. L. B. Namier once said that "the crowning attainment of historical study" is to achieve "an intuitive sense of how things do not happen."[2] It is precisely this kind of awareness that the paranoid fails to develop. He has a special resistance of his own, of course, to such awareness, but circumstances often deprive him of exposure to events that might enlighten him. We are all sufferers from history, but the paranoid is a double sufferer, since he is afflicted not only by the real world, with the rest of us, but by his fantasies as well.

---

[2] L. B. Namier: "History," in Fritz Stern (ed.): *The Varieties of History* (New York, 1956), p. 375.

THE PSEUDO-CONSERVATIVE REVOLT—1954

In the spring of 1954 I was invited by the directors of the American Civilization Program of Barnard College to speak on some aspect of American dissent. Since the McCarthyist movement was then at its peak, I chose to speak on right-wing or, as I called it, pseudo-conservative dissent. In defining the right-wing movement, which was so fond of designating itself "conservative," as being in some sense of movement of *dissent*, I tried to pose the problem around which my argument was built. The lecture was later published in the Winter 1954–5 issue of *The American Scholar*. I have written nothing else of comparable brevity that aroused more attention or drew more requests for quotation or reprinting.

It soon became apparent that several writers, working independently and simultaneously, were arriving at roughly similar approaches to McCarthyism and related phenomena. Daniel Bell, in *The New American Right* (1955), collected and introduced the relevant pieces, which had been written by David Riesman and Nathan Glazer, Seymour M. Lipset, Talcott Parsons, and Peter Viereck; these essays are now most conveniently available, along with the editor's and authors' afterthoughts and new essays by Alan F. Westin and Herbert H. Hyman, in *The Radical Right* (1963), which puts the earlier analysis into the context of the 1960's. Inevitably, the authors, despite significant differences in their political and social views, have come to be regarded as a school; but in commenting on our convergent ideas in the subsequent essays, I can speak only for myself.

On some counts I no longer hold with what I wrote in 1954. But it proved impossible to take adequate account of the limitations of this essay merely by revising it; and since it serves as a record of how things looked to some of us in 1954 and as a useful way of opening up a dialogue between the present and the recent past, it still seemed desirable to include it here. I therefore reprint it with only minor textual changes and a few added monitory footnotes. The task of correcting and extending it I have left to the two subsequent essays. The first of these restates the issues, and the second shows how pseudo-conservative politics were exemplified in the Goldwater campaign of 1964.

TWENTY years ago the dynamic force in American political life came from the side of liberal dissent, from the impulse to reform the inequities of our economic and social system and to change our ways of doing things, to the end that the sufferings of the Great Depression would never be repeated. Today the dynamic force in our political life no longer comes from the liberals who made the New Deal possible. By 1952 the liberals had had at least the trappings of power for twenty years. They could look back to a brief, exciting period in the mid-1930's when they had held power itself and had been able to transform the economic and administrative life of the nation. After twenty years the New Deal liberals have quite unconsciously taken on the psychology of those who have entered into possession. Moreover, a large part of the New Deal public, the jobless, distracted, and bewildered men of 1933, have in the course of the years found substantial places in society for themselves, have become homeowners, suburbanites, and solid citizens. Many of them still have the emotional commitments to the liberal dissent with which they grew up politically, but their social position is one of solid comfort. Among them the dominant tone has become one of satisfaction, even of a kind of conservatism. Insofar as

Adlai Stevenson stirred their enthusiasm in 1952, it was not in spite of but in part because of the air of poised and reliable conservatism that he brought to the Democratic convention. By comparison, Harry Truman's impassioned rhetoric, with its occasional thrusts at "Wall Street," seemed passé and rather embarrassing. The change did not escape Stevenson himself. "The strange alchemy of time," he said in a speech at Columbus, "has somehow converted the Democrats into the truly conservative party of this country—the party dedicated to conserving all that is best, and building solidly and safely on these foundations." What most liberals now hope for is not to carry on with some ambitious new program, but simply to defend as much as possible of the old achievements and to try to keep traditional liberties of expression that are threatened.

There is, however, a dynamic of dissent in America today. Representing no more than a modest fraction of the electorate, it is not so powerful as the liberal dissent of the New Deal era, but it is powerful enough to set the tone of our political life and to establish throughout the country a kind of punitive reaction. The new dissent is certainly not radical—there are hardly any radicals of any sort left—nor is it precisely conservative. Unlike most of the liberal dissent of the past, the new dissent not only has no respect for nonconformism, but is based upon a relentless demand for conformity. It can most accurately be called pseudo-conservative—I borrow the term from *The Authoritarian Personality*, published in 1950 by Theodore W. Adorno and his associates—because its exponents, although they believe themselves to be conservatives and usually employ the rhetoric of conservatism, show signs of a serious and restless dissatisfaction with American life, traditions, and institutions. They have little in common with the temperate and compromising spirit of true conservatism in the classical sense of the word, and they are far from pleased with the dominant practical conservatism of the moment as it is represented by the Eisenhower administration. Their political reactions express rather a profound if largely unconscious hatred of our society and its ways—a hatred which one would hesitate to impute to them if one did not have suggestive evidence both from clinical techniques and from their own modes of expression.

From clinical interviews and thematic apperception tests, Adorno and his co-workers found that their pseudo-conservative subjects, although given to a form of political expression that combines a curious mixture of largely conservative with occasional radical notions, succeed in concealing from themselves impulsive tendencies that, if released in action, would be very far from conservative. The pseudo-conservative, Adorno writes, shows "conventionality and authoritarian submissiveness" in his conscious thinking and "violence, anarchic impulses, and chaotic destructiveness in the unconscious sphere. . . . The pseudo-conservative is a man who, in the name of upholding traditional American values and institutions and defending them against more or less fictitious dangers, consciously or unconsciously aims at their abolition."[1]

Who is the pseudo-conservative, and what does he want? It is impossible to identify him by social class, for the pseudo-conservative impulse can be found in practically all classes in society, although its power probably rests largely upon its appeal to the less-educated members of the middle classes. The ideology of pseudo-conservatism can be characterized but not defined, because the pseudo-conservative tends to be

---

[1] Theodore W. Adorno et al.: *The Authoritarian Personality* (New York, 1950), pp. 675–6. While I have drawn heavily upon this enlightening study, I have some reservations about its methods and conclusions. For a critical review, see Richard Christie and Marie Jahoda (eds.): *Studies in the Scope and Method of "The Authoritarian Personality"* (Glencoe, Ill., 1954), particularly the penetrating comments by Edward Shils.

more than ordinarily incoherent about politics. The lady who, when General Eisenhower's victory over Senator Taft had finally become official in 1952, stalked out of the Hilton Hotel declaiming: "This means eight more years of socialism," was probably a fairly good representative of the pseudo-conservative mentality. So also were the gentleman who, at the Freedom Congress held at Omaha over a year ago by some "patriotic" organizations, objected to Earl Warren's appointment to the Supreme Court with the assertion: "Middle-of-the-road thinking can and will destroy us"; the general who spoke to the same group, demanding "an Air Force capable of wiping out the Russian Air Force and industry in one sweep," but also "a material reduction in military expenditures";[2] the people who a few years ago believed simultaneously that we had no business to be fighting communism in Korea and that the war should immediately be extended to an Asia-wide crusade against communism; and the most ardent supporters of the Bricker Amendment. Many of the most zealous followers of Senator McCarthy are also pseudo-conservatives, although his appeal clearly embraces a wider public.

The restlessness, suspicion, and fear shown in various phases of the pseudo-conservative revolt give evidence of the anguish which the pseudo-conservative experiences in his capacity as a citizen. He believes himself to be living in a world in which he is spied upon, plotted against, betrayed, and very likely destined for total ruin. He feels that his liberties have been arbitrarily and outrageously invaded. He is opposed to almost everything that has happened in American politics in the past twenty years. He hates the very thought of Franklin D. Roosevelt. He is disturbed deeply by American participation in the United Nations, which he can see only as

---

[2] On the Omaha Freedom Congress, see Leonard Boasberg: "Radical Reactionaries," *The Progressive*, December 1953.

45

a sinister organization. He sees his own country as being so weak that it is constantly about to fall victim to subversion; and yet he feels that it is so all-powerful that any failure it may experience in getting its way in the world—for instance, in the Orient—cannot possibly be due to its limitations but must be attributed to its having been betrayed.[3] He is the most bitter of all our citizens about our involvement in the wars of the past, but seems the least concerned about avoiding the next one. While he naturally does not like Soviet communism, what distinguishes him from the rest of us who also dislike it is that he shows little interest in, is often indeed bitterly hostile to, such realistic measures as might actually strengthen the United States vis-à-vis Russia. He would much rather concern himself with the domestic scene, where communism is weak, than with those areas of the world where it is really strong and threatening. He wants to have nothing to do with the democratic nations of Western Europe, which seem to draw more of his ire than the Soviet Communists, and he is opposed to all "giveaway programs" designed to aid and strengthen these nations. Indeed, he is likely to be antagonistic to most of the operations of our federal government except congressional investigations, and to almost all its expenditures. Not always, however, does he go so far as the speaker at the Freedom Congress who attributed the greater part of our national difficulties to "this nasty, stinking 16th [income tax] Amendment."

A great deal of pseudo-conservative thinking takes the form of trying to devise means of absolute protection against that betrayal by our own officialdom which the pseudo-conservative feels is always imminent. The Bricker Amendment, indeed, might be taken as one of the primary symptoms of pseudo-conservatism. Every dissenting movement brings

---

[3] See the comments of D. W. Brogan in "The Illusion of American Omnipotence," *Harper's Magazine,* December 1952, pp. 21–8.

its demand for constitutional changes; and the pseudo-conservative revolt, far from being an exception to this principle, seems to specialize in constitutional revision, at least as a speculative enterprise. The widespread latent hostility toward American institutions takes the form, among other things, of a flood of proposals to write drastic changes into the body of our fundamental law. In June 1954, Richard Rovere pointed out in a characteristically astute piece that Constitution-amending had become almost a major diversion in the Eighty-third Congress.[4] About a hundred amendments were introduced and referred to committee. Several of these called for the repeal of the income tax. Several embodied formulas of various kinds to limit non-military expenditures to some fixed portion of the national income. One proposed to bar all federal expenditures on "the general welfare"; another, to prohibit American troops from serving in any foreign country except on the soil of the potential enemy; another, to redefine treason to embrace not only persons trying to overthrow the government but also those trying to "weaken" it, even by peaceful means. The last proposal might bring the pseudo-conservative rebels themselves under the ban of treason: for the sum total of these amendments could easily serve to send the whole structure of American society crashing to the ground.

As Mr. Rovere points out, it is not unusual for a large number of constitutional amendments to be lying about somewhere in the congressional hoppers. What is unusual is the readiness the Senate has shown to give them respectful consideration, and the peculiar populistic arguments some of its leading members have used to justify referring them to the state legislatures. While the ordinary Congress hardly ever has occasion to consider more than one amendment, the

---

[4] Richard Rovere: "Letter from Washington," *The New Yorker*, June 19, 1954, pp. 67–72.

Eighty-third Congress saw six constitutional amendments brought to the floor of the Senate, all summoning simple majorities, and four winning the two-thirds majority necessary before they can be sent to the House and ultimately to the state legislatures. It must be added that, with the possible exception of the Bricker Amendment itself, none of the six amendments so honored can be classed with the most extreme proposals. But the pliability of the senators, the eagerness of some of them to pass the buck and defer to "the people of the country," suggests how strong they feel the pressure to be for some kind of change that will give expression to the vague desire to repudiate the past which underlies the pseudo-conservative revolt.

One of the most urgent questions we can ask about the United States in our time is: Where did all this sentiment arise? The readiest answer is that the new pseudo-conservatism is simply the old ultra-conservatism and the old isolationism heightened by the extraordinary pressures of the contemporary world. This answer, true though it may be, gives a deceptive sense of familiarity without much deepening our understanding, for the particular patterns of American isolationism and extreme right-wing thinking have themselves not been very satisfactorily explored. It will not do, to take but one example, to say that some people want the income-tax amendment repealed because taxes have become very heavy in the past twenty years: for this will not explain why, of three people in the same tax bracket, one will grin and bear it and continue to support social-welfare legislation as well as an adequate military establishment, while another responds by supporting in a matter-of-fact way the practical conservative leadership of the moment, and the third finds his feelings satisfied only by the angry accusations of conspiracy and extreme demands of the pseudo-conservative.

No doubt the circumstances determining the political style

of any individual are complex. Although I am concerned here to discuss some of the neglected social-psychological elements in pseudo-conservatism, I do not wish to appear to deny the presence of important economic and political causes. I am aware, for instance, that wealthy reactionaries try to use pseudo-conservative organizers, spokesmen, and groups to propagate their notions of public policy, and that some organizers of pseudo-conservative and "patriotic" groups often find in this work a means of making a living—thus turning a tendency toward paranoia into a vocational asset, probably one of the most perverse forms of occupational therapy known to man. A number of other circumstances—the drastic inflation and heavy taxes of our time, the imbalance in our party system, the deterioration of American urban life, considerations of partisan political expediency—also play a part. But none of these things seems to explain the broad appeal of pseudo-conservatism, its emotional intensity, its dense and massive irrationality, or some of the peculiar ideas it generates. Nor will they explain why those who profit by the organized movements find such a ready following among a large number of people, and why the rank-and-file janizaries of pseudo-conservatism are so eager to hurl accusations, write letters to congressmen and editors, and expend so much emotional energy and crusading idealism upon causes that plainly bring them no material reward.

Elmer Davis, seeking to account for such sentiment in his recent book *But We Were Born Free*, ventures a psychological hypothesis. He concludes, if I understand him correctly, that the genuine difficulties of our situation in the face of the power of international communism have inspired a widespread feeling of fear and frustration, and that those who cannot face these problems in a more rational way "take it out on their less influential neighbors, in the mood of a man who, being afraid to stand up to his wife in a domestic argument, relieves his feelings by kicking the cat."[5] This suggestion has the merit of both simplicity and plausibility, and it may begin to account for a portion of the pseudo-conservative public. But while we may dismiss our curiosity about the man who kicks the cat by remarking that some idiosyncrasy in his personal development has brought him to this pass, we can hardly help but wonder whether there are not, in the backgrounds of the hundreds of thousands of persons who are moved by the pseudo-conservative impulse, some commonly shared circumstances that will help to account for their all kicking the cat in unison.

All of us have reason to fear the power of international communism, and all our lives are profoundly affected by it. Why do some Americans try to face this threat for what it is, a problem that exists in a world-wide theater of action, while others try to reduce it largely to a matter of domestic conformity? Why do some of us prefer to look for allies in the democratic world, while others seem to prefer authoritarian allies or none at all? Why do the pseudo-conservatives express such a persistent fear and suspicion of *their own government*, whether its leadership rests in the hands of Roosevelt, Truman, or Eisenhower? Why is the pseudo-conservative impelled to go beyond the more or less routine partisan argument that we have been the victims of considerable misgovernment during the past twenty years to the disquieting accusation that we have actually been the victims of persistent conspiracy and betrayal—"twenty years of treason"? Is it not true, moreover, that political types very similar to the pseudo-conservative have had a long history in the United States, and that this history goes back to a time when the Soviet power did not loom nearly so large on our mental horizons? Was the Ku Klux Klan, for instance, which was responsibly estimated

---

[5] Elmer Davis: *But We Were Born Free* (New York, 1954), pp. 35–6; cf. pp. 21–2 and passim.

to have had a membership of from 4,000,000 to 4,500,000 persons at its peak in the 1920's, a phenomenon totally dissimilar to the pseudo-conservative revolt?

What I wish to suggest—and I do so in the spirit of one setting forth nothing more than a speculative hypothesis—is that pseudo-conservatism is in good part a product of the rootlessness and heterogeneity of American life and, above all, of its peculiar scramble for status and its peculiar search for secure identity. Normally there is a world of difference between one's sense of national identity or cultural belonging and one's social status. However, in American historical development, these two things, so easily distinguishable in analysis, have been jumbled together in reality, and it is precisely this that has given such a special poignancy and urgency to our status strivings. In this country a person's status—that is, his relative place in the prestige hierarchy of his community—and his rudimentary sense of belonging to the community—that is, what we call his "Americanism"—have been intimately joined. Because, as a people extremely democratic in our social institutions, we have had no clear, consistent, and recognizable system of status, our personal status problems have an unusual intensity. Because we no longer have the relative ethnic homogeneity we had up to about eighty years ago, our sense of belonging has long had about it a high degree of uncertainty. We boast of "the melting pot," but we are not quite sure what it is that will remain when we have been melted down.

We have always been proud of the high degree of occupational mobility in our country—of the greater readiness, as compared with other countries, with which a person starting in a very humble place in our social structure could rise to a position of moderate wealth and status, and with which a person starting with a middling position could rise to great eminence. We have looked upon this as laudable in principle, for it is democratic, and as pragmatically desirable, for it has served many a man as a stimulus to effort and has, no doubt, a great deal to do with the energetic and effectual tone of our economic life. The American pattern of occupational mobility, while often much exaggerated, as in the Horatio Alger stories and a great deal of the rest of our mythology, may properly be credited with many of the virtues and beneficial effects that are usually attributed to it. But this occupational and social mobility, compounded by our extraordinary mobility from place to place, has also had its less frequently recognized drawbacks. Not the least of them is that this has become a country in which so many people do not know who they are or what they are or what they belong to or what belongs to them. It is a country of people whose status expectations are random and uncertain, and yet whose status aspirations have been whipped up to a high pitch by our democratic ethos and our rags-to-riches mythology.[6]

In a country where physical needs have been, by the scale of the world's living standards, on the whole well met, the luxury of questing after status has assumed an unusually prominent place in our civic consciousness. Political life is not simply an arena in which the conflicting interests of various social groups in concrete material gains are fought out; it is also an arena into which status aspirations and frustrations are, as the psychologists would say, projected. It is at this point that the issues of politics, or the pretended issues of politics, become interwoven with and dependent upon the personal

---

[6] Cf. in this respect the observation of Tocqueville: "It cannot be denied that democratic institutions strongly tend to promote the feeling of envy in the human heart; not so much because they afford to everyone the means of rising to the same level with others as because these means perpetually disappoint the persons who employ them. Democratic institutions awaken and foster a passion for equality which they can never entirely satisfy." Alexis de Tocqueville: *Democracy in America*, ed. by Phillips Bradley (New York, 1945), I, 201.

problems of individuals. We have, at all times, two kinds of processes going on in inextricable connection with each other: *interest politics*, the clash of material aims and needs among various groups and blocs; and *status politics*, the clash of various projective rationalizations arising from status aspirations and other personal motives. In times of depression and economic discontent—and by and large in times of acute national emergency—politics is more clearly a matter of interests, although of course status considerations are still present. In times of prosperity and general well-being on the material plane, status considerations among the masses can become much more influential in our politics. The two periods in our recent history in which status politics has been particularly prominent, the present era and the 1920's, have both been periods of prosperity.

During depressions, the dominant motif in dissent takes expression in proposals for reform or in panaceas. Dissent then tends to be highly programmatic—that is, it gets itself embodied in many kinds of concrete legislative proposals. It is also future-oriented and forward-looking, in the sense that it looks to a time when the adoption of this or that program will materially alleviate or eliminate certain discontents. In prosperity, however, when status politics becomes relatively more important, there is a tendency to embody discontent not so much in legislative proposals as in grousing. For the basic aspirations that underlie status discontent are only partially conscious; and, even so far as they are conscious, it is difficult to give them a programmatic expression. It is more difficult for the old lady who belongs to the D.A.R. and who sees her ancestral home swamped by new working-class dwellings to express her animus in concrete proposals of any degree of reality than it is, say, for the jobless worker during a slump to rally to a relief program. Therefore, it is the tendency of status politics to be expressed more in vindictiveness, in sour memories, in the search for scapegoats, than in realistic proposals for positive action.[7]

Paradoxically the intense status concerns of present-day politics are shared by two types of persons who arrive at them from opposite directions. The first are found among some types of old-family, Anglo-Saxon Protestants, and the second are found among many types of immigrant families, most notably among the Germans and Irish, who are very frequently Catholic. The Anglo-Saxons are most disposed toward pseudo-conservatism when they are losing caste, the immigrants when they are gaining.[8]

Consider first the old-family Americans. These people, whose stocks were once far more unequivocally dominant in America than they are today, feel that their ancestors made and settled and fought for this country. They have a certain inherited sense of proprietorship in it. Since America has always accorded a certain special deference to old families—so many of our families are *new*—these people have considerable

---

[7] Cf. Samuel Lubell's characterization of isolationism as a vengeful memory. *The Future of American Politics* (New York, 1952), Ch. 7. See also the comments of Leo Lowenthal and Norbert Guterman on the right-wing agitator: "The agitator seems to steer clear of the area of material needs on which liberal and democratic movements concentrate; his main concern is a sphere of frustration that is usually ignored in traditional politics. The programs that concentrate on material needs seem to overlook that area of moral uncertainties and emotional frustrations that are the immediate manifestations of malaise. It may therefore be conjectured that his followers find the agitator's statements attractive not because he occasionally promises to 'maintain the American standard of living' or to provide a job for everyone, but because he intimates that he will give them the emotional satisfactions that are denied them in the contemporary social and economic set-up. He offers attitudes, not bread." *Prophets of Deceit* (New York, 1949), pp. 91–2.

[8] Every ethnic group has its own peculiar status history, and I am well aware that my remarks in the text slur over many important differences. The status history of the older immigrant groups like the Germans and the Irish is quite different from that of ethnic elements like the Italians, Poles, and Czechs, who have more recently arrived at the point at which they are bidding for wide acceptance in the pro-

claims to status by descent, which they celebrate by membership in such organizations as the D.A.R. and the S.A.R. But large numbers of them are actually losing their other claims to status. For there are among them a considerable number of the shabby genteel, of those who for one reason or another have lost their old objective positions in the life of business and politics and the professions, and who therefore cling with exceptional desperation to such remnants of their prestige as they can muster from their ancestors. These people, although very often quite well-to-do, feel that they have been pushed out of their rightful place in American life, even out of their neighborhoods. Most of them have been traditional Republicans by family inheritance, and they have felt themselves edged aside by the immigrants, the trade unions, and the urban machines in the past thirty years. When the immigrants were weak, these native elements used to indulge themselves in ethnic and religious snobberies at their expense.[9] Now the

---

fessional and white-collar classes, or at least for the middle-class standards of housing and consumption enjoyed by these classes. The case of the Irish is of special interest, because the Irish, with their long-standing prominence in municipal politics, qualified as it has been by their relative non-acceptance in many other spheres, have an unusually ambiguous status. In many ways they have gained, while in others, particularly insofar as their municipal power has recently been challenged by other groups, especially the Italians, they have lost some status and power. The election of 1928, with its religious bigotry and social snobbery, inflicted upon them a status trauma from which they have never fully recovered, for it was a symbol of the Protestant majority's rejection of their ablest leadership on grounds quite irrelevant to merit. This feeling was kept alive by the breach between Al Smith and F.D.R., followed by the rejection of Jim Farley from the New Deal succession. A study of the Germans would perhaps emphasize the effects of uneasiness over national loyalties arising from the Hitler era and the Second World War, but extending back even to the First World War.

[9] One of the noteworthy features of the current situation is that fundamentalist Protestants and fundamentalist Catholics have so commonly subordinated their old feuds (and for the first time in our history) to unite in opposition to what they usually describe as "godless" elements.

immigrant groups have developed ample means, political and economic, of self-defense, and the second and third generations have become considerably more capable of looking out for themselves. Some of the old-family Americans have turned to find new objects for their resentment among liberals, left-wingers, intellectuals, and the like—for in true pseudo-conservative fashion they relish weak victims and shrink from asserting themselves against the strong.

New-family Americans have had their own peculiar status problem. From 1881 to 1900 over 8,800,000 immigrants came here, and during the next twenty years another 14,500,000. These immigrants, together with their descendants, constitute such a large portion of the population that Margaret Mead, in a stimulating analysis of our national character, has persuasively argued that the characteristic American outlook is now a third-generation point of view.[1] In their search for new lives and new nationality, these immigrants have suffered much, and they have been rebuffed and made to feel inferior by the "native stock," commonly being excluded from the better occupations and even from what has bitterly been called "first-class citizenship." Insecurity over social status has thus been mixed with insecurity over one's very identity and sense of belonging. Achieving a better type of job or a better social status and becoming "more American" have been practically synonymous, and the passions that ordinarily attach to social position have been vastly heightened by being associated with the need to belong.[2]

The problems raised by the tasks of keeping the family to-

---

[1] Margaret Mead: *And Keep Your Powder Dry* (New York, 1942), Ch. 3.

[2] Addendum, 1965: Much of the following paragraph now seems to me to be gratuitously speculative, and I think the emphasis on authoritarianism in immigrant as opposed to native families questionable. That the pseudo-conservative mentality is characterized by a disorder in relation to authority, however, still seems to me to be a central point.

gether, disciplining children for the American race for success, trying to conform to unfamiliar standards, protecting economic and social status won at the cost of much sacrifice, holding the respect of children who grow American more rapidly than their parents, have thrown heavy burdens on the internal relationships of many new American families. Both new and old American families have been troubled by the changes of the past thirty years—the new because of their striving for middle-class respectability and American identity, the old because of their efforts to maintain an inherited social position and to realize under increasingly unfavorable social conditions imperatives of character and personal conduct deriving from nineteenth-century Yankee-Protestant-rural backgrounds. The relations between generations, being cast in no stable mold, have been disordered, and the status anxieties of parents have been inflicted upon children.[3] Often parents entertain status aspirations that they are unable to gratify, or that they can gratify only at exceptional psychic cost. Their children are expected to relieve their frustrations and redeem their lives. They become objects to be manipulated to that end. An extraordinarily high level of achievement is expected of them, and along with it a tremendous effort to conform and be respectable. From the standpoint of the children these expectations often appear in the form of an exorbitantly demanding authority that one dare not question or defy. Resistance and hostility, finding no moderate outlet in give-and-

---

[3] See Else Frenkel-Brunswik's "Parents and Childhood as Seen Through the Interviews," in Adorno: op. cit., Ch. 10. The author remarks (pp. 387–8) concerning subjects who were relatively *free* from ethnic prejudice that in their families "less obedience is expected of the children. Parents are less status-ridden and thus show less anxiety with respect to conformity and are less intolerant toward manifestations of socially unaccepted behavior. . . . Comparatively less pronounced status-concern often goes hand in hand with greater richness and liberation of emotional life. There is, on the whole, more affection, or more unconditional affection, in the families of unprejudiced subjects. There is less surrender to conventional rules."

take, have to be suppressed, and reappear in the form of an internal destructive rage. An enormous hostility to authority, which cannot be admitted to consciousness, calls forth a massive overcompensation which is manifest in the form of extravagant submissiveness to strong power. Among those found by Adorno and his colleagues to have strong ethnic prejudices and pseudo-conservative tendencies, there is a high proportion of persons who have been unable to develop the capacity to criticize justly and in moderation the failings of parents and who are profoundly intolerant of the ambiguities of thought and feeling that one is so likely to find in real-life situations. For pseudo-conservatism is among other things a disorder in relation to authority, characterized by an inability to find other modes for human relationship than those of more or less complete domination or submission. The pseudo-conservative always imagines himself to be dominated and imposed upon because he feels that he is not dominant, and knows of no other way of interpreting his position. He imagines that his own government and his own leaders are engaged in a more or less continuous conspiracy against him because he has come to think of authority only as something that aims to manipulate and deprive him. It is for this reason, among others, that he enjoys seeing outstanding generals, distinguished Secretaries of State, and prominent scholars browbeaten.

Status problems take on a special importance in American life because a very large part of the population suffers from one of the most troublesome of all status questions: unable to enjoy the simple luxury of assuming their own nationality as a natural event, they are tormented by a nagging doubt as to whether they are really and truly and fully American. Since their forebears voluntarily left one country and embraced another, they cannot, as people do elsewhere, think of nationality as something that comes with birth; for them it is a matter of *choice*, and an object of striving. This is one reason why problems of "loyalty" arouse such an emotional response in many Americans and why it is so hard in the American climate of opinion to make any clear distinction between the problem of national security and the question of personal loyalty. Of course, there is no real reason to doubt the loyalty to America of the immigrants and their descendants, or their willingness to serve the country as fully as if their ancestors had lived here for three centuries. Nonetheless, they have been thrown on the defensive by those who have in the past cast doubts upon the fullness of their Americanism. Possibly they are also, consciously or unconsciously, troubled by the thought that since their forebears have already abandoned one country, one allegiance, their own national allegiance might be considered fickle. For this I believe there is some evidence in our national practices. What other country finds it so necessary to create institutional rituals for the sole purpose of guaranteeing to its people the genuineness of their nationality? Does the Frenchman or the Englishman or the Italian find it necessary to speak of himself as "one hundred per cent" English, French, or Italian? Do they find it necessary to have their equivalents of "I Am an American Day"? When they disagree with one another over national policies, do they find it necessary to call one another un-English, un-French, or un-Italian? No doubt they too are troubled by subversive activities and espionage, but are their countermeasures taken under the name of committees on un-English, un-French, or un-Italian activities?

The primary value that patriotic societies and anti-subversive ideologies have for their exponents can be found here. They provide additional and continued reassurance both to those who are of old-American ancestry and have other status grievances and to those who are of recent American ancestry and therefore feel in need of reassurance about their nation-

59

ality. Veterans' organizations offer the same satisfaction—
what better evidence can there be of the genuineness of
nationality and *earned* citizenship than military service under
the flag of one's country? Of course, such organizations, once
they exist, are liable to exploitation by vested interests that
can use them as pressure groups on behalf of particular measures and interests. (Veterans' groups, since they lobby for the
concrete interests of veterans, have a double role in this respect.) But the cement that holds them together is the status
motivation and the desire for an identity.

Sociological studies have shown that there is a close relation
between social mobility and ethnic prejudice. Persons moving
downward in the social scale, and even upward under many
circumstances, tend to show greater prejudice against such
ethnic minorities as the Jews and Negroes than commonly
prevails in the social strata they have left or are entering.[4]
While the existing studies in this field have been focused upon
prejudice rather than the kind of hyper-patriotism and hyper-
conformism that I am most concerned with, I believe that the
typical prejudiced person and the typical pseudo-conservative
dissenter are usually the same person, that the mechanisms at
work in both complexes are quite the same,[5] and that it is
merely the expediencies and the strategy of the situation
today that cause groups that once stressed racial discrimina-
tion to find other scapegoats. Both the displaced old-American type and the new ethnic elements that are so desperately
eager for reassurance of their fundamental Americanism can
conveniently converge upon liberals, critics, and nonconform-

---

[4] Cf. Joseph Greenblum and Leonard I. Pearlin: "Vertical Mobility
and Prejudice," in Reinhard Bendix and Seymour M. Lipset (eds.):
Class, Status and Power (Glencoe, Ill., 1953), pp. 480–91; Bruno Bet-
telheim and Morris Janowitz: "Ethnic Tolerance: A Function of
Personal and Social Control," *American Journal of Sociology*, IV
(1949), 137–45.

[5] The similarity is also posited by Adorno: op. cit., pp. 152 ff., and
by others (see the studies cited by him, p. 152).

ists of various sorts, as well as Communists and suspected Communists. To proclaim themselves vigilant in the pursuit of those who are even so much as accused of "disloyalty" to the United States is a way not only of reasserting but of advertising their own loyalty—and one of the chief character-istics of American super-patriotism is its constant inner urge toward self-advertisement. One notable quality in this new wave of conformism is that its advocates are much happier to have as their objects of hatred the Anglo-Saxon, Eastern, Ivy League intellectual gentlemen than they are to have such bedraggled souls as, say, Julius and Ethel Rosenberg. The reason, I believe, is that in the minds of the status-driven it is no special virtue to be more American than the Rosenbergs, but it is really something to be more American than Dean Acheson or John Foster Dulles—or Franklin Delano Roose-velt.[6] The status aspirations of some of the ethnic groups are actually higher than they were twenty years ago—which suggests one reason (there are others) why, in the ideology of the authoritarian right wing, anti-Semitism and other blatant forms of prejudice have recently been soft-pedaled. Anti-Semitism, it has been said, is the poor man's snobbery. We Americans are always trying to raise the standard of living, and the same principle now seems to apply to standards of hating. So during the past fifteen years or so, the authoritar-ians have moved on from anti-Negroism and anti-Semitism to anti-Achesonianism, anti-intellectualism, anti-nonconformism, and other variants of the same idea, much in the same way as the average American, if he can manage it, will move on from a Ford to a Buick.

---

[6] I refer to such men to make the point that this animosity extends to those who are guilty of no wrongdoing. Of course, a person like Alger Hiss, who has been guilty, suits much better. Hiss is the hostage the pseudo-conservatives hold from the New Deal generation. He is a heaven-sent gift. If he did not exist, the pseudo-conservatives would not have been able to invent him.

Such status strivings may help us to understand some of the otherwise unintelligible figments of the pseudo-conservative ideology—the incredibly bitter feeling against the United Nations, for instance. Is it not understandable that such a feeling might be, paradoxically, shared at one and the same time by an old Yankee-Protestant American, who feels that his social position is not what it ought to be and that these foreigners are crowding in on his country and diluting its sovereignty just as "foreigners" have crowded into his neighborhood, and by a second- or third-generation immigrant who has been trying so hard to de-Europeanize himself, to get Europe out of his personal heritage, and who finds his own government mocking him by its complicity in these Old World schemes?

Similarly, is it not status aspiration that in good part spurs the pseudo-conservative on toward his demand for conformity in a wide variety of spheres of life? Conformity is a way of guaranteeing and manifesting respectability among those who are not sure that they are respectable enough. The nonconformity of others appears to such persons as a frivolous challenge to the whole order of things they are trying so hard to become part of. Naturally it is resented, and the demand for conformity in public becomes at once an expression of such resentment and a means of displaying one's own soundness. This habit has a tendency to spread from politics into intellectual and social spheres, where it can be made to challenge almost anyone whose pattern of life is different and who is imagined to enjoy a superior social position—notably, as one agitator put it, those in the "parlors of the sophisticated, the intellectuals, the so-called academic minds."

Why has this tide of pseudo-conservative dissent risen to such heights in our time? To a considerable degree, we must remember, it is a response, however unrealistic, to realities. We do live in a disordered world, threatened by a great power and a powerful ideology, a world of enormous potential violence, which has already shown us the ugliest capacities of the human spirit. In our own country there has indeed been espionage, and laxity over security has in fact allowed some spies to reach high places. There is just enough reality at most points along the line to give a touch of credibility to the melodramatics of the pseudo-conservative imagination.

However, a number of developments in our recent history make this pseudo-conservative uprising more intelligible. For two hundred years and more, various conditions of American development—the process of settling the continent, the continuous establishment of new status patterns in new areas, the arrival of continuous waves of new immigrants, each pushing the preceding waves upward in the ethnic hierarchy —made it possible to satisfy a remarkably large part of the extravagant status aspirations that were aroused. There was a sort of automatic built-in status elevator in the American social edifice. Today that elevator no longer operates automatically, or at least no longer operates in the same way.[7]

Second, the growth of the mass media of communication and their use in politics have brought politics closer to the people than ever before and have made politics a form of entertainment in which the spectators feel themselves involved. Thus it has become, more than ever before, an arena into which private emotions and personal problems can be readily projected. Mass communications have made it possible to keep the mass man in an almost constant state of political mobilization.

Third, the long tenure in power of the liberal elements to which the pseudo-conservatives are most opposed and the wide variety of changes that have been introduced into our

---

[7] Addendum, 1965: The substantive point may still be a good one, but it occurs to me that this paragraph might be taken to mean that social mobility in the United States has been decreasing; the evidence points to the contrary.

social, economic, and administrative life have intensified the sense of powerlessness and victimization among the opponents of these changes and have widened the area of social issues over which they feel discontent. There has been, among other things, the emergence of a wholly new struggle: the conflict between businessmen of certain types and the New Deal bureaucracy, which has spilled over into a resentment of intellectuals and experts.

Finally, unlike our previous postwar periods, ours has been a period of continued crisis, from which the future promises no relief. In no foreign war of our history did we fight so long or make such sacrifices as in the Second World War. When it was over, instead of being able to resume our peacetime preoccupations, we were very promptly confronted with another war. It is hard for a certain type of American, who does not think much about the world outside and does not want to have to do so, to understand why we must become involved in such an unremitting struggle. It will be the fate of those in power for a long time to come to have to conduct the delicate diplomacy of the cold peace without the sympathy or understanding of a large part of their own people. From bitter experience, Eisenhower and Dulles are learning today what Truman and Acheson learned yesterday.

These considerations suggest that the pseudo-conservative political style, while it may already have passed the peak of its influence, is one of the long waves of twentieth-century American history and not a momentary mood. I do not share the widespread foreboding among liberals that this form of dissent will grow until it overwhelms our liberties altogether and plunges us into a totalitarian nightmare. Indeed, the idea that it is purely and simply fascist or totalitarian, as we have known these things in recent European history, is to my mind a false conception, based upon the failure to read American developments in terms of our peculiar American constellation of political realities. (It reminds me of the people who, because they found several close parallels between the N.R.A. and Mussolini's corporate state, were once deeply troubled at the thought that the N.R.A. was the beginning of American fascism.) However, in a populistic culture like ours, which seems to lack a responsible elite with political and moral autonomy, and in which it is possible to exploit the wildest currents of public sentiment for private purposes, it is at least conceivable that a highly organized, vocal, active, and well-financed minority could create a political climate in which the rational pursuit of our well-being and safety would become impossible.

PSEUDO-CONSERVATISM
REVISITED
—1965

I

THE Goldwater campaign showed that the ultra-right has grown considerably in organization and influence, if not in numbers, over the past ten years, and the effort to understand it has lost none of its urgency. Although a decade of experience and inquiry, climaxed by the Goldwater movement, which is itself almost an ideal test case for the nature of pseudo-conservatism, has confirmed some of the suggestions advanced in "The Pseudo-Conservative Revolt" and similar ventures in explanation, these ideas appear at other points to need revision.

There are four general matters on which I believe my own essay now demands qualification or correction. The first and most complex has to do with the place of status anxieties and status resentments in the right-wing ferment of the McCarthyist era. At the time I wrote, the status factor had been largely ignored and therefore needed emphasizing, but I have no doubt that an essay devoted rather single-mindedly to this one element in a complex situation inevitably had the effect of giving it disproportionate weight. Also, the term "status" was used in an uncommonly wide sense, and needed more definition than it got. But this is not to be taken as a retraction of what I had to say about the importance of status considerations; it is a preface to some refinements of my original statement. The distinction made in the earlier essay between status politics and interest politics seems to me to be of fundamental significance, and to have a general usability in understanding our political history that goes far beyond the issues of the 1950's which it was invoked to explain.

The other points are more easily dealt with. I think that in portraying the pseudo-conservative type, my essay overstressed clinical findings by failing to supplement them sufficiently with a more conventional historical analysis of the rhetoric, arguments, and tactics of the pseudo-conservatives. I hope I have made amends in the next essay, which deals with the Goldwater campaign. Again, I believe now that I overstated the role of certain ethnic minorities in the right wing. To be sure, these were present, as additional data have since shown; but they have turned out to be more a receding than an advancing element, and it is probably the native American side of the right wing that demands our primary attention. Finally—and this point is related to the preceding one—I made only passing reference in a footnote to the role of fundamentalism, and it is plain that this is one of the salient elements in the right wing, an element whose importance has become increasingly evident in the past decade.

The last two points can best be discussed in connection with the significant changes that have recently taken place in the right wing, which, despite some continuity in ideas and in leadership, render any static account of it somewhat misleading. In this respect, my emphasis on ethnic factors in the pseudo-conservatism of 1954 now seems to me analogous to the strategy of generals who are prepared to fight the last war. What was true about it, I believe, is that the extreme right did draw somewhat on the older isolationism, in which the attitudes of German and Irish Americans were important, and also, to a degree, upon the feelings of Americans linked to Eastern European countries under Soviet domination.[1] Our role in the Second World War temporarily stirred the feeling of national dislocation and the Anglophobia of these groups, feelings which were duly exploited by McCarthy. But the radical rightism of the 1960's is predominantly a movement of white Anglo-Saxon Protestant Republicans, with only a fringe of ethnic support. German Anglophobia now appears to be of less consequence than it once was and the election of an Irish Catholic President in 1960 may have helped to quiet the sense of incomplete cultural acceptance that has troubled the American Irish since 1928. In retrospect, it seems that even by 1954 ethnic factors in American pseudo-conservatism were waning, not rising.

Over the past three decades, right-wing movements have appealed to segments of the public which, though overlapping, have been significantly different. In the 1930's the chief vehicle of right-wing discontent was Father Coughlin's Social Justice movement, a depression phenomenon drawing the bulk of its support from those who suffered most from bad times—the working class and the unemployed, farmers and some of the lower middle class. Its tone was more pseudo-radical than psuedo-conservative. It played on old Populist themes, attacked international bankers, demanded free silver and other changes in the money and credit system, and resorted to an anti-Semitic rhetoric far more virulent than anything the Populists would have dreamed of. It was stronger in rural areas and small towns than in cities, and

---

[1] For some confirmation, see Seymour M. Lipset: "Three Decades of the Radical Right," in Daniel Bell (ed.): *The Radical Right* (New York, 1963), pp. 336–8. In what follows I am much indebted to Lipset's analysis of survey data.

much stronger among Catholics, particularly Irish Catholics, than among Protestants. Its isolationist and Anglophobic note drew support from Germans, both Catholic and Lutheran. It was strongest in two areas: the West Central states, where its appeal was both ethnic and agrarian, and in New England, where it attracted Irish Catholics. That Coughlin had little strength in the South is perhaps an interesting token of surviving religious prejudice; also, up to the time of Huey Long's assassination, the South had its own native and more appealing messiah.

Coughlinism died with the war and the subsequent prosperity. The new right wing of the McCarthy era showed both continuity and discontinuity with Coughlinism. McCarthy, as an Irish Catholic, picked up much of the ethnic and religious following that had once been Coughlin's, as well as some support from ethnic groups drawn from the "captive" nations of Eastern Europe. But as a phenomenon of prosperity McCarthyism was almost entirely devoid of economic content and had no economic program. Since McCarthy appealed both to Republicans who resented their party's continuing domination by its eastern wing and to those in both parties who were swept up by the anti-Communist passions of the cold war, his following was much greater than Coughlin's. On the whole, he received a measure of support disproportionate to their numbers in the general population from Catholics and from the ill-educated, but also from Republicans, Irish Americans, the lower classes, and the aged. Along with economic issues, McCarthy abruptly dropped the old right-wing appeal to anti-Semitism.

Part of McCarthy's strength lay in his ability to combine a mass appeal with a special appeal to a limited stratum of the upper classes. As compared with Coughlin, whose following had been almost entirely a low-status public, McCarthy was able to win considerable support from the middle and upper ranks of society, mobilizing Republicans who had never accepted the changes brought by the New Deal and whose rage at the long exclusion of the party from presidential power was reaching a peak. There is evidence also that McCarthy had a special appeal to the postwar newly rich. Most prophetic too of the future of the right wing was his strong appeal for fundamentalist-oriented Protestants, who now took a significant place along with their Catholic counterparts.[2]

This is strikingly illustrated by the changing views of Baptists. Probably because of Coughlin's priestly vocation, Baptists had ranked low among the evangelical denominations that supported him, but McCarthy, though a lay Catholic, commanded more support from them than from any other Protestant denomination. It is in the McCarthyist era that the anti-Communist issue becomes so salient for members of this evangelical denomination (and presumably others) that they abandon their traditional anti-Catholic animus in order to take part in right-wing ecumenical anti-Communism.

The right wing of the 1960's, whose leadership has fallen to the John Birch Society, continues to move up the socioeconomic ladder. With its strong commitment to ultra-

---

[2] McCarthyism, it must also be remembered, was a phenomenon of much broader significance than the far right itself. During 1953 and 1954, when McCarthy was at the peak of his influence, there was no poll in which less than 34 per cent of the public was found approving him, and at one point, January 1954, the figure rose to 50 per cent. No sensible observer has ever imagined that extreme right-wing ideas command the loyalty of one third, much less one half, of the American public. In July 1964, for example, at a time of great right-wing ferment, a major national poll found that only 4 per cent of the public would be influenced to vote for a presidential candidate because he was endorsed by the John Birch Society, as against 47 per cent who would be more disposed to vote against him; the remainder would have been unaffected or expressed no opinion. *The New York Times*, July 31, 1964. Characteristically, from about 5 to 10 per cent of the public will express approval of the Birch Society (see Bell (ed.): op. cit., pp. 201–2, 349–63), though right-wing positions often receive the endorsement of as much as 15 per cent of the public.

conservative economic ideas, the Birch Society makes little appeal to the economically deprived. It is primarily an organization of well-educated, middle- and upper-status Republicans who are deviants among the educated strata in several ways—including a greater disposition to ethnic prejudice than the population as a whole.[3] As an elite corps, the Birch Society is, of course, much better educated than the members of other right-wing groups. It has also brought out an interesting polarity within the educated upper classes of American society, which is related to party affiliation. Among Democrats, increasing education is correlated with increasing disapproval of the Birch Society; but among Republicans, increasing education is correlated with increasing support for the society.

Although the Birch Society as a whole draws its most vital public support from affluent Republican Protestants, it has some special appeal, when party affiliation is held constant, to Catholics. Its sociological profile is that of a group enjoying a strong social position, mainly well-to-do and educated beyond the average, but manifesting a degree of prejudice and social tension not customarily found among the affluent and the educated.

Although it is doubtful that extreme rightists in the 1960's are any more numerous than they were in the McCarthyist period, the right wing has learned the secret of organization, which largely accounts for its greater successes. Coughlinism and McCarthyism were largely the creation of astute and voluminous publicity on the radio and in the press, which was not matched by their organizational efforts. Coughlin's organ-

---

[3] Birchite prejudice, it should be said, is directed more significantly against Negroes, Mexicans, and Orientals than it is against Jews. Birchites are a shade *less* prejudiced against Catholics than anti-Birchites. (Lipset: op. cit., p. 361.) Though all polls agree on the relatively high level of formal education among Birchites, they do not provide information about the kind of colleges they attended, and it would be interesting to know to what extent these were the great cosmopolitan universities and colleges or denominational institutions.

ized groups were of relatively little consequence, and Mc-Carthy could barely organize his own files, much less a national movement. The John Birch Society, with only a fraction of McCarthy's support among the public, has won its successes through tightly organized and militant cadres of workers, operating in a manner resembling that of Communist cells, and linked to the Republican party not through publicity but by active work in district, precinct, and community organizations where ideological affinities can be translated into power.

At the grass roots the extreme right now draws its primary support from two basic (and at points overlapping) social types: first, the affluent (perhaps newly affluent) suburban educated middle class, largely outside the Northeast, which responds to ultra-conservative economic issues as well as to militant nationalism and anti-communism, and which seeks to win a place in the political structure proportionate to the secure place it has won in society; and second, a large lower middle class, somewhat less educated and less charmed than the first group by old-fashioned economic liberalism but even more fearful of communism, which it perceives rather abstractly in the light of a strong evangelical-fundamentalist cast of thought.

I I

THE RE-EMERGENCE of fundamentalism in politics, invigorated by the conditions of the cold war and the stimulus of the affluent society, is a notable development of the past fifteen years. Of necessity I use the term "fundamentalism" in a rather extended way to describe a religious style rather than firm doctrinal commitments, since no one knows how many evangelical right-wingers adhere to a literal view of Scripture and other fundamentalist tenets. Two other qualifications should be made: first, there are large numbers of fundamentalists who interpret their religious commitment as a reason to withdraw from worldly politics, in which they see no more hope than they do in the other things of this world; and second, many fundamentalists have inherited generous views on domestic economic reforms which they do not easily give up. But on certain issues of cultural politics fundamentalists have always been rigid, and when such issues become more salient the fundamentalists become more responsive to the blandishments of pseudo-conservative prophets. Moreover, the Manichean and apocalyptic style of thought prevalent in the fundamentalist tradition can easily be carried over into secular affairs and transmuted into a curiously crude and almost superstitious form of anti-communism.

Not only is the entire right-wing movement infused at the mass level with the fundamentalist style of mind, but the place in its ranks of fundamentalist preachers, ex-preachers, and sons of preachers is so prominent as to underline the mutual congeniality of thought. Leading right-wing spokesmen have brought into politics the methods and the style of the evangelical revivalists, just as many preachers have discovered that they can arouse more fervor and raise more cash by politicizing their message than they can by appealing solely to the religious sensibilities of their audiences.[4]

---

[4] This is not the first period in our history in which fundamentalist leaders, anguished over the general repudiation of their beliefs and values, lent their energies to political reaction. During the 1920's they gave heavy support to the Ku Klux Klan, particularly in the South. During the years 1922 to 1928, 26 of 39 anti-Catholic lecturers employed by the Klan were Protestant ministers of the fundamentalist type, and 16 of such ministers were Klan officials. Klansmen were regularly entertained in the homes of such ministers, and churches were used for Klan meetings. The two chief leaders of the new Klan had fundamentalist backgrounds—its initiator, Colonel William J. Simmons, had been a religious camp meeting exhorter, and its most successful promoter, Edward Y. Clarke, went into the fundamentalist

73

Under the aegis of right-wing politics, rigid Protestants of a type once intensely anti-Catholic can now unite with Catholics of similar militancy in a grand ecumenical zeal against communism and in what they take to be a joint defense of Christian civilization. The malevolent energy formerly used in the harassment of Catholics can now be more profitably spent in the search for Communists, or even in attacks on the alleged subversiveness of liberal Protestant denominations. The Manichean conception of life as a struggle between absolute good and absolute evil and the idea of an irresistible Armageddon have been thinly secularized and transferred to the cold war. The conflict between Christianity and communism is conceived as a war to the death, and Christianity is set forth as the only adequate counterpoise to the communist credo.

Fundamentalist leaders play a part in right-wing organizations far out of proportion to the strength of fundamentalism in the population at large. Among them are Robert H. Welch, Jr., the founder of the John Birch Society; Dr. Fred C. Schwarz, the head of the Christian Anti-Communism Crusade; and Reverend Billy Hargis, of the Christian Crusade, which flourishes in the Southwest.[5]

---

movement after giving up his efforts in the Klan. In return, the Klan often fought for passage of the anti-evolution laws. On the relation between the preachers of certain denominations and Klan activities, see Michael Williams: *The Shadow of the Pope* (New York, 1932), pp. 317 ff. On the limitations of this connection and Protestant opposition to the Klan, see Robert Moats Miller: "A Note on the Relation Between the Protestant Churches and the Revival of the Klan," *Journal of Southern History*, XXII (August 1956), 355–68.

[5] Welch, who was raised as a pious fundamentalist Baptist in North Carolina, chose to name his organization after a young fundamentalist Baptist preacher from Macon, Georgia, who was killed by the Chinese Communists. As a prosperous candy manufacturer, once very active in the National Association of Manufacturers, Welch embodies the union of fundamentalist inspiration and small-business parochial conservatism that animates the extreme right. Schwarz is the son of an Australian pentecostal preacher; he had considerable experiences in

A large part of the rise of fundamentalist ultra-conservatism may be linked with the astonishing growth of the Southern Baptist Church, which increased from 2,300,000 members in 1936 to 10,000,000 in 1962. A comparable growth has also been enjoyed by the right-wing Churches of Christ. The increase in these groups has far outstripped that of more moderate Protestant denominations in the same period.[6] Such church groups have created a vast religious public, once poor and depression-ridden but now to a large degree moderately prosperous, whose members sometimes combine the economic prejudices of the newly well-to-do with the moral prejudices of the revolt against modernity.

We know more, of course, about the role of fundamentalist leaders in right-wing groups than we do about fundamentalism among the mass following. The presence of two kinds of subcultures in the Christian Anti-Communism Crusade is suggested in a study by Raymond E. Wolfinger and his associates of a sample of its members in Oakland, California. Their findings point to a bifurcation between a relatively affluent, edu-

---

his native country as a lay preacher before coming to the United States on the invitation of some anti-modernist preachers. He began his American career with an evangelical-style tour. Preachers and ex-preachers figure prominently in the "faculty" he has recruited for his anti-Communist "schools." Hargis moved on from evangelism to right-wing politics in much the same way as such predecessors as Gerald L. K. Smith, Gerald Winrod, and J. Frank Norris. He is the product of Ozark Bible College in Arkansas and of the Disciples of Christ, though his ministry is now independent. Another successful southwestern leader is Dr. George Benson, a former Church of Christ missionary in China, now president of the church-affiliated Harding College in Searcy, Arkansas. This organization still holds forth against Darwin, but its main claim to fame is its role as the source of right-wing political radio broadcasts and films, on the strength of which it has attracted munificent contributions from businessmen. In the East, the Reverend Carl McIntire of the Bible Presbyterian Church in Collingswood, New Jersey, reaches large audiences with his radio broadcasts. A former disciple of the highbrow fundamentalist H. Gresham Machen, McIntire set up on his own after being expelled from the General Assembly of the Presbyterian Church, and he has been vociferous in fighting modernist Christianity and the ecumenical

cated, and "sophisticated" wing, concerned most intensely with the economic content of ultra-conservatism, and a more deeply religious wing, leaning toward fundamentalism, primarily concerned with religious and moral issues. Among 308 people who consented to be interviewed, persons belonging to fundamentalist churches constituted 20 per cent (they would be a larger proportion in southern California). Those who reported that they came to the "schools" of this right-wing movement because of church influence differed from the whole sample in important respects: they were more fundamentalist, more active as church members, less affluent, less educated, and less active in politics. They were more favorably disposed than other respondents to such reforms as medicare and federal aid to education, and were more willing to accept the legitimacy of trade unions. Their more intense Christian convictions were perhaps also reflected in their taking a less sympathetic view than other members of the South's position on racial integration. But they were more anti-evolution, more disturbed about the threat of communism to theistic belief, and more anxious about the alleged internal threat of communism to the nation.[7] An impressionistic study by

---

movement. Finally, there is the Church League of America, founded in 1937 to fight liberal Protestantism but now a right-wing organization managed by Edgar Bundy, a minister ordained in the Southern Baptist Convention.

[6] Kenneth K. Bailey: *Southern White Protestantism in the Twentieth Century* (New York, 1964), p. 152. See Chs. 3 and 4 of this work on the fundamentalist background in the South. On internal tensions that have come with this fantastic growth, see Samuel S. Hill, Jr.: "The Southern Baptists," *Christian Century*, LXXX (January 1963), 39–42.

[7] Wolfinger et al.: "America's Radical Right: Politics and Ideology," in David E. Apter (ed.): *Ideology and Discontent* (Glencoe, Ill., 1964), pp. 281–3. This study does not purport to be a representative sample. Among other difficulties was the hostility of a large proportion of members to student interviewers. Their refusal to be interviewed or to answer mailed questionnaires suggest that the Wolfinger group's respondents represent the less extreme members of the movement. The Crusaders were drawn, out of proportion to their

participant observers of the membership of the same movement in a small midwestern industrial city found the members predominantly Baptist-fundamentalist, educated, with few exceptions, only to the high-school level, aggressively anti-intellectual, anxious about the preservation of the old-fashioned moral virtues, and rather disposed to see the world in the paranoid style.[8]

III

ONE WAY of adding to our understanding of the politics of the 1950's and 1960's is to compare it with that of the 1920's. During the 1920's our political life was profoundly affected, and at times dominated, by certain cultural struggles, which were interrupted and deflected by the depression, the New Deal, and the war, but which have in a measure reasserted themselves in the different setting of the postwar decades. Both the 1920's and the postwar years, as periods of relative prosperity, saw some diminution in the force of economic issues and an upsurge in the issues of status politics—issues of religion, morals, personal style, and culture. It is significant that the election campaign which, of all the campaigns in our history, was most completely dominated by status politics was the Smith-Hoover campaign of 1928, conducted when the ill-fated boom of the twenties was nearing its peak. In 1964,

---

numbers in the population, from professional and technical workers and business managers, from income brackets over $10,000, and from those who had graduated from or attended college. Their average age was also somewhat higher than that of the general population of the Bay area. Their profile bears a fairly close resemblance to those approving the Birch Society in a national sample. See Lipset: op. cit., p. 350.

[8] Mark Chesler and Richard Schmuck: "Participant Observation in a Super-Patriot Discussion Group," *Journal of Social Issues,* XIX (April 1963), 18–30.

again under prosperous conditions, the issues of status politics once more played an unusually significant part.

During the 1920's small-town and rural Protestants were waging a vigorous defense of their cultural values against their rapidly gaining foes—the advancing Catholics and minority ethnic groups on one side and the modernists in religion and secularists in intellectual culture on the other. The Ku Klux Klan, Prohibitionism, the campaign against evolution in the schools, anti-Catholicism and the whispering campaign against Al Smith were all aspects of this struggle. On one count, immigration restriction, the old guard scored an important and permanent victory, and on another, Prohibition, they scored a gratifying if temporary success. But on the others they continued to lose ground. They substantially lost the fight against teaching evolution in the public schools, which exposed them to humiliating ridicule throughout the world. Lost, too, was the fight against modern relaxation in manners, morals, and censorship. Again the effort to contain the influence of immigrants in politics was lost within the Democratic party. The rural Protestant Democrats fought in 1924 to keep their party free of urban ethnic domination, and the two factions nearly tore the Democratic party apart at its 1924 convention. By 1928 the enemy was in control and Smith was nominated. He paid a heavy price for his religion and his defiance of establishment manners and morals, but he did succeed, partly by mobilizing the ethnic Catholic vote, in rehabilitating his party and raising it from the desperate condition it had reached in the two previous elections. The Democratic party became the coalition party of the new urban polyglot America. What Smith had begun, Roosevelt completed; F.D.R.'s consolidation of the ethnic and working-class elements in the country into an effective political force was almost as important as his economic reforms.

The problems of the depression and the Second World

War somewhat eclipsed these cultural antagonisms, though they were often visible beneath the surface. Fundamentalist-evangelical America was, in fact, so long divided or quiescent as a political force that many intellectuals have forgotten that it still exists. Nor has it surrendered its commitment to Prohibitionism or its dislike of evolution in popular education.[9] Even as recently as 1959, according to a Gallup poll, 34 per cent of all Protestants favored national Prohibition. Three-fifths of all Protestant farmers and two-fifths of all Protestants living in towns of less than 10,000 population took this view.[1] Again, only a few years earlier, another survey showed the effects of a resolute if quiet effort being made to protect the young against Darwinism and secularism. In a poll of adolescents based on an unusually large sample, only 35 per cent responded by checking "Yes" alongside the statement: "Man was evolved from lower forms of animals." As many as 40 per cent marked "No," and 24 per cent "Don't know."[2]

Now the point of all this is not to say that the old cultural issues of the 1920's are important manifest issues under present conditions, but rather that ascetic Protestantism remains a significant undercurrent in contemporary America, and that its followers have found newfangled ways of re-affirming some of their convictions. They cannot bring back Prohibition or keep evolution entirely out of the schools. They have been unable even to defend school prayer or prevent *Life* magazine from featuring the topless bathing suit. But they can recriminate against and punish the new America that outrages them, and they have found powerful leaders to

---

[9] I have tried to account for the background of the revolt against modernity in *Anti-intellectualism in American Life* (New York, 1963), esp. Ch. 5.

[1] Seymour M. Lipset: "Religion and Politics in the American Past and Present," in Robert Lee and Martin Marty (eds.): *Religion and Social Conflict* (New York, 1964), pp. 114–15.

[2] H. H. Remmers and D. H. Radler: *The American Teenager* (Indianapolis, 1957).

79

echo their views.[3] As the old fight against immigration has waned in significance, the Negro "revolution" has frightened many of them, and has given a new focus to ethnic conflict. The participants in this revolt against modernity are no longer rubes and hicks, and they have gained something both in sophistication and in cohesiveness through modern urbanization. They too live in the cities and the suburbs, at closer and more irritating range to the things that disturb them, but also closer to each other, and more susceptible to organization.

Above all, they have found a fighting issue that helps them to surmount their previous isolation, an issue on which at last they have common ground with all America: they are implacably and consumingly anti-Communist, and in the grand ecumenicism of their anti-Communist passion they welcome all allies. They are particularly happy to have made terms with the Catholics and to accept members of minority ethnic groups as comrades-in-arms. That the Whore of Babylon now sits in Moscow, not Rome, is to their incalculable advantage, for they have been able to turn a powerful domestic foe, the Church, into an ally, and in its former place they have installed the impotent American Communist. Nor does it trouble them that genuine Communists are all but impossible to find. Liberals, pacifists, beatniks, agitators for racial justice, radicals of other persuasions—what Robert Welch calls "comsymps"—will do as well.

People who share this outlook have a disposition to interpret issues of secular politics as though they were solely moral and spiritual struggles. They are less concerned with the battle against communism in the world theater than they are with the alleged damage it does to politics and morals at home. The cold war serves as a constant source of recriminations about our moral and material failure, but as an objective

---

[3] For example, see below, pp. 116–24.

struggle in the arena of world politics it is less challenging to them than it is as a kind of spiritual wrestling match with the minions of absolute evil, who, as is so often the case with Satanic powers, exercise an irresistible attractiveness. Those who look at the world in this way see their fundamental battle as one to be conducted against other Americans at home, and they respond eagerly to the notion, so pervasive in the right wing, that the worst enemy of American liberties is to be found in Washington. Moreover, whereas in the past only an occasional wealthy crank was interested in subsidizing attacks on Catholicism, the anti-Communist crusade brings lavish outpourings from right-wing foundations and from some of the nation's large business firms.

Though many Americans with fundamentalist leanings have traditionally been sympathetic to economic and social reforms, there is one aspect of right-wing thought that invariably attracts them—the moralistic quality of its economic ideas. Christian economic moralism, to be sure, has often buttressed benevolence and inspired social reform. But it has another side: insofar as economic life is regarded as a sphere for the fulfillment of the ascetic Protestant virtues, Christian moralism has worked for right-wing discontent. One strain in Protestant thinking has always looked to economic life not just for its efficacy in producing goods and services but as a vast apparatus of moral discipline, of rewards for virtue and industry and punishments for vice and indolence. In the past, vocational life was supposed to inculcate prudence, economy, and diligence—and many writers seem to have felt that economic discipline would be more effective in this task than sermons and exhortations. The vocational life was a moral testing ground. Today these assumptions have been flouted. The modern economy, based on advertising, lavish consumption, installment buying, safeguards to social security, relief to the indigent, government fiscal manipulation, and unbalanced

81

budgets, seems reckless and immoral, even when it happens to work. In the intellectual synthesis of contemporary ultra-conservatism, the impulses of Protestant asceticism can thus be drawn upon to support business self-interest and the beautiful mathematical models of neo-classical economists.

I V

WE CAN now return to our original interest: to what extent are the newly affluent, the fundamentalist, and the other constituent elements of the modern American right animated by status resentments and anxieties? This question does not seem to have the same urgency it had ten years ago, because the point which the various authors of *The Radical Right* then sought to make has been widely accepted. At that time we were all struck by a salient fact: the literature of the American right was a literature not of those who felt themselves to be in possession but of those who felt dispossessed—a literature of resentment, profoundly anti-establishment in its impulses.[4] We were all struck by the flimsiness of its pretensions to conservatism, and by its profound hostility to the culture and institutions by which it was surrounded.

If the essays in *The Radical Right* dwelled on status resentments, it was not because the authors thought they had found a final, single explanation of the right-wing line of thought, but because we had come upon a hitherto neglected and unexplained side of the movement. Our ideas were offered as an

---

[4] One is struck also by the disparity between the actual social position of these segments of the population and the intensity of their discontent. As Daniel Bell observes, they come from disparate groups many of which are doing very well. "In identifying 'the dispossessed,' it is somewhat misleading to seek their economic location, since it is not economic interest alone that accounts for their anxieties." Bell (ed.): op. cit., p. 19.

addition to the store of what was already known about the right wing, not as an attempt to displace the undeniable structural and historical setting in which the right wing arose. We were, in short, not trying to deny the obvious, but to go beyond it.

Our emphasis, then, on certain social and psychological forces at work in American society was not intended to deny the plurality of circumstances that gave birth to the right-wing resurgence—the shock of the Korean War, the failures of our foreign policy, the frustrations of Republicans too long defeated in presidential politics, the traditional irritations of big money, the continued high taxes, the impact of inflation, revelations of Communist espionage and of political corruption, the long-standing pent-up resentment against the New Deal and the social reforms it had established, the dislike of the type of national leadership that it had installed. We were trying to bring to the surface the additional sociological and psychological forces that helped all these circumstances come to a center and find a rhetorical form, and that gave to their anti-establishment animus its particular edge. We were impressed by the way in which the processes of prosperity yield their own kind of discontent, which, if not so widely shared as that of hard times, is nonetheless as bitter.

The emphasis given to status resentments and anxieties in the essays in *The Radical Right* was based partly on inferences from poll data about the socio-economic status and the education of McCarthyists, partly from impressionistic observation of contemporary social changes, and partly from the rhetoric of McCarthyism and the social objects against which its grievances were directed. What seemed important was not only the wrongs the McCarthyist right-wingers thought had been committed but who they thought had committed them; and repeated denunciations of "striped-pants diplomats," Ivy League graduates, high-ranking generals, college presidents, intellectuals, the Eastern upper classes, Harvard professors, and members of Phi Beta Kappa seemed to be serving psychological purposes which had little to do with arriving at a realistic historical account of the nation's difficulties and failures.[5] As McCarthy put it in his famous speech at Wheeling, the nation had been sold out by "those who have had all the benefits that the wealthiest nation on earth has to offer—the finest homes, the finest college education, and the finest jobs in Government. . . . The bright young men who are born with silver spoons in their mouths are the ones who have been worst."[6]

This seemed to voice certain status resentments, but it was hard to gauge them quantitatively or to measure their place among the many forces that were at work. To my knowledge only one study has been made to try to define felt status grievances in such a way as to put the notion to the test, and it reports a modest confirmation of the hypothesis of *The Radical Right*.[7] Other empirical studies have stressed quite correctly the large number of variables that have gone into the making of the right wing, but have not effectively argued that status resentments should be excluded from them.[8]

---

[5] See Immanuel Wallerstein: "McCarthyism and the Conservative," unpublished M.A. essay, Columbia University (1954), pp. 46 ff.

[6] *Congressional Record*, 81st Cong., 2nd. sess. (February 20, 1950), p. 1954.

[7] Robert Sokol: "Status Inconsistency," unpublished doctoral dissertation, Columbia University (1961), esp. pp. 87–95, 120–5, 175, 198–200.

[8] The best evaluation, I believe, of available information from various sources remains that of Seymour Lipset in "Three Decades of the Radical Right," esp. pp. 326–48.

The study most frequently cited as having effectively contradicted the status hypothesis is Martin Trow's survey of McCarthyist opinion in Bennington, Vermont, in 1954, "Small Businessmen, Political Tolerance, and Support for McCarthy," *American Journal of Sociology*, LXIV (November 1958), 270–81. Why it is so construed I do not understand. Though it differs clearly enough on a rather marginal point, it puts strong emphasis on the anti-conservative, anti-establishment element in McCarthyism, finds it directed "precisely against the

The essays in *The Radical Right* were prompted by a curiosity about certain facts hitherto taken for granted. We wanted to know why Americans who were affected in a similar way by many events reacted to them so differently. Of course, party affiliation, socio-economic status, and geographical region always affect political opinions, but in this case the aggregate of these readily perceptible factors did not yield a satisfactory or exhaustive answer. There was a wide range of reaction to the events of the 1950's, for example, among people in the same social class and in the same political party. People responded to political events, as they always do, not merely with profoundly different opinions about the policies that should be pursued but in strikingly different mental and rhetorical styles. It was understood that the Korean War and the overlong exclusion of Republicans from the White House had much to do with the temper of the times, but why did some Republicans welcome the peace in Korea while others branded the Republican President who made it as a traitor? Again, millionaires cannot be expected to like progressive taxation, but how could we account for the political differences

---

conservative authorities and institutions—the 'big shots,' the 'stuffed shirts,' the 'bureaucrats,' " sees support for McCarthy as "the channeling of certain dissatisfactions with aspects of the social, economic, and political order," finds McCarthyists "angrily confused and deeply resentful of a world that continually offends their deepest values," and reports them animated by resentment and indignation that has "no effective and institutionalized channels of expression" and by a "generalized fear of the dominant currents and institutions of modern society"—and in this respect offers an analysis not remarkably dissimilar to that of the authors it is held to refute. See esp. pp. 273, 276, 277. In any case, there was no reason to believe that Bennington was a good or representative place to study McCarthyism, and, as Lipset has pointed out, some of its key findings were not replicated by national data. "Three Decades of the Radical Right," pp. 340–1.

Two of the most valuable studies of the extreme right that have raised serious questions about the status hypothesis are those of Nelson W. Polsby: "Towards an Explanation of McCarthyism," *Political Studies*, VIII (1960), 250–71, and Wolfinger: op. cit. But some of the difficulties of the subject are exemplified in their positive

between a first- or second-generation oil millionaire in Texas and a third-generation oil millionaire in New York? Why did taxpayers enjoying the same income and belonging to the same political party have such profoundly different views of the social reforms inherited from the New Deal?

I confess to mixed feelings about the term "status politics" as a means of explaining the discontents animated by the right wing. On one hand, I have no desire to overstate the role of status, narrowly defined, in the right wing of the 1950's or of today. There are a large number of factors, social and economic, that enter into the composition of the right wing, and, like any other single explanation, this one is bound to have its limitations. Yet I should be sorry if, because of its limited utility in this context, the fundamental importance of the distinction between status politics and interest politics should be lost. I chose the term "status politics" because I was looking for a way to designate an impulse held in common by a variety of discontented elements. If there is something misleading in the word "status," it is because its meaning is somewhat too specific to account for what it attempts to describe, and takes the part for the whole. Few critics have denied the presence

---

conclusions. Polsby dwells (p. 258) on "the rather heavy evidence supporting the hypothesis that McCarthy succeeded at the grass roots primarily among Republicans," and he is echoed by Wolfinger in his study of right-wing Christian Crusaders of the 1960's, which finds as "the most salient fact about the Crusaders: whatever else they may be, they are not Democrats." The scarcity of Democrats, he says, was "the most striking single characteristic of our sample" (pp. 285, 288). These conclusions—that McCarthy appealed more to Republicans than to Democrats and that the right-wingers of the 1960's are overwhelmingly Republican in partisan affiliation—have the great advantage that they are likely to go ringing down the corridors of time unchallenged and unimpaired. They have an attractive solidity, but they do not offer an arresting new idea to our store of understanding. What would be most pertinent would be to find out just what characteristics divide those Republicans who have joined the extreme right from those who believe that it is a menace to the body politic, and what were the social characteristics of the rather substantial number of Democrats who were pro-McCarthy.

or significance of what is intended, but it has been suggested that such terms as "cultural politics" and "symbolic politics" will serve better.

In my original essay I used the term "status politics" to refer to three things that are related but not identical: first is the problem of American identity, as it is complicated by our immigrant origins and the problems of ethnic minorities; second, the problem of social status, defined as the capacity of various groups and occupations to command personal deference in society; and, finally, the effort of Americans of diverse cultural and moral persuasions to win reassurance that their values are respected by the community at large. The purpose of the term was to heighten our awareness of a constant political struggle arising not out of the real or imagined contest for gain that is familiar in our interest-group politics—that is, the historical struggles for cheap land, cheap credit, higher farm prices, larger profits, market protection of various kinds, more jobs, more bargaining power, economic security—but out of commitments to certain other values, which are taken by the persons who share them to be ultimate moral goals, disinterestedly pursued. Such persons believe that their prestige in the community, even indeed their self-esteem, depends on having these values honored in public. Besides their economic expectations, people have deep emotional commitments in other spheres—religion, morals, culture, race relations—which they also hope to see realized in political action. Status politics seeks not to advance perceived material interests but to express grievances and resentments about such matters, to press claims upon society to give deference to non-economic values. As a rule, status politics does more to express emotions than to formulate policies. It is in fact hard to translate the claims of status politics into programs or concrete objectives (national Prohibition was an exception, though ultimately an unsuccessful one); and for the most part

87

the proponents of such politics, being less concerned with the uses of power than with its alleged misuse, do not offer positive programs to solve social problems. The operative content of their demands is more likely to be negative: they call on us mainly to prohibit, to prevent, to censor and censure, to discredit, and to punish.

The most useful attempt to apply the concept of status politics to an aspect of our history is Joseph R. Gusfield's recent book on the temperance movement, *Symbolic Crusade: Status Politics and the Temperance Movement.* Defining status politics rather sharply as "political conflict over the allocation of prestige," he argues that its importance "lies precisely in identifying non-economic segments as crucial in certain social and political conflicts."[9] Gusfield distinguishes between the political aims of those he calls "cultural fundamentalists" and "cultural modernists"—the fundamentalists having a character more rigidly and exclusively oriented toward production, work, and saving, while the modernists are more concerned with consumption and enjoyment. The fundamentalists are "locals" in Robert Merton's terminology: that is, they take their values from the traditions of local society; the modernists are "cosmopolitans" in that they are more *au courant* with what is going on in the nation-wide mass soci-

---

[9] *Symbolic Crusade* (Urbana, Ill., 1963), p. 18. "A political issue becomes one of status when its tangible, instrumental consequences are subordinated to its significance for the conferral of prestige . . . The argument is less over the effect of the proposed measures on concrete actions than it is over the question of whose culture is to be granted legitimacy by the public action of government" (p. 148).

Gusfield is gratifyingly careful to avoid the reductionist fallacy: he recognizes the profoundly genuine concern of temperance advocates with the moral issues, and does not try to reduce it to a preoccupation with their status. He shows how their moral commitment comes to affect their status, and offers much evidence that in the end they become quite aware of this process. (See esp. Ch. 5.) In his book the concern with status is treated not as something that displaces the substantive purpose of the movement but as an important additional aspect of it. See pp. 57–60.

ety, whether or not they approve of it. Both are engaged with
politics, but the fundamentalists have a special edge because
they want to restore the simple virtues of a bygone age and
they feel themselves to be fighting in a losing cause.

This is exemplified by the temperance movement, whose
political commitments Gusfield traces from the early days of
the Republic to recent times. The temperance movement of
the late nineteenth and the early twentieth century, he points
out, was often associated with progressive causes—feminism,
Christian pacifism, the Progressive movement of the Roose-
velt-Wilson era—but as its members have felt an increasing
sense of alienation from modernity, and as its more moderate
adherents have been drawn away into the orbit of cosmopolitan society, temperance advocates have become more and
more embittered. They know that they are regarded as
oddities and that the most respectable and honored people no
longer support their cause. Since the New Deal—a heavily
urban and cosmopolitan administration—gave the *coup de
grâce* to national Prohibition, the members of the movement
have moved to the political right. The Prohibition party no
longer attempts, as it did a generation ago, to appeal to
reformers and liberals, but, as Gusfield concludes, "has moved
toward an open appeal to the right-wing elements of both
major parties."

In many areas of life, the style of status politics has been
shaped in large measure by rigid moral and religious attitudes,
and those who are moved by the issues of status politics transfer these attitudes to social and economic questions. On many
occasions they approach economic issues as matters of faith
and morals rather than matters of fact. For example, people
often oppose certain economic policies not because they have
been or would be economically hurt by such policies, or even
because they have any carefully calculated views about
their economic efficacy, but because they disapprove *on*

moral grounds of the assumptions on which they think the policies rest.

A prominent case in point is the argument over fiscal policy. Deficit spending is vehemently opposed by great numbers of people in our society who have given no serious thought—indeed, are hardly equipped to do so—to the complex questions bearing on its efficacy as an economic device. They oppose it because their personal experience or training in spending, debts, and prudential management leads them to see in deficit spending a shocking repudiation of the moral precepts upon which their lives have been based. As a matter of status politics, deficit spending is an affront to millions who have been raised to live (and in some cases have been forced by circumstances to live) abstemious, thrifty, prudential lives. As a matter of interest politics, deficit spending might work to their advantage; but the moral and psychological effect, which is what they can really understand and feel, is quite otherwise: when society adopts a policy of deficit spending, thrifty small-businessmen, professionals, farmers, and white-collar workers who have been managing their affairs by the old rules feel that their way of life has been officially and insultingly repudiated.

Historians and social critics of the present generation have a particularly urgent need for such an analytical instrument as status politics: it serves to keep their conception of political conflict from being imbued with the excessive rationalism that infused the work of the two preceding generations of historians and political scientists. Under the guidance of such writers as Charles A. Beard, Frederick Jackson Turner, V. L. Parrington, Arthur F. Bentley, and others, we used to think of political man basically as a rational being who reckons as well as he can what his economic interests are, forms pressure groups and parties to advance these interests, and as a citizen casts his vote in order to see them realized.

Of course, the writers of this school understood that men can make miscalculations as to the nature of their interests and the best ways of pursuing them, and they also knew that at times non-economic factors entered significantly into political behavior. But they persisted in seeking fundamental economic motives in almost all political conflict. When they dealt with non-economic factors, as their sense of reality compelled them to do, they tended to discount the significance of these factors and to look upon them as momentary aberrations, and felt no need to develop a theory that would take adequate account of them. They were strongest when writing about those political conflicts that did in fact rest squarely on economic issues, and weakest when other issues came to the foreground. Their conceptions of historical change were least suited to deal with the kind of discontents that have developed during prosperity and which to a significant degree cut across class lines.

This rationalistic bias has very largely broken down in our time, partly under the impact of political events, partly because of what has been learned through public-opinion polling and depth psychology.[1] A conception of politics which dealt with the public largely as a set of economic blocs had no adequate way of coping with the variety of other factors that have entered into our political history—among them the sheer weight of habit and party loyalty, ethnic origins and tradi-

---

[1] Even the pollsters, however, were slow to break away from the older pattern of thought. The realization that socio-economic status was a fundamental category was at the very foundation of commercial polling, but the importance of religious affiliation was not realized. George Gallup found it hard to believe when Paul Lazarsfeld first told him that religious affiliation has a powerful and independent relation to voting habits; and even as recently as 1959 Elmo Roper asserted that there is no relation between religious affiliation and voting. Lipset: "Religion and Politics in the American Past and Present," already cited, p. 70. On religion as an independent force in American politics, and on the conservative drive of ascetic Protestantism, see Benton Johnson: "Ascetic Protestantism and Political Preference," *Public Opinion Quarterly*, XXVI (Spring 1962), 35–46.

tions, religious affiliations and religious styles, racial and ethnic prejudices, attitudes toward liberty and censorship, feelings about foreign policy quite unrelated to commercial goals and of dubious relationship to the national interest. In American history the combined effect of such forces has been singularly large. The wealth of the country and the absence of sharp class-consciousness have released much political energy for expression on issues not directly connected with economic conflict; and our unusually complex ethnic and religious mixture has introduced a number of complicating factors of great emotional urgency.

Significantly, the periods in which status politics has been most strikingly apparent have been the relatively prosperous 1920's and the 1960's. In periods of prosperity, when economic conflicts are blunted or subordinated, the other issues become particularly acute. We have noticed that whereas in depressions or during great bursts of economic reform people vote for what they think are their economic interests, in times of prosperity they feel free to vote their prejudices. In good times, with their most severe economic difficulties behind them, many people feel that they can afford the luxury of addressing themselves to larger moral questions, and they are easily convinced that the kind of politics that results is much superior to the crass materialism of interest politics. They have fewer inhibitions about pressing hard for their moral concerns, no matter how demanding and ill-formulated, as an object of public policy, than they have in pressing for their interests, no matter how reasonable and realistically conceived. In the following essay, I will try to show that Barry Goldwater was one campaigner who saw with considerable clarity the distinction between interest politics and status politics, and went out of his way in his campaign to condemn the immorality of the first and to call for an intensification of the second.

GOLDWATER AND PSEUDO-CONSERVATIVE POLITICS

I

GOLDWATER's capture of the Republican nomination was the triumphal moment of pseudo-conservatism in American politics. One may say that it was an accident, in that it was out of scale with right-wing Republican strength and could happen only because of a series of failures and misadventures among moderate Republicans which are not likely to recur. But in another sense it was far from accidental: it resulted from the chronic, frustrating impotence of the minority party and from the efficient organization that the right wing had quietly built up inside it.

If Goldwater is accepted on his own terms as a conservative, he baffles understanding, but if he is taken as a product of the pseudo-conservative revolt, his ideas fall into place. Questioning his conservatism may seem gratuitous, but there is more at stake here than an empty issue or a suitable label. What is at stake, as Robert J. Donovan puts it, is whether the Republican party can learn to make "a distinction between the conservatism represented by Senator Goldwater and his supporters and the conservatism that conserves."[1]

---

[1] *The Future of the Republican Party* (New York, 1964), p. 127.

Unquestionably Goldwater's ideas do retain some shreds and scraps of genuine conservatism, but the main course of his career puts him closer to the right-wing ideologues who were essential to his success, who shaped his tactics, who responded to his line of argument, and whose extremism he chose to defend at the vital moment of his career. Without invoking these formative affiliations, how are we to explain the character of a "conservative" whose whole political life has been spent urging a sharp break with the past, whose great moment as a party leader was marked by a repudiation of our traditional political ways, whose followers were so notable for their destructive and divisive energies, and whose public reputation was marked not with standpattism or excessive caution but with wayward impulse and recklessness?

Goldwater's brand of conservatism has its most recognizable American roots in those thinkers, quite numerous in this country, who imagine conservatism to be almost identical with economic individualism. Here he has responded more fervently to the nostalgic reveries and the pronouncements of perennial truths that mark ideological conservatism than he has to the tradition of shrewd and subtle manipulation, concession, and conciliation that has characterized American conservatism in practice. Most conservatives are mainly concerned with maintaining a tissue of institutions for whose stability and effectiveness they believe the country's business and political elites hold responsibility. Goldwater thinks of conservatism as a system of eternal and unchanging ideas and ideals, whose claims upon us must be constantly asserted and honored in full.[2] The difference between conservatism as a set

---

[2] "The laws of God, and of nature, have no date-line. The principles on which the Conservative political position is based have been established by a process that has nothing to do with the social, economic, and political landscape that changes from decade to decade and from century to century. These principles are derived from the nature of man, and from the truths that God has revealed about His

of doctrines whose validity is to be established by polemics, and conservatism as a set of rules whose validity is to be established by their usability in government, is not a difference of nuance, but of fundamental substance.

It is instructive how far Goldwater's devotion to eternal truths brought him beyond the position of such a Republican predecessor as Eisenhower, and how far it took him even beyond the conservatism of Robert A. Taft. Many of Eisenhower's statements both before and after his presidency could lead one to conclude that his social thinking was more similar to Goldwater's than different. Eisenhower too spoke often for the old-fashioned prudential virtues and against growing federal bureaucracy, and his cabinet incorporated at least two members, George Humphrey and Ezra Taft Benson, who fully shared the right-wing philosophy. But in practice Eisenhower was faithful to the opportunistic traditions of American conservatism. Though a mediocre politician with little enthusiasm for the political game, he was nonetheless so intuitively an "insider" in the American political tradition that he instinctively took the working politician's approach to the split mentality of American conservatism. He knew that many conservatives yearn for the days of untrammeled enter-

---

creation. Circumstances do change. So do the problems that are shaped by circumstances. But the principles that govern the solution of the problems do not. . . . The challenge is not to find new or different truths, but how to apply established truths to the problems of the contemporary world." Barry Goldwater: *The Conscience of a Conservative* (New York, Macfadden ed., 1960), "Foreword," p.3. (It may be necessary to add, since Goldwater has been exceptionally candid about the extent to which his books were ghost-written, that I have used them on the assumption that he read them carefully before he signed them, and that they do indeed represent his views as of the time that they were written.)

Again: "The basic problems are no different in our times than under Lincoln or Washington. . . . We have merely changed the horse for the tractor, the hand tools for a machine." A speech before the Utah State Convention of the Junior Chamber of Commerce in 1960, quoted in *The New Republic*, March 27, 1961, p. 14.

prise, uncomplicated foreign problems, and negligible taxes, but also that they can usually recognize the complexity of the contemporary world, the difficult obligations the country has taken on, and the irreversibility of the historical process that has brought us from simple agrarian conditions to the complex conditions of modern urban life and corporate organization. When Eisenhower spoke in philosophical terms, therefore, he often gave voice to their wistfulness about old ideals, but in administrative practice he usually bowed to what he thought were the necessities of the hour.

Here the strategies of three of our leading politicians are instructive. Eisenhower believed, at least with half his mind, in the old pieties, but concluded, with whatever misgivings, that they could not be taken as rules for action. Goldwater not only believed in them, but believed that they ought to be followed unerringly. Lyndon Johnson presumably does not believe in them at all; but understands that since they are widely believed in by honest men, some symbolic gestures are desirable in order to show such men that he at least respects their values. His talk of economy, and his much-publicized gesture of turning out the lights in the White House to save money, are gestures of this sort. Among cynical men they are naturally taken to be cynical. But they may also be taken as a humane effort to give symbolic comfort to those to whom, in the nature of things, more substantial forms of comfort cannot be given.

In any case, to ultra-conservatives, for whom the old pieties are binding moral principles, the Eisenhower administration was worse than a disappointment, it was a betrayal. It did not repeal the New Deal reforms, do away with high taxes, kill foreign aid, or balance the budget. In fact, its primary historical function seemed to be to legitimate what had been done under Roosevelt and Truman: when it left certain domestic and foreign policies intact, it made them more generally

96

acceptable by passing them, so to speak, through the purifying fire of eight years of Republicanism and thus confirming that they represented, after all, a bipartisan consensus. The right-wing minority saw all this not as a clue to the nature of our national problems but as further evidence that the conspiracy originally set in motion by the Democrats was being carried on by the Eastern Republicans behind Eisenhower. McCarthy, for example, had been quick to strike at Eisenhower and to change his slogan, "Twenty years of treason," to a more inflammatory one: "Twenty-one years of treason." Again, one of Eisenhower's budgets prompted Goldwater to brand his administration as "a dime-store New Deal." On a later occasion he said with fervor: "One Eisenhower in a generation is enough."[3]

Goldwater's deviation from Taft Republicanism also marks him off from the established moderate conservative wing of his party. Unlike Goldwater, Taft came from a family with long seasoning in public affairs; and, again unlike Goldwater, he took an active part on Capitol Hill in framing legislation. His brand of conservatism was modified by several concessions to the demands of expediency and responsibility. Though he had a profound dislike of change and a passionate bias toward fiscal conservatism and decentralized administration, Taft accepted the idea that the federal government should concern itself with "seeing that every family has a minimum standard of decent shelter," should "assist those states desiring to put a floor under essential services in relief, in medical care, in housing, and in education," should underwrite the states in providing "a basic minimum education to every child," sustain minimum-wage laws "to give the unorganized worker some protection" comparable to that given to organized workers by the unions, persist in a steeply gradu-

---

[3] *Time*, July 24, 1964, p. 27.

ated income tax, maintain minimum farm prices, and through its social security program (which he held to be woefully inadequate) "assure to every citizen 65 years of age and over a living wage."

These commitments, made in various speeches from 1943 to 1951, accept the reality of the welfare state. They stand in sharp contrast to Goldwater's notion that economic individualism can still be ruthlessly applied to American life. Before Goldwater found it necessary to modify a few of his positions for the sake of his primary and presidential campaigns in 1964, his beliefs came straight out of nineteenth-century laissez-faire doctrine and the strictest of strict constructionism. Governmental activities in "relief, social security, collective bargaining, and public housing," he thought, had caused "the weakening of the individual personality and of self-reliance." He asked for "prompt and final termination of the farm subsidy program," declared himself against "every form of federal aid to education," denounced the graduated income tax as "confiscatory," and asserted that the country had "no education problem which requires any form of Federal grant-in-aid programs to the states." The government, he said "must begin to withdraw from a whole series of programs that are "outside its constitutional mandate," including "social welfare programs, education, public power, agriculture, public housing, urban renewal. . . ."[4] Collectively, such statements called for the dismantling of the welfare state. "My aim is not to pass laws but to repeal them," Goldwater once boasted, and on another occasion he said: "I fear Washington and centralized government more than I do Moscow."[5] These are the

---

[4] *The Conscience of a Conservative*, p. 43; *Congressional Record*, 87th Cong., 1st sess. (June 21, 1961), p. 10971; ibid., 88th Cong., 1st sess. (September 3, 1963), p. 16222; statement to Senate Subcommittee on Education, Senate Committee on Labor and Public Welfare, April 30, 1963 (*Hearings*, I, 279).

[5] *Fortune*, May 1961, p. 139; *Look*, April 21, 1964; cf. *The Conscience of a Conservative*, p. 22.

characteristic accents of the pseudo-conservative agitators, who are convinced that they live in a degenerate society and who see their main enemy in the power of their own government.

Goldwater's departure from the Republican pattern was compounded by his position on civil rights. One of the oldest, though hardly the most efficacious, of the traditions of many conservatives in the North—and even to a degree in the South as well—has been a certain persistent sympathy with the Negro and a disposition to help him in moderate ways to relieve his distress. This tradition goes back to the Federalist party; it was continued by the Whig gentry; it infused the early Republican party. By adopting "the Southern strategy," the Goldwater men abandoned this inheritance. They committed themselves not merely to a drive for a core of Southern states in the electoral college but to a strategic counterpart in the North which required the search for racist votes. They thought they saw a good mass issue in the white backlash, which they could indirectly exploit by talking of violence in the streets, crime, juvenile delinquency, and the dangers faced by our mothers and daughters.

Eisenhower, like Goldwater, had been unmoved by noble visions of progress toward racial justice, but he at least gave lip service to the ideal and thought it important to enforce the laws himself and to speak out for public compliance. But Goldwater arrived at the position, far from conservative in its implications, that the decisions of the Supreme Court are "not necessarily" the law of the land.[6] Of course, the decisions of the Court have always had political content and they have often been highly controversial; there is no reason why they should suddenly be regarded with whispered reverence. But it is only in our time, and only in the pseudo-conservative movement, that men have begun to hint that disobedience to

---

[6] *The Conscience of a Conservative*, p. 37; cf. *The New York Times*, November 24, 1963.

the Court is not merely legitimate but is the essence of conservatism.

It is not the authority and legitimacy of the Court alone that the pseudo-conservative right calls into question. When it argues that we are governed largely by means of near-hypnotic manipulation (brainwashing), wholesale corruption, and betrayal, it is indulging in something more significant than the fantasies of indignant patriots: it is questioning the legitimacy of the political order itself. The two-party system, as it has developed in the United States, hangs on the common recognition of loyal opposition: each side accepts the ultimate good intentions of the other. The opponent's judgment may be held to be consistently execrable, but the legitimacy of his intent is not—that is, in popular terms, his Americanism is not questioned. One of the unspoken assumptions of presidential campaigns is that the leaders of both parties are patriots who, however serious their mistakes, must be accorded the right to govern. But an essential point in the pseudo-conservative world view is that our recent Presidents, being men of wholly evil intent, have conspired against the public good. This does more than discredit them: it calls into question the validity of the political system that keeps putting such men into office.

A man like Goldwater, who lives psychologically half in the world of our routine politics and half in the curious intellectual underworld of the pseudo-conservatives, can neither wholly accept nor wholly reject such a position. He disdains and repudiates its manifest absurdities (Eisenhower as a Communist agent), but he lives off the emotional animus that gives birth to them. This ambiguity makes it more understandable why, on the night of his defeat, he so flagrantly violated the code of decorum governing the conduct of losing presidential candidates. The code requires a message of congratulation, sent as soon as the result is beyond doubt, so worded that it emphasizes the stake of the whole nation in the successful administration of the victor, and reasserts the loser's acceptance of the public verdict. In withholding his congratulations until the morning after the election, and then in hinting at Johnson's incapacity to solve the acute problems gratuitously enumerated in his telegram, Goldwater did something more than show bad manners. By complying with the code, but grudgingly and tardily, he expressed his suspicion that the whole American political system, with its baffling ambiguities and compromises, is too soft and too equivocal for this carnivorous world.

II

ALTHOUGH THE ULTRAS usually speak with nostalgia about the supposed virtues of our remote past, they have a disposition to repudiate the more recent past, and it was in character for Goldwater to write off as unacceptable the Republican conservatism of recent years. But in return, he and his followers were unable to win acceptance from the major centers of genuinely conservative power. Businessmen, to be sure, gave Goldwater a narrow margin of support, but they gave him far less than any other Republican in recent history. The press also broke from its normal pattern: for the first time in memory a Democrat was favored by newspapers with an aggregate circulation much larger than those endorsing his opponent. Conservative chains like the Hearst and Scripps-Howard newspapers backed Johnson, as did establishment Republican papers like the New York *Herald Tribune*. Old centers of Republican conservatism such as rural New England turned their backs on Goldwater, and he became the first Republican presidential candidate to lose Vermont. The conservative voters of the normally Republican states of the wheat belt also deserted in large numbers. Repeatedly the pollsters who found Republican voters expressing doubt about Goldwater or open opposition to him noticed a recurrent explanation: "He's too radical for me." The American public is not notably sophisticated about ideological labels, and its use of the term "radical" rarely shows much precision; but this response registers a sounder sense of the situation than that of the highbrow conservatives who acclaimed the Arizonan as their own. Whatever tag Goldwater chose to wear, a large part of the public saw in him an excessively sharp deviation from the pattern of American politics and they found it frightening.

Goldwater's deviation is as much marked in his conduct as in his ideas. American politics is run mainly by professionals who have developed over a long span of time an ethos of their own, a kind of professional code. In emphasizing how completely Goldwater, and even more his followers, departed from the professional code, it is important to be clear that one is not making a substantive criticism of what they stood for but an attempt to compare their ways historically with our normal conservative practice. The professional code is not a binding moral imperative for anyone—not even for politicians. At one time or another most politicians have broken it. On occasion we admire them for breaking it in the interest of what they believe to be a higher principle. Finally, it should be conceded that Goldwater, at certain moments of his career, observed it handsomely, and that he too was victimized at times when the code was broken by others.[7]

---

[7] For example, Goldwater observed the code conspicuously in his conduct toward Nixon in 1960 and again momentarily in 1964 when he expressed some sympathetic understanding for the position of Republicans who could not afford to be fully identified with him. His opponents broke it at the Cow Palace when they circulated the famous Scranton letter, which, in its denunciation of his ideas and alleged tactics, went far beyond the usual etiquette of intra-party dispute.

The point, however, is that the professional code, for all its limitations, is an American institution embodying the practical wisdom of generations of politicians. It seems ironic that the most unqualified challenge ever made within a major party to this repository of the wisdom of our ancestors should have been made by a self-proclaimed conservative, and that Goldwater's advisers in 1964 brought him as close as any presidential candidate has ever come to subverting the whole pattern of our politics of coalition and consensus.

Professional politicians want, above all, to win, and their conduct is shaped by this pragmatic goal. Moreover, they know that if they win they have to govern; and their behavior in dealing with opposing factions in their own party, with the opposition party, and with the electorate is constantly molded and qualified by the understanding that they have to organize a government capable of coping with the problems of the moment. Both their ideas and their partisan passions are modified by the harsh corrective of reality. They are quite aware, for example, that their promises, which express rather what they think they should offer to do than what they think they can do, cannot be perfectly fulfilled. They are also aware that their denunciation of the opposing party in the conduct of election campaigns must be followed by the attempt to work with the opposition in Washington. Under the heated surface of our political rhetoric, therefore, there exists a certain sobriety born of experience, an understanding that what sounds good on the banquet circuit may not make feasible policy, that statements, manifestos, and polemics are very far from pragmatic programs; that these have to be *translated* into programs for the solution of our

---

On the requirements of American coalition politics as they bear on convention behavior, and on their repudiation by the Goldwater forces, see my essay: "Goldwater and His Party," *Encounter*, XXIII (October 1964), 3–13.

domestic and foreign problems; and that even then these programs have to undergo still further modification in the legislative mill before they can become reality.

Goldwater's career is distinguished by its lack of training for this code. Before his entry into national politics, his experience had given him responsibility for no national organization and had required an attention to administrative demands no more complex than those of his inherited department store. As a member of the Senate, he assumed no important role, involved himself with no legislation on major national problems. His main business there was simply to vote No. He made no outstanding contributions to debate or to the consideration of legislative details (as, for example, Taft had done); he was not prominent in committee work, and his busy speech-making program made him a frequent absentee. He did not, as a working senator, command the ear of fellow senators, not even of those who shared his views. In the framework of practical politics, he remained an "outsider," and as a presidential candidate he continued to make decisions that reflected the outsider's cast of mind.[8]

But to say this of Goldwater's legislative role is not to deny that he worked hard to earn his position in his party: it is simply that he rose to it not by making contributions to government but through his partisan activity, which for years was dedicated and tireless. He was chairman of the Republi-

---

[8] For a shrewd statement of the differences between the political mentality of the outsider and that of the insider, see the contrast drawn by Eric L. McKitrick between Andrew Johnson and Abraham Lincoln in *Andrew Johnson and Reconstruction* (Chicago, 1960), esp. Ch. 4.

Oddly enough, the externals of John F. Kennedy's senatorial career correspond with Goldwater's. However, the difference in their cast of mind, not to speak of their intellectual caliber, was beyond reckoning. It was only one aspect of these differences that JFK was, by family training, education, and social position—one suspects also, as it were, by instinct—an insider.

can Senatorial Campaign Committee. He was constantly available to fellow Republicans everywhere, giving substantial help to their campaign efforts and their fund-raising. His arduous round of speechmaking on the banquet circuit gave him a chance to bring his "conservative" message to thousands of rank-and-file party workers and to put many party leaders in his debt. His role, then, was that of the partisan exhorter and organizer, a speaker and ideologue for whom preaching a sound philosophy was more interesting than addressing himself to the problems of state. But in this role he was constantly speaking to audiences already largely or wholly converted to his point of view, unlike the legislator on Capitol Hill who must constantly deal with shrewd and informed men who differ with him. Resounding applause no doubt confirmed his conviction of the validity and importance of his "conservatism," and persuaded him that an irresistible conservative revival was astir in the country, but it did not enlarge his capacity to conciliate or persuade those who differed with him—still less to learn from an exchange of views. The habits of mind thus shaped were carried into his campaign, during which he once again brought salvation to the already converted.[9]

Goldwater, then, made up for his lack of stature as a legislative leader by his outstanding success as a partisan evangelist who particularly mobilized those Republicans whose discontent was keenest, whose ideological fervor was strongest, those most dissatisfied with the bland and circumspect Eisenhower legacy. At the grass roots large segments of the Republican party were taken over by dedicated enthusiasts, hitherto

---

[9] "With one exception, and that a slip-up apparently, he held no press conferences during the campaign. When he visited the cities he generally avoided the crowds, the slums, and the ghettos and appeared only in halls filled with militant conservatives who needed no persuasion by him. There was precious little effort on the senator's part to take his case to the unconvinced." Donovan: op. cit., p. 55.

political amateurs, with a bent for unorthodox ideas and new departures. Reporters at San Francisco were impressed by the preponderance of unfamiliar faces among the Goldwater delegates.[1] Victory won with the help of these new-idea delegates was followed by the creation of a Goldwater staff in which professionals and cosmopolitans were entirely overshadowed by amateurs and provincials—a staff the press called "the Arizona Mafia."

Goldwater's advisers and enthusiasts, being new to major-party politics, found it easy to abandon the familiar rules of political conduct. Party workers raised on the professional code want above all to find winners, to get and keep office, to frame programs on which they can generally agree, to use these programs to satisfy the major interests in our society, and to try to solve its most acute problems. If they find that they have chosen a loser, they are quick to start looking for another leader. If they see that their program is out of touch with the basic realities, they grope their way toward a new one.

But Goldwater's zealots were moved more by the desire to dominate the party than to win the country, concerned more to express resentments and punish "traitors," to justify a set of values and assert grandiose, militant visions, than to solve actual problems of state. More important, they were

---

[1] Robert D. Novak remarks that these were "not merely the run-of-the-mill party workers under the command and the bidding of regular party leaders. Here was a new breed of delegate, most of whom had never been to a national convention before. . . . They were going there for one purpose: to vote for Barry Goldwater. To woo them away to another candidate would be as difficult as proselytizing a religious zealot." *The Agony of the G.O.P. 1964* (New York, 1965), pp. 345–6.

Cf. Richard Rovere: "They are a new breed. It has been said—quite proudly—by the Goldwater people that this was the first Convention for more than half of them. . . . There was youth on every hand." "Letter from San Francisco," *The New Yorker*, July 25, 1964, p. 80.

immune to the pressure to move over from an extreme position toward the center of the political spectrum which is generally exerted by the professional's desire to win. Their true victory lay not in winning the election but in capturing the party—in itself no mean achievement—which gave them an unprecedented platform from which to propagandize for a sound view of the world.

Since the major parties in the United States have always been coalitions of disparate and even discordant elements, the professional leaders of major parties have always had to forge out of their experience the techniques of consensus politics that are adapted to holding such coalitions together and maintaining within them a workable degree of harmony. The art of consensus politics, in our system, has to be practiced not only in coping with the opposition party but internally, in dealing with one's partisans and allies. The life of an American major party is a constant struggle, in the face of serious internal differences, to achieve enough unity to win elections and to maintain it long enough to develop a program for government. Our politics has thus put a strong premium on the practical rather than the ideological bent of mind, on the techniques of negotiation and compromise rather than the assertion of divisive ideas and passions, and on the necessity of winning rather than the unqualified affirmation of principles, which is left to the minor parties.

The perennial task of coalition building has resulted in a number of rituals for party conventions, which Goldwater and his followers either ignored or deliberately violated at San Francisco. A candidate who enters a convention with the preponderant and controlling strength that Goldwater had in 1964 has at his disposal a number of effective devices to conciliate and incorporate the opposition. One is to write a conciliatory platform, which makes concessions to the defeated side or which hedges on disputed matters. Party platforms are often vague, they are usually long and tedious, and they remain unread; but their significance lies precisely in showing the ability of all factions and candidates to agree at least on a statement of policy. Their very vagueness proves that party leaders do not consider it necessary to fight issues out or to reach clear statements of principle and policy. Bitter or prolonged platform fights, such as those waged by the Democrats in 1896 and 1924, are always signs of a fatal absence of basic unity.

The winning candidate has other placatory devices available. One is the choice of a running mate: he may pick his leading opponent for this role, as Kennedy did in 1960, or he may turn to someone who represents the main opposing tendency in the party. He may go out of his way to arrive at an understanding, as Eisenhower did with Taft in 1952 or Nixon with Rockefeller in 1960. In his acceptance address he will almost invariably do the graceful thing and dwell upon conciliatory themes, stressing the commitments and sentiments that unite the party rather than those that divide it. In return, some corresponding rituals are expected of the loser: he, or one of his close associates, usually presents a motion to make the nomination unanimous. If he speaks, he minimizes the issues that have divided his party, denounces the opposition party with renewed vigor, and promises to support the victor with all his might. Normally he keeps this promise, as Goldwater himself did for Nixon in 1960.[2]

This traditional placatory ritual was flouted at every point by the Goldwater organization at San Francisco. To begin,

---

[2] Goldwater's break with the professional code in 1964 did not come from failure to understand its easily mastered general principles but from his constant gravitation toward the doctrinaires. "We are a big political party," he declared in a speech on September 11, 1963, "and there is all kinds of room for a difference of opinion. But in differing, we need not beat the hides off those we differ with." Novak: op. cit., p. 232. It was this message that got lost at San Francisco.

their platform in effect repudiated many recent Republican policies. Then, proposed amendments endorsing civil rights, reasserting civilian control over nuclear weapons, and condemning extremist groups were crushed, and in the debate over the last of these, Governor Rockefeller was interrupted unmercifully by booing from the galleries. (The Goldwater managers, disturbed by this outburst, were able to prevent their delegates from persisting in the demonstration but could not stop their partisans in the galleries from giving vent to their feelings.) In the choice of a running mate, Goldwater again had an opportunity to soften the conflict by taking some eminent man from the large moderately conservative middle band of the party who would have been acceptable on all sides, but he settled on an obscure provincial, William E. Miller—professional enough, to be sure, but undistinguished except by belligerent partisanship. The effects of this choice were in no way mollified by the selection of his fellow Arizonan Dean Burch as national chairman—"a politician of limited experience who had never even been a county chairman and who was a complete stranger to hundreds of eminent Republicans around the country."[3] Finally, to top it all, Goldwater's acceptance speech, far from sounding the conciliatory note so necessary after the acrimony of the proceedings, said that "those who do not care for our cause we don't expect to enter our ranks in any case," and flung his famous challenge: "I would remind you that extremism in the defense of liberty is no vice. And let me remind you also that moderation in the pursuit of justice is no virtue!"—a two-sentence manifesto approved by a dozen top members of his staff and written by a hard-core right-winger whom Goldwater found congenial and kept by his side as a speechwriter throughout the campaign.

---

[3] Donovan: op. cit., p. 92.

Most presidential candidates try to look their best at the strategic moment when their party convention acclaims them. For Goldwater this was impossible. His moment of victory at the Cow Palace found him firmly in the hands of his ecstatic pseudo-conservative followers. For the past few years his own presidential prospects had done much to draw them into active politics, and it was their money and hard work which had built the Goldwater movement. In precinct after precinct and county after county they had fought and ousted old-line Republicans.[4] They were now prominent among his delegates —an official of the John Birch Society claimed that more than a hundred of the Goldwater delegates were Birchites. The Goldwater campaign had given focus to the right-wing movement, and had brought into prominence such exponents of the paranoid style as John A. Stormer and Phyllis Schlafly, whose books were sold and given away by the millions, and whose conspiratorial views articulated the mental heat behind pseudo-conservatism more fully than Goldwater's more equivocal utterances. Schlafly's *A Choice Not an Echo* expressed the animus of Midwestern Republicans against "the secret New York kingmakers" who had repeatedly stolen the Republican nomination "to insure control of the largest cash market in the world: the Executive Branch of the United States Government." It was reminiscent of the same bias which a few years earlier had inspired Goldwater to suggest that "this country would be better off if we could just saw off the Eastern Seaboard and let it float out to sea." Stormer's

---

[4] The procedure by which Goldwater and his followers conducted their campaign for delegates was not one calculated to develop their talents for conciliation. As Novak puts it, Goldwater repealed "the rule of preconvention politics that required a candidate to appease the uncommitted rather than titillate his own committed followers. . . . Rather than appease the uncommitted, Goldwater was destroying them. And this required keeping his own committed followers in a state of high titillation. . . . He was conquering, not convincing, the Republican party." Op. cit., p. 353.

None Dare Call It Treason, which took its title from a couplet attributed to Sir John Harrington:

> Treason doth never prosper, what's the reason?
> For if it prosper, none dare call it treason,

was a masterful piece of folkish propaganda, which continued the McCarthyist and Birchite line of accusation without committing the bizarre verbal indiscretions that have caused people to make fun of Robert Welch. It drew up a thoroughgoing indictment of Eisenhower Republicanism without in so many words calling Eisenhower a traitor.[5]

To be fully faithful to this clientele, Goldwater had to be graceless to many fellow Republicans; yet it would have been graceless too to spurn the people whose work had won his victory. But, in fact, he saw nothing wrong with them. While he could hardly take Robert Welch seriously, he had said more than once that the John Birch Society was a fine organization,[6] and now he would neither repudiate nor offend its members. This meant that the path to the customary procedures of our politics was closed off, since the right-wingers scorned them. The convention showed the nation for the first time how well organized the right-wing movement was, but it

---

[5] Phyllis Schlafly: *A Choice Not an Echo* (Alton, Ill., 1964), p 5; John A. Stormer: *None Dare Call It Treason* (Florissant, Mo., 1964), esp. pp. 33–53, 196–8, 224–5. These young writers represent the militant younger generation of conservatives that was attracted to Goldwater. Stormer was chairman of the Missouri Federation of Young Republicans, and Schlafly president of the Illinois Federation of Republican Women and a Goldwater delegate at the Cow Palace.

[6] "A lot of people in my home town have been attracted to the [Birch] society," Goldwater said in 1961, "and I am impressed by the type of people in it. They are the kind of people we need in politics." On another occasion he called them "the finest people in my community," and still later, when it had become clear that they might be a serious campaign liability, he stood by them, insisting that as a group they should not be called extremists. "They believe in the Constitution, they believe in God, they believe in Freedom." *Time,* April 7, 1961, p. 19; ibid., June 23, 1961, p. 16; *The New York Times,* July 18, 1964.

also proved, as the subsequent campaign was to prove again, that the right wing, though brilliantly organized for *combat*, was not organized to conciliate or persuade. Having convinced themselves that the forces they were fighting were conspiratorial and sinister, not to say treasonous, they found it impossible to shake off the constricting mental framework of the paranoid style. The sudden and startling outburst of wild applause, the jeers and fist-shaking at the broadcast booths and press stands, which came when Eisenhower made a mildly hostile reference to some unidentified columnists, was a key to the prevailing mood. Animated by a profound resentment, and now at last on the verge of a decisive victory over their tormentors, the Goldwater zealots were filled with the desire to punish and humiliate, not to appease and pacify.[7] The acceptance speech showed that this desire extended upward into Goldwater's own staff.

The shock inflicted by San Francisco was so severe that some gesture seemed imperative; and for a moment it seemed that Goldwater would make the usual effort at rapprochement when the Hershey Conference was held in August. Indeed he did say there many of the expected things, and some in strong terms; but the damage had been done, and Goldwater's announcement to reporters at the close of the conference that "this is no conciliatory speech at all. It merely reaffirms what I've been saying all through the campaign," canceled much of the conciliatory effect. The wounds had been covered over, not healed, and although Goldwater won

---

[7] Cf. Richard Rovere's report from San Francisco (p. 80). For the most part, he found the Goldwater delegates young and affluent, "smartly dressed, well organized, and well spoken. And they were as hard as nails. The spirit of compromise and accommodation was wholly alien to them. They did not come to San Francisco merely to nominate their man and then rally his former opponents behind him; they came for a total ideological victory and the total destruction of their critics. . . . They wished to punish as well as to prevail."

the dutiful support of a number of moderates, including his main opponent, Scranton, he went on to conduct a right-wing campaign in which they were inevitably out of key.[8] By now it was not altogether a matter of his being unwilling to offer reassurance. What had happened was that he had been so extreme so long that neither the Republican moderates nor a large, strategic segment of the electorate had confidence that further reassurances from him would have any meaning.

Overwhelming defeat in the election—a thing which the professional politician always takes as a spur to rethink his commitments and his strategy—had no such effect on the Goldwater camp. His enthusiasts were more disposed to see the event as further evidence of the basic unregeneracy of the country, or worse, of the conspiracy by which they had been thwarted all along. The old right-wing myth, that there was an enormous conservative "silent vote" that would pour out to the polls if the party would only nominate a proper right-winger, was exploded, but it seems to have been replaced by a new one: that Goldwater was defeated so badly largely because he was sabotaged by the party moderates and liberals.[9]

---

[8] It was impossible after San Francisco to put the pieces together again. Scranton made many strong campaign speeches, as the code required, for Goldwater, and acted as his host at a great rally in Pittsburgh near the end of the campaign. In his introduction he made a casual reference to the fact that he did not always agree with Goldwater. At this he was met by such a chorus of boos from the faithful that he hurried through to a perfunctory and cool conclusion. See Novak: op. cit., p. 5.

[9] As is often the case, there is a modest portion of truth in this myth: the battle with the moderates in the primaries and at San Francisco helped to fix an image of Goldwater in the public mind that was never erased. But after San Francisco, it was not true that Goldwater was a loser because the moderates deserted him, but rather that the moderates, with their survival in mind, had to desert him because he was a loser. After the Hershey Conference, most of them were prepared to obey the professional code (as, for example, Scranton handsomely did), but many of those who were running for office found it too dangerous to their chances. This effect was not confined to the moderates. The ultra-conservative senatorial candidate

It must be conceded that if one's underlying purpose is not to win elections or affect the course of government but to propagandize for a set of attitudes, the right-wing enterprise of 1964 can be considered something of a success. It was so taken by many Goldwater ideologues, and on the far right the post-election mood was one of cheer, if not elation. One of its spokesmen said that the election marked "the defeat not of conservatism but of the Republican party"—a clear confession that the fate of an ideology was taken as being far more important than the well-being of the institution; and Goldwater remarked in a revealing statement: "I don't feel the conservative cause has been hurt. Twenty-five million votes are a lot of votes and a lot of people dedicated to the concept of conservatism."[1]

If one accepts the point of view of political doctrinaires and amateurs, whose primary aim in politics is to make certain notions more popular, this statement has its validity: for a generation, no politician has been able to preach Goldwater's brand of ultra-right-wing individualism and aggressive nationalism to so wide an audience from so exalted a platform. However, a practical conservative politician, more concerned with consequences than with doctrine, might see the matter in a different light. He would observe that Goldwater's overwhelming defeat and the consequent collapse of Republican party strength in Congress have smashed the legislative barriers that for more than twenty-five years have blocked major advances in the welfare state. He would note that the preponderance in Congress has been overwhelmingly shifted toward the liberals, that legislative seniority, the makeup of

---

in California, George Murphy, also found it expedient to keep his distance from Goldwater, and this strategy may have been an element in his success.

[1] *The New York Times*, November 5, 1964. Goldwater's figure represented the current state of the vote count, which was not complete.

the House Rules Committee, the composition indeed of all
the committees, were so changed that a new flood of welfare
legislation of the kind so fervently opposed by Goldwater
was made possible; that medicare, a major extension of federal
aid to education, a new voting-rights bill, a wider coverage
for the minimum-wage act, regional aid for the Appalachian
states, and a general anti-poverty program—all policies which
the Goldwater forces considered dangerous in the extreme—
were brought much closer to enactment; and that beyond
these lay the further improved chances of a new immigration
act with quota changes, urban transporation measures, the
creation of a national arts foundation, even repeal of the
"right to work" section of the Taft-Hartley Act.

From this point of view, liberals could be grateful to Goldwater. No other Republican could have made such a startling
contribution to the first really significant and general extension of the New Deal since the 1930's. It was his campaign
that broke the back of our postwar practical conservatism.

III

THE CONDUCT of Goldwater's campaign is no less interesting
than his convention strategy. Americans, always ready to forget failure and write off defeat, may be disposed to say that
this campaign is dead and should be forgotten, except insofar
as it may serve working politicians of all shades of opinion as a
model of how not to do things. But it will also serve as a good
case history of the pseudo-conservative mentality in action.

On both domestic and foreign policy, Goldwater was
encumbered by the many impulsive utterances he had made
during the previous years. His campaign engaged him in the
unenviable task of trying to disavow the starker implications
of these utterances and to give the public some reassurance as

to his stability without at the same time sacrificing his entire political identity and the allegiance of his true believers.[2] Although these efforts led to some preposterous inconsistencies, I believe a rigid consistency would in this case have been more discreditable. His inconsistencies represent at least Goldwater's effort—too little, too hesitant, and too late—to transform himself from a right-wing ideologue to a major-party leader in the American tradition, and he would have been more vulnerable to criticism if he had made no effort of this kind.[3] What is most extraordinary about his campaign is not these negative and unsuccessful disclaimers, but his positive strategy, which rested upon an appeal to moral uneasiness and discontent.

In his opening campaign speech at Prescott, Arizona, Goldwater struck his major theme: "There is a stir in the land. There is a mood of uneasiness. We feel adrift in an uncharted and stormy sea. We feel we have lost our way." In later speeches he cited the evidences of this "drift and decay" that had overcome the country: "wave after wave of crime in our streets and in our homes . . . riot and disorder in our cities . . . a breakdown of the morals of our young people. . . .juvenile delinquency. . . . obscene literature. . . . corruption." All these evils had mounted because "the moral fiber of the American people is beset by rot and decay."[4] Decay particularly

---

[2] I have tried to establish in a rough way the implications of Goldwater's search for a suitable image at various steps in his career in "A Long View: Goldwater in History," *The New York Review of Books*, October 8, 1964, pp. 17–19.

[3] Goldwater's one significant gesture at refashioning his doctrinaire right-wing posture actually came early in 1961, but he was barraged by protests from the right wing and he withdrew. From that point on his basic commitment never changed. See Novak: op. cit., Ch. 3, for this episode.

[4] Quotations in this and the following paragraphs from Goldwater's campaign speeches are from mimeographed news releases of the Republican National Committee. The speeches I have drawn on are those of September 3 (Prescott), October 7 (Newark), 9

afflicted the young, and this was something more profound and significant than the "normal pranks and rebellion of youth coming of age. . . . something much more fundamental is at work. Something basic and dangerous is eating away at the morality, dignity, and respect of our citizens—old as well as young, high as well as low." And he suggested that this was a poor time in our nation's history "for the Federal Government to ban Almighty God from our school rooms"—a reference to the Supreme Court's school-prayer decision. Not only was the Democratic party platform silent on the question of a constitutional amendment allowing for the restoration of prayer, but "you will search in vain for *any* reference to God or religion in the Democratic platform." Almost his entire speech at Salt Lake City was given over to the theme of religion and "the moral crisis of our time." At Topeka and elsewhere he linked President Johnson to this moral crisis— among other things, he said, Johnson "visited church after church and city after city in a political travesty of the Lord's day" and turned "Sunday into a day of campaign chaos."

Beyond this, however, as Goldwater made clear in a television appearance on October 9, the deterioration of home, family, and community, of law and order and good morals, was "the result of thirty years of an unhealthy social climate. I refer to the philosophy of modern 'liberalism,' the dominant philosophy of the opposition party." It was the modern liberal, he argued, who fosters permissiveness in the school and the home, who regards discipline and punishment as "barbaric relics of a discredited past," who seeks to eliminate religious sentiment from every aspect of public life, who cares more

---

(ABC-TV network), 10 (Salt Lake City), 13 (Topeka and Milwaukee), 15 (Houston), and 16 (Sioux Falls). Where three dots of elision appear, they do not represent omissions from the text but reproduce the punctuation adopted for these releases. Four dots represent cuts of my own.

for the criminal than for his victims, who "frowns on the policeman and fawns on the social psychologist." He went on to link these things with modern economics and sociology—their discovery of poverty and unemployment and the equality of human rights, and their well-intentioned but ill-conceived efforts to do something about them. Up to a point, he too was in favor of such efforts, but what he opposed was the constant expansion of spending, the planning of new controls, the presence of "a government establishment that is preparing to nationalize our society while paying for it with the fruits of private industry." The failures of internal prudence and candor which he saw connected with these policies, he linked to our foreign affairs and the lack of respect with which America is regarded in the world. "I'm talking about the re-establishment of the dignity of the American people . . . the pride of the individual American."

The element, then, that unified Goldwater's foreign and domestic campaign themes was the argument that domestic demoralization, foreign failures, and the decline in our prestige abroad were together the consequence of a failure of the old virtues and the old moral fiber. In response, he urged a twofold stiffening of the moral backbone: first, "take the bureaucratic shackles off," put "our main reliance on individuals, on hard work, on creativity, investment, and incentive"; then, reassert American power overseas. *"Stop the spread of socialism at home and Communism abroad."*

The rhetoric of these speeches, so far as they dwell on America's internal condition, resounds with the fundamentalist revolt against the conditions of modernity: the call for "hard work, creativity, investment, and incentive," the emphasis on symptoms of "a sickness in our society," "shattered prestige," the demand for "common purpose . . . moral responsibility for our individual actions," the call for "greatness of soul—to restore inner meaning to every man's life in a time

118

too often rushed, too often obsessed by petty needs and material greeds," the fear of "the erosion of individual worth by a growing Federal bureaucracy." The whole election, Goldwater said in his Prescott speech, was not a question of political personalities, or promises or programs: "It is a choice of what sort of people we want to be."

One of Goldwater's many difficulties was that of opposing an incumbent President at a time of high and sustained prosperity. But this difficulty, seen in a larger context, is only one manifestation of a nagging problem confronting ultra-right spokesmen. As they see it, we have been committed for many years, for decades, to economic policies which are wrong morally and wrong as expedients, destructive of enterprise, and dangerous to the fabric of free society. At the same time, every informed person recognizes that we have become much richer doing all these supposedly wrong and unsound things than we were when we had hardly begun to do them. Moreover, the portion of the public that responds to appeals to economic discontent is relatively small, and Goldwater knew that the really significant part of that public—the mass of those not sharing in the general prosperity—was already in Johnson's camp. Goldwater's appeal then, like those of the ultra-right generally, had to be addressed to the kind of discontents that appear in an affluent society, and this he did with unusual self-awareness and clarity. He distinguished between interest politics and status politics, and showed why, from his vantage point, the usual practice of interest politics should be regarded as morally discreditable and vastly inferior to status politics.

These matters were best dealt with in his national television program of October 9. He conceded the realities of American affluence: Gross national product was up—so were wages, housing, savings, automobiles. "Yes, more people have more *things* than ever before." But the same thing was true almost everywhere—in England, France, Germany, Nigeria, Japan, even behind the Iron Curtain. The point was that in the United States other things were also up: crime, juvenile delinquency, divorce, illegitimacy, mental illness, school dropouts, drug addiction, pornography, riots, and hoodlumism. These were the terrifying things with which he proposed to deal, and one could infer from this that his campaign on the moral realities was even more significant than anything he had to say about economic policy.

Here he boldly characterized his entire campaign in words that deserve quotation at length:

> You have probably been reading and hearing about some of the unorthodox things I have been doing.
>
> I have gone into the heart of Appalachia . . . and there I have *deliberately* attacked this administration's phony war on poverty.
>
> I have gone into the heart of Florida's retirement country . . . and there I have *deliberately* warned against the outright hoax of this administration's medicare scheme.
>
> I have gone into the heart of our farm area . . . and there I have *deliberately* called for the gradual transition from a controlled to a free agriculture.
>
> I have gone into an area of rapid urban growth . . . and there I have *deliberately* leveled against the Supreme Court the charge that they have no business attempting to draw the map of our state legislative districts.
>
> I have done all these things *deliberately* . . . for a reason that is clear in my own mind . . . and I want to make it clear to you tonight. *I will not attempt to buy the votes of the American people . . . I will not treat any of you as just so many special interests . . . I will not appeal to you as if you were simply pocketbooks . . . surrounded on all sides by self-serving concerns.*
>
> And of this I am deeply convinced: The American people won't sell their votes. They won't *sell* their freedom . . . not for any cheap political appeals.

Having gone thus far to flout the time-honored methods of American campaigning, which he charged his opponent exemplified in an egregious way, Goldwater went bravely on to underline the non-political quality of his own politics:

> It's not your partisan approval that I'm seeking tonight: What I want is your undivided attention. Because I want to ask you this question . . . *What place does politics have in a campaign for the Presidency?*
>
> You heard me right: What does *politics* . . . the ward heeler politics of something for everyone . . . have to do with the American Presidency?

This speech, and the campaign strategy which it correctly describes, must surely be classed among the most adventurous episodes in our recent politics, and it underlines the paradox that if we are in search of tradition-breakers we are most likely to find them among the ideological conservatives. Old-line professionals might shake their heads in dismay at a campaigner who would appear before the old folks and attack medicare, criticize TVA in the heart of TVA country, and attack the poverty program in Appalachia, but Goldwater was acting in consonance with his belief that interest politics should not merely be supplemented by status politics but displaced by it. As he saw it, the venerable tradition of appealing separately to a variety of special interests in the course of a campaign and then trying to act as broker among them in the actual process of governing was an ignoble kind of politics, vastly inferior to a politics that would address itself to realizing the religious and moral values of the public and to dealing with "the moral crisis of our time." He wanted, in short, to drive the politics out of politics. Goldwater was taking his stand in the hope that the American people (even though their moral fiber was "beset by rot and decay") would somehow reject the kind of interest-appeals they had always responded to in the past and vote for men who could meet the moral crisis.

A vital difficulty, of course, is that Goldwater was not

consistent in this effort to surmount interest politics. There is no record, I believe, of his appearing before the National Association of Manufacturers to urge them to be less solicitous about their tax burdens or of his appearing before segregationist audiences to urge that they move over and make some place for the Negro. The abandonment of interest politics, then, is a rather one-sided affair. One need not question Goldwater's sincerity to see that politics, as he practiced it, would leave certain favored interests free to continue to seek their advancement through political action while encouraging large masses of the people to commit themselves entirely to the more abstract effort to fulfill high moral ideals. Confronted with this kind of political imbalance, most Americans, who do not pretend to be as "conservative" as Goldwater, preferred to stay closer to the wisdom of our ancestors, who believed that under the American system a plurality of interests, vigorously pursued, would end by providing a rough counterpoise to each other, which would be more likely to yield satisfactory results than a general appeal to human virtue.

It is important to be clear as to what we find odd and out-of-pattern in Goldwater's campaign appeals. There is nothing singular in believing that there is a moral crisis in our time, or in saying so in a presidential campaign. There is nothing wrong in suggesting that such problems as juvenile delinquency, drug addiction, or crime in the streets might legitimately be made the objects of national discussion or of action by the federal government. Even the view that the moral fiber of the American people is beset by rot and decay is not peculiar to Barry Goldwater—the same view has been regularly expressed by many American intellectuals. What was substantially out of the American political pattern was the concerted attempt to exploit these difficult problems largely for their divisive content (most people understood what Goldwater was getting at when he complained that American women are not safe on the streets).

It is especially odd that they should have been stressed in a presidential campaign by a man whose whole theory of federal-state relations denied that the federal government can or should intervene in the solution of these "local" problems. It was, in short, the non-programmatic character of Goldwater's approach to these issues that stood out as singular. His main solution to the moral crisis, set forth many times during the campaign, was, to put it charitably, ingenuous: he would restore "domestic tranquillity," as he said in his Newark speech, first of all "by example at the top," because it was the moral example of the presidency more than anything else that was really at the root of all the evils. Remove from the White House the bad example of Lyndon B. Johnson and such attendant lords as Bobby Baker, Billie Sol Estes, and Matt McCloskey, and the problems of law enforcement would be relatively simple to solve. The arrogance of the suggestion that Goldwater and Miller, by the purity of their superior moral example, would turn the tide, is only incidental. What is important is the style of thought underlying the suggestion: the moral problems in question—which are in fact the great and pervasive social problems of modern industrial urban life and of mass culture—Goldwater saw largely as problems of "law enforcement," and the key to law enforcement he saw in a stiffening of the moral backbone, and the replacement of a bad example by a good example. We are, in short, to lift ourselves up by our moral bootstraps. The conclusion reached by many of us that the problems are intrinsically difficult, that they involve complex economic, sociological, and psychological calculations, is swept away—indeed, it was precisely Goldwater's conception that the inquiring and humane spirit behind modern sociology and psychology has not helped to solve but has produced our difficulties.

The root notion here is what linked Goldwater so closely to

the fundamentalist right wing and the more paranoid reaches of the pseudo-conservative mentality: it is the same devil theory of social ills found in all the familiar rhetoric about treason and conspiracy. The devil in 1964 was personified by Lyndon B. Johnson, as in earlier years it had been by Truman, Dewey, Acheson, Marshall, Eisenhower, and the Eastern establishment. Ultimately, as this view of the world has it, our problems are only moral; but more than that: the moral life itself is not complex and difficult and full of trial and confusion, it is basically simple. Is this a caricature? Perhaps, but in his Memphis speech Goldwater asserted: "A lot of my enemies call me simple. The trouble with the so-called liberal today is that he doesn't understand simplicity. The answers to America's problems are simple." For Goldwater this was a heartfelt cry. At Salt Lake City he departed from the prepared text of his address to declare with more fervor than grammar: "Many Americans don't like simple things. That is why they are against we conservatives."

It is against the background of this conception of the world that one can best understand the choice of a Goldwater campaign slogan that rests its appeal on simple intuition: "In your heart you know he's right."

I V

GOLDWATER'S VIEWS on foreign policy, which were more damaging to him than his views on domestic affairs, required even more strenuous efforts to undo the existing image of him as a reckless adventurer. In his opening speech at Prescott he used the word "peace" twenty times, and for his foreign-policy slogan he adopted the relatively inoffensive "Peace through strength." Many times during the campaign he reiterated that he did not *want* a general war—an assurance

124

which even his critics should have credited but which it was dangerous for a politician to have to offer—and he frequently emphasized the argument that the Republican party had been the historic peace party rather than his own well-known dissatisfaction with some of its recent peaceful policies.

By the autumn of 1964, however, Goldwater was the prisoner of his previous utterances on foreign affairs. The views he had expressed went far beyond what might be called the "hard line" in the cold war. The hard line, which has always been arguable in theory and which has had some successes in practice, views the imperatives of the cold war as an ineluctable challenge, has encouraged a skeptical view of the limits of negotiation, and has placed its primary trust in ample reserves of strength. The pseudo-conservative line is distinguishable from this not alone in being more crusade-minded and more risk-oriented in its proposed policies but also in its conviction that those who place greater stress on negotiation and accommodation are either engaged in treasonable conspiracy (the Birch Society's view) or are guilty of well-nigh criminal failings in moral and intellectual fiber (Goldwater's).

The characteristic note in Goldwater's damaging pre-1964 statements was a certain robust impatience with negotiation and compromise, a resolution to do away with uncertainty and ambiguity, a readiness to believe that large and complex questions of state could somehow be swept off the board by some sudden and simple gesture of violent decision. It was this state of mind that had led him to declare that a policy of coexistence was wholly impossible, to urge on more than one occasion that we withdraw from the United Nations and break off diplomatic relations with Russia and that we flatly declare ourselves against disarmament, to suggest that nuclear defoliation might be considered as a tactic in Vietnam, and to vote against the test-ban treaty.

It can be argued that occasional indiscretions, which were

125

finally qualified or repudiated, were used unfairly to Goldwater's disadvantage. Far more damaging than such indiscretions, however, was the militant conception of the cold war, never repudiated, but embodied in the argument and the title of Goldwater's book *Why Not Victory?* This book denies systematically and articulately a view of the situation that has gradually come to prevail in Washington and Moscow but not in Peking or Phoenix. The prevailing view assumes that in the thermonuclear age the losses in a general war, because it would destroy the peoples and societies on both sides of the Iron Curtain, are monstrously and unacceptably disproportionate to what could conceivably be gained by the military "victory" of either side; and that therefore both sides must conduct the cold war under restraints, both mutually imposed and self-imposed, and hardly less vital for being experimental and ill defined, which it is hoped will prevent conflict in limited theaters from escalating into a general conflict. What makes men circumspect today is their awareness that "victory" gained in such a conflict would be without meaning.

The hope of the peoples of the West has been that the uncomfortable but bearable equipoise made possible by this view will endure, at least until we have reached some less dangerous modus vivendi. And it was the basic message of Goldwater's philosophy of foreign policy that this hope is self-deceptive and cowardly. As he saw it, we are engaged in a relentless life-or-death struggle which makes coexistence meaningless. "Victory is the key to the whole problem," he wrote, "the only alternative is—obviously—defeat." The struggle against communism he saw not simply as the necessary and tragic burden of our time but as the great imperative of our existence; and there were passages in which he appeared to lament the time we find for other things. ("And yet, we still go about our everyday business, being good neighbors, providing comforts for our families, worshiping

God, and stubbornly refusing to admit the enormity of the conspiracy which has been created to destroy us.") He was troubled by the thought that "the free world," frightened by nuclear war and too much influenced by unrealistic intellectuals, "is gradually accepting the notion that anything is better than fighting." "A craven fear of death is entering the American consciousness," he wrote in 1960, "so much so that many recently felt that honoring the chief despot himself was the price to pay to avoid nuclear destruction," and he followed this melancholy observation with a strange one-sentence affirmation of faith: "We want to stay alive, of course; but more than that we want to be free." He was among those, he said disquietingly in *Why Not Victory?*, who believe "that armed conflict *may* not be necessary to defeat communism"—the italics are mine.[5]

Goldwater's approach to the world-wide strategic problems of the United States went far beyond the old isolationism, which, arrogant and chauvinist though it could be, was also infused with a strong spirit of pacifism. To the isolationists, our withdrawal from a corrupt world was meant at least to serve the interests of our own peace. Goldwater, though taking a dim view of most kinds of foreign aid, stood for the broadest interpretation of our commitments outside our borders. As he once put it, he stood for neither isolationism nor internationalism but for "a new form of nationalism" which underwrites the resistance of free nations to communism and avows as a national goal a final victory over the Communists.[6]

---

[5] *Why Not Victory?* (New York, Macfadden ed., 1963), pp. 16, 19, 22; *The Conscience of a Conservative*, pp. 90, 94.

[6] *Why Not Victory?*, pp. 90–1. It was significant that Goldwater, with a certain show of justice, should have denounced Johnson's acceptance speech to the 1964 Democratic convention as "isolationist" because of its failure to deal with the issues of foreign policy. It is also instructive to compare his views with those of Robert A. Taft, which were much affected by the older isolationism. Taft, while hardly deficient in nationalist enthusiasm, was always much more

Thus far Goldwater was not remote from the American consensus, but his unyielding and unchanging conception of the cold war represented a breach of the continuity that had on the whole pervaded the administrations of Truman, Eisenhower, and Kennedy. Goldwater looked upon the cold war as a series of relentless confrontations between ourselves and the Communists on various fronts throughout the world. If we maintain superior strength we can emerge victorious from all these confrontations, and in time the whole Communist world (which should be treated uniformly as a bloc, whatever its apparent internal differences) will crack under the stress of repeated defeats. The goal of our policies cannot be limited to peace, security, and the extension of our influence, but must go on to ultimate total victory, the ideological and political extermination of the enemy. "Our objective must be the destruction of the enemy as an ideological force possessing the means of power. . . . We will never reconcile ourselves to the Communists' possession of power of any kind in any part of the world."[7] Thus to the pseudo-conservative the ambiguous world in which we have lived for twenty years is reduced to a fleeting illusion; what is ultimately real is total victory or total

---

concerned with the prospect that war would completely destroy democracy, local self-government, and private enterprise in America. To the best of my knowledge, this concern has never been expressed by Goldwater in his significant statements on foreign policy. Taft's views, as they had developed to 1951, are stated in his book *A Foreign Policy for Americans* (New York, 1952); but for an excellent factual survey of his changing positions, see Vernon Van Dyke and Edward Lane Davis: "Senator Taft and American Security," *Journal of Politics*, XIV (May 1952), 177–202.

Although Taft's real fear of war and his understanding of its threat to free enterprise have disappeared from most right-wing thinking, there is also a strong point of continuity: Taft himself was among those Republicans who changed the debate on our foreign policy from an argument over political judgment to an argument over "treason." See Richard Rovere: "What's Happened to Taft?" *Harper's Magazine*, April 1952, pp. 38–44.

[7] *Why Not Victory?*, p. 118.

defeat, and it is this upon which we must insist. There can be no middle ground.[8] We are not merely preserving our own security; we are engaged in an attempt to stamp out an idea, in every corner of the globe, by the force of arms.

The question has been repeatedly raised whether the attempt to press every crisis to a victorious solution, especially with the avowed ultimate aim of the utter ideological extermination of the enemy, might not bring on a general war. But to raise this question is felt by right-wingers to be tainted with an unforgivable lack of manhood. Goldwater's answer was to promise that the Soviets, faced with our superiority in weapons, will never strike. But of course this is a promise on which no American can deliver, and for whose fulfillment we must depend upon Moscow, and ultimately Peking. Moreover, there is a curious passage in *Why Not Victory?* in which Goldwater flatly admitted that such fulfillment is not to be expected. The Communist world, he said, is likely to resort to general war only under one of two conditions. One, of course, is if we invite their attack by political weakness and military disarmament. But the other is "if there is a decisive switch in world affairs to the point where it is obvious they are going to lose."[9] And it is, of course, precisely to this point that Goldwater has always urged that they be pushed. The central dilemma of total victory, as expounded by Goldwater, is thus made to seem more ominous and insoluble than the many perplexing dilemmas of coexistence.

It was his casual view of nuclear warfare, and not his occasional indiscretions, that made Goldwater seem dangerous to many conservative Americans. What had become clear by 1964, and what could not be undone in the campaign, was the public impression that Goldwater's imagination had never

---

[8] For Goldwater's objection to the idea that total victory cannot be rendered meaningful in our time, see ibid., pp. 106-9.

[9] Ibid., p. 82.

confronted the implications of thermonuclear war. For a man who was so gravely distressed by violence in the streets, he seemed strangely casual about the prospect of total destruction. The final spiritual Armageddon of the fundamentalists, their overarching moral melodrama, the dream of millennial crusading and decisive conflict, plainly stirred his mind, but the hard realities of the current world seemed more remote. He could no more recognize that nuclear weaponry had created a new age of diplomacy than he could admit that modern urban industrialism had created a new environment. "I do not subscribe to the theory," he wrote, "that nuclear weapons have changed everything. . . . We have in the nuclear bomb an advance in weaponry, and terrible though that advance is, it still is merely a more efficient means of destruction. In a historical and relative sense, it can be compared with the advance made in military operations by the invention and adaption [*sic*] of gunpowder to war-making and the development of aerial warfare and strategic bombing missions."[1]

As a concession to campaign opportunism, Goldwater sometimes soft-pedaled his approach to the problems of foreign policy, contenting himself mainly with appeals to the restlessness of the people over the inability of the country to resolve its foreign crises or maintain its prestige in the world: "Are you proud of our fight for freedom? Are you proud of Panama? Are you proud of the burned effigy in Greece? Are you proud when no country is too small to pull Uncle Sam's whiskers and get away with it? Are you proud of wheat deals with the destroyers of liberty?" An interesting aspect of this appeal, since it sheds light not simply on the pseudo-conservative mentality but on the dynamics of American politics today, is its resemblance to Kennedy's appeal in the campaign of 1960. Like Goldwater, Kennedy had protested that we

---

[1] Ibid., pp. 83–4.

were seriously underarmed—and his admirers remember the bogus "missile gap" issue with chagrin. Like Goldwater, Kennedy had stressed the theme that the United States had lost prestige abroad, and dwelled on the establishment of Castro in Cuba only ninety miles from our shores.

Thus the Kennedy and Goldwater campaigns were both vigorously nationalist, appealing to public uneasiness over the indecisiveness of the cold war. That two men so different in outlook should have had this much in common as campaigners underlines the force of a persistent issue that opposition candidates will find it hard to resist. Both campaigns signify the deep perplexity of the American public over our foreign policies. The weakness of the pseudo-conservative appeal is that it strikes at only one side of complex public feelings: it shows an utter lack of tenderness for the pervasive American desire to continue in peace. In its appeal to toughness and frontier hardihood and its call for a fundamentalist all-out struggle with absolute evil, it runs up against both the pacific yearnings and the basic hedonism of the public, for which pseudo-conservatives have an ill-concealed contempt. But the strength of the pseudo-conservative position lies in its appeal to the American bafflement before the ambiguities and compromises in our foreign dealings. The American public pays heavy taxes to maintain an immensely expensive military machine with vast and unprecedented powers of destruction and to sustain military and economic operations around the globe; and yet year by year it finds that its expenditures and efforts yield neither decisive victories nor final settlements. The roll of inconclusive negotiations, sorties, and stalemates, symbolized by the names of Yalta, Korea, Berlin, Cuba, and Vietnam, seems to stretch out indefinitely.

All attempts to explain that this frustrating situation is not simply the product of execrable statecraft—not to speak of treason—run up against a fundamental fact of American history and a basic fixture in the American imagination. Many years ago, in an illuminating essay, D. W. Brogan pointed to a state of mind which he called "the illusion of American omnipotence"—defined as "the illusion that any situation which distresses or endangers the United States can only exist because some Americans have been fools or knaves."[2] The best illustration, he suggested, was our response to the Chinese Revolution, toward which Americans had neither historical awe nor historical curiosity, preferring to regard it as no more than a problem in our foreign and domestic policy. The oldest civilization in existence, comprising about a fifth of the human race, situated six thousand miles from the Pacific coast of the United States and having a contiguous frontier with Russia, had taken a turn—presumably for reasons deeply rooted in its history and geography, its traditions and problems—which was understandably very unwelcome to Americans. Instead of concluding that this was a response to massive strategic and economic realities largely beyond our control, millions of Americans were apparently convinced that this enormous country had been in our pocket, and had been lost or stolen only because of the mistakes (or treachery) of Roosevelt, Marshall, and Acheson, mistakes which could easily have been rectified by greater statesmen like Walter Judd or Senator Jenner.[3] Roosevelt was anathematized for having "permitted" Russia to become a Pacific power at Yalta, although Russia had been a Pacific power before the United States existed. It was all too lightly assumed, Brogan prophetically remarked, that Russia had "taken over" China as she had taken over Poland. Moreover, the persistent faith that American intervention could have changed Chinese history was accompanied

---

[2] "The Illusion of American Omnipotence," *Harper's Magazine*, December 1952, pp. 21–8.

[3] Cf. Stormer: "About 600-million Chinese were betrayed into communist slavery. It was all done by a handful of American traitors and their liberal dupes." Op. cit., p. 31.

by the faith that this involved nothing more than the choice of a few sound alternative policies, without demanding of the American people the massive sacrifices necessary to sustain a major commitment in China.

The difficulty many Americans have in understanding that their power in the world is not unlimited—a difficulty shared by no other people—Brogan explained by observing that in one very real sense the Americans had only recently been confronted by a situation long since familiar to the rest of the human race. The trying responsibilities and insoluble problems now confronting the United States were, he remarked, "a new story for the United States but . . . an old one for Europe. What the American people are enduring now is what the French, the English, the Russian peoples, even the Spanish and Italian peoples, suffered in the process of extending or trying to retain their empires."

The American frame of mind was created by a long history that encouraged our belief that we have an almost magical capacity to have our way in the world, that the national will can be made entirely effective, as against other peoples, at a relatively small price. We began our existence without world-wide territorial aspirations or responsibilities, but as a continental power with basically continental aspirations. From the beginning of our national life, our power to attain national goals on which we were determined was in effect irresistible —*within* our chosen, limited continental theater of action. Our chief foes—Indians, Mexicans, the decaying Spanish Empire—were on the whole easily vanquished. It is true that in fighting the British in 1812 we became engaged with a vastly greater power, but at a time when the British were in mortal combat with Napoleon and their American effort was a sideshow. Even then, though we did rather badly—our invasions of Canada were repulsed, our capital was burned, and our shipping was bottled up—a curious stroke of luck at New

Orleans made it possible for us to imagine that the stalemate peace we concluded represented some kind of victory.[4] The only time the American land was truly ravaged by the horrors of war was during our own Civil War when our wounds were self-inflicted. Europe's quarrels, which in the twentieth century have become an American problem, were during the nineteenth an American advantage. The achievement of independence with national boundaries stretching westward to the Mississippi, the bargain purchase of the enormous territory of Louisiana, the easy acquisition of the Floridas without war, the assertion of our place in the world's carrying trade, the annexation of Texas and the seizure of immense western territories from Mexico—all these were accomplished at the cost of troubled, preoccupied, or weak nations, and at a minimum expenditure of our blood and treasure. In our own hemisphere, which was our only center of territorial aspirations, our preponderance tempted Secretary of State Olney to say in 1895: "Today the United States is practically sovereign on this continent and its fiat is law on the subjects to which it confines its interposition." A few years later our entry into the imperial game of the nineteenth century came at the expense of a befuddled and bankrupt Spain, incapable of offering us serious opposition.[5]

---

[4] The smashing victory scored by the Americans under Jackson at New Orleans came only after the terms of peace, in which none of our demands was met, were already signed. The news of New Orleans, however, circulated about the country more or less simultaneously with the news of the peace—a fortunate conjuncture for the American imagination.

[5] Goldwater, who is reported to read a good deal in the history and antiquities of Arizona, but not in world history, had a different version of this: "It was this independence—strong, virile, and unafraid —that led us to challenge a much mightier Spain and call her to her account for her tyranny over our Western Hemispheric neighbors." *Why Not Victory?*, p. 54. This is a delusion not shared by any American historian. Nor was it shared by informed American contemporaries. See my essay "Cuba, the Philippines, and Manifest Destiny," below, esp. p. 162.

While expansion was won so cheaply, the United States, thanks largely to its continental position, was enjoying, as C. Vann Woodward has pointed out, virtually free security—which, he suggests, should be given a place among the great shaping forces of our history alongside the free land of our continental interior.[6] Fenced in behind the Atlantic, Pacific, and Arctic oceans, the United States was in a position to spare itself expensive armies and elaborate chains of fortifications. Even naval protection came cheap, since the navy that policed and defended the Atlantic was maintained, to our considerable benefit, by the British. In 1861, as Woodward points out, the United States maintained the second-largest merchant marine in the world without having a battle fleet—there were only 7,600 men in our navy as compared with over ten times that number in the British navy. A luxurious penury also affected our military establishment. At the outbreak of the Civil War the United States army numbered only a few more than 16,000 men, occupied mainly at posts on the Indian frontier. Even by 1914, when the nation had been launched upon its imperial career and had reorganized its military establishment, the proportion of its military appropriations to national income was only one-fourth of that paid by the British people, about one-sixth of that paid by the French, Japanese, and Germans, and about one-eighth of that paid by the Russians.

Free security, easy expansion, inexpensive victories, decisive triumphs—such was almost our whole experience with the rest of the world down to the twentieth century. The First World War, which we entered triumphantly in its closing phases, gave us a glimpse, but only the glimpse of an outsider, of what the rest of the world endured. It was only after the major effort of the Second World War, when we found our-

---

[6] "This Age of Reinterpretation," *American Historical Review*, XLVI (October 1960), 2–8.

selves not presiding over a pacified and docile world, but engaged in a world-wide stalemate and a costly and indecisive struggle in Korea, that the American people first experienced the full reality of what all the other great nations have long known—the situation of limited power. The illusion of American omnipotence remained, but the reality of American preponderance was gone. It is this shock to the American consciousness to which Goldwater and others appealed when they cried: "Why not victory?" Why not, indeed, when one remembers all those facile triumphs? In this light it becomes possible to understand how Goldwater thought he could promise unremitting victories in the cold war along with balanced budgets and lower taxes.

"Until 1950," Goldwater wrote in *Why Not Victory?*, "America had never lost a shooting war," but within the next ten years we had suffered "repeated defeats."[7] This situation, in his view, is not to be accounted for by the fact that we now have world-wide aspirations going far beyond our early strategic goals or that our free security is gone because of technological changes; it is not because we are for the first time situated, as many peoples have been before us, in a position of limited power, or because we are counterposed to great and numerous peoples with a nuclear weaponry comparable to our own. It is because we have been ruled by the foolish and the incompetent, and perhaps, as his more ardent admirers boldly proclaim, by the treasonous as well. For those who conceive of history not as a sequence of related events but as a moral melodrama, such imputations seem plausible enough. And when one ponders how much the world position of America has changed within the past fifty years, what seems most remarkable is not that many should respond wholeheartedly to the pseudo-conservative interpretation of events, but

---

[7] Pp. 23–4.

136

that our statesmanship has been as restrained as it has usually been and that this restraint has won preponderant public support.

V

THE RIGHT-WING ENTHUSIASTS were justified, I believe, in the elation they expressed, even in defeat, over the Goldwater campaign. They had less than nothing to show in practical results, but it is not practical results that they look for. They have demonstrated that the right wing is a formidable force in our politics and have given us reason to think that it is a permanent force. Writing in 1954, at the peak of the McCarthyist period, I suggested that the American right wing could best be understood not as a neo-fascist movement girding itself for the conquest of power but as a persistent and effective minority whose main threat was in its power to create "a political climate in which the rational pursuit of our well-being and safety would become impossible."[8] This still seems to be the true potential of the pseudo-conservative right; it is a potential that can be realized without winning the White House, even without again winning the Republican nomination.

That the right-wingers are actually increasing in numbers is doubtful; but their performance in 1964 shows how much leverage they can achieve, whatever their numbers, with dedication and organization. The tally of over 27 million votes for a candidate of pronounced right-wing views is delusive, but to them it is delusive in a heartening and invigorating way. A post-election poll suggested that at the most generous estimate only about 5.4 million Goldwater voters—or one-fifth of the whole—can be counted as hard-core Goldwater enthusiasts, a

---

[8] See above, p. 65.

finding which fits roughly with his standing in the pre-nomination Gallup polls and with those primaries in which he was rated by Republican voters against the whole field of moderate and liberal candidates.[9] But so long as their zeal and gifts for organization are as powerful as they have been in recent years, the right-wingers still stand in a position to make themselves effective far out of proportion to their numbers. The professionals who have already repossessed the party apparatus have not yet had a final reckoning with its right wing. Moreover, Goldwater's views, though far from predominant among the party's voters, were much more popular among its activist personnel—among those who do its hard work and supply its funds and who won him his delegates at the Cow Palace.

The largest single difficulty facing the right wing as a force within the Republican party is its inability to rear and sustain national leaders. Most Republican governors belong to the party's moderate wing. The roll call of the right wing's senatorial heroes is a list of the dead or the departed: Taft, McCarthy, Knowland, Bricker, Bridges, Jenner, and now Goldwater—and today not a single right-wing senator remains who is both secure in his seat and well known to the public. Although this is a serious liability in practical politics, it is less serious in the arena which the right wing regards as most important, the arena of "conservative education." At the

---

[9] *The New York Times*, December 18, 1964; cf. the pre-election polls and primaries at various stages in the nomination fight, reported in Novak: op. cit., pp. 263, 325, 326, 332, 375, 379, 380, 389, 396. Louis H. Bean and Roscoe Drummond, however, estimate that only 2.5 to 3 million of Goldwater's votes were those of true believers and that the rest was simply a Republican party vote. They arrive at this estimate partly by measuring the proportion of Republicans who preferred Goldwater in polls to other Republicans against the total number of declared Republicans. They have checked this against his actual performance at the polls, as compared with more typical Republican candidates in the past. See "How Many Votes Does Goldwater Own?" *Look*, March 23, 1965, pp. 75–6.

level of party leadership, the right-wingers do well. In many parts of the country the most ardent Republicans are ultra-conservative. Often they are the heads of small businesses or independent professionals who can find the time and spend the money to make their views felt. Moderate Republicans are more likely to be officers or employees of large corporations whose positions leave them less time for partisan activity. Hence the party in some sections of the country has gravitated into the hands of a leadership that is considerably more conservative than its voters. The great middle band of the party, which is by far its largest portion, is conservative enough to be susceptible to some of the right-wing notions, even though it does not share the partisan rage and the conspiratorial suspicions of the Goldwaterites.

In the battle for public opinion, the right wing has ample funds at its disposal, and certain advantages that accrue from its rough-and-tumble tactics. The conservative label and the nationalist animus of the far right are handsome advantages: it can wrap itself in the symbols of respectability and Americanism, and yet it has no inhibitions about gaining what it can through intimidation, which it brings to bear with great effectiveness upon schoolteachers and school administrators, librarians, advertisers in the press and mass media, local merchants, and working politicians. It gets a bad press in the sophisticated national media which it so ardently resents, but the journalists and intellectuals in the cosmopolitan centers readily forget how frightening right-wing pressures can be in smaller communities.

Even the seemingly permanent minority position of the Republican party, which in one sense sets a limit to the operations of the far right, is in another sense one of its assets. Over the years the number of American voters who identify themselves in polls as Republicans has shrunk proportionately to a point at which it is now only half as large as the number of

Democrats—a situation reflected quite precisely in the present ratio between the two parties in Congresss. The Democratic party, with its broad centrist position, has come to embrace so large a part of the American political consensus that moderate Republican leaders find it all but impossible to discover a constructive issue upon which they can forge an independent identity and relieve themselves of the onus of "me-tooism" with which the right wing, on the whole quite correctly, charges them. The very destruction that Goldwater has wreaked within the party has its compensations for the right-wingers. It is true that this immediately cost them the control of the party; but so long as the party continues in its present helpless minority position, the possibility remains that, even without a repetition of the Goldwater takeover, the right-wingers can prevent the moderates from refurbishing the party as a constructive opposition.

But, above all, the far right has become a permanent force in the political order because the things upon which it feeds are also permanent: the chronic and ineluctable frustrations of our foreign policy, the opposition to the movement for racial equality, the discontents that come with affluence, the fevers of the culturally alienated who practice what Fritz Stern has called in another connection "the politics of cultural despair." As a movement, ironically enough, the far right flourishes to a striking degree on what it has learned from the radicals. Their forces, as men like Fred C. Schwarz and Stephen Shadegg have urged, have been bolshevized—staffed with small, quietly efficient cadres of zealots who on short notice can whip up a show of political strength greatly disproportionate to their numbers. The movement now uses the techniques it has taken from the radicals while it spends the money it gets from the conservatives. Finally, it moves in the uninhibited mental world of those who neither have nor expect to win responsibility. Its opponents, as men who carry the burdens

140

of government, are always vulnerable to the discontents aroused by the manifold failures of our society. But the right-wingers, who are willing to gamble with the future, enjoy the wide-ranging freedom of the agitational mind, with its paranoid suspicions, its impossible demands, and its millennial dreams of total victory.

Part II

Some Problems
of the Modern Era

CUBA, THE PHILIPPINES, AND MANIFEST DESTINY

This essay, now considerably revised, was originally written in 1951 as one of a series of fourteen lectures given by various writers at Bennington College and published in 1952 under the editorship of Daniel Aaron in *America in Crisis*. Each of the lecturers undertook to analyze a focal episode in the development of the American public consciousness, in the hope that a common exploration of such episodes would shed some light on the American manner of responding to crises.

My assignment was to analyze the decision made when our entry into and retention of the Philippine Islands after the war with Spain caused the nation to turn from its traditional continental policies and launch itself on a course of world imperialism. What were the issues, what were the consequences for the national mentality, when a democratic country, committed by its creed and its very origins to self-government and self-determination, was confronted with the prospect of taking by conquest distant territory inhabited by an alien and all but unknown people?

The more one looked at it, the clearer it became that the debate set off by the issue of "imperialism" from 1898 to 1900 could not be considered apart from the entire crisis in foreign policy that came with the Spanish-American War. The most striking thing about that war was that it originated not in imperialist ambition but in popular humanitarianism. It started with our desire to free Cuba and ended with our domination over the Philippines. The war was not begun with the intention of taking either Cuba or the Philippines. The Teller Resolution, appended to the declaration of war and adopted without debate, expressly disclaimed any American intention to acquire Cuba, and its promise was kept. As for the Philippines, occupation was never at any time the subject of public discussion or interest, or even of concern among the ruling elites. Before the outbreak of the war no one would have dared to propose the conquest and retention of these islands as an object of national policy. Except for a few naval strategists concerned with a strike at the Spanish navy there, no one thought about the Philippines at all, and Dewey's sudden victory in Manila Bay confronted even policy-makers with an unexpected decision. Little wonder that the people themselves were quickly persuaded that "destiny" had imposed upon them a new and unwelcome duty: destiny or no, they had been confronted with a *fait accompli*.

Yet it was true that the sudden fact of overseas conquest was absorbed by American opinion leaders and by the public itself without extraordinary anguish and by some with enthusiasm. The humanitarian impulse behind the war was strangely coupled with a taste for battle; similarly the imperialist impulse that led to ready acceptance of annexation was also coupled with and softened by much talk of duty and responsibility, which in fact foreshadowed later American policies in the Philippines. Both the humane feelings and the urge to combat and conquest seem to stem from a prevalent state of mind that had come into being in the 1890's, and the primary concern of my essay turned out to be not so much the easily won argument over keeping the islands as the relationship between an observable crisis in the national consciousness and the events of the war. Some readers have been disposed to see in this an attempt to offer a psychological alternative to an economic interpretation of the origins of American imperialism. I consider it less psychological than institutional; less an alternative than a necessary supplement to any economic interpretation that is to avoid running aground on certain stubborn facts. The general depression of the 1890's, the widespread anxieties and discontents of the era, clearly had important bearings on questions of war and empire, and must be seen as major instrumentalities of history.

Two important full-scale studies of the roots of American

imperialism have appeared since the original version of this essay was written. Neither is entirely in accord with my analysis, but there is common ground on some points. Walter La Feber, in *The New Empire*, emphasizes—I believe quite rightly—how long and purposeful a preparation the imperialism of the 1890's had, and he looks upon expansion as a response to the industrial revolution of the latter half of the nineteenth century. He stresses the demand for new markets, the propaganda of navalists and expansionists, the creation of the new navy—all of which were well-developed trends before the crisis of the 1890's. He also remarks, however, that "the depression of 1893 acted as the catalyst to these developments of a half century," and it is precisely this catalytic process with which I am concerned. Ernest R. May, whose views of the age likewise differ from mine in significant respects, concurs in finding the source of the war in a crisis of the national consciousness. "The nation," he writes of the 1890's in his *Imperial Democracy*, "was in a state of upset"; and after enumerating some of the sources of this upset, he concludes: "In some irrational way, all these influences and anxieties translated themselves into concern for suffering Cuba. For the people as for the government, war with monarchical, Catholic, Latin Spain had no purpose except to relieve emotion." Whatever else may be said about it, the entire episode is indeed an instructive case study in the dynamics of national emotion.

I

T HE taking of the Philippine Islands from Spain in 1899 marked a major historical departure for the American people, a breach in their traditions and a shock to their established values. To be sure, from their national beginnings they had constantly engaged in expansion, but almost entirely into contiguous territory. Now they were extending themselves to distant extra-hemispheric colonies. They were abandoning a strategy of defense hitherto limited to the continent and its appurtenances, in favor of a major strategic commitment in the Far East. Thus far their expansion had been confined to the spread of a relatively homogeneous population into territories planned from the beginning to develop self-government; now control was to be imposed by force on millions of ethnic aliens. The acquisition of the islands, therefore, was understood by contemporaries on both sides of the debate, as it is readily understood today, to be a turning point in our history.

To discuss the debate in isolation from other events, however, would be to deprive it of its full significance. America's entrance into the Philippine Islands was a by-product of the Spanish-American War. The Philippine crisis is inseparable from the war crisis, and the war crisis itself is inseparable from a larger constellation that might be called "the psychic crisis of the 1890's."

Central in the background of the psychic crisis was the great depression that broke in 1893 and was still very acute when the agitation over the war in Cuba began. Severe depression, by itself, does not always generate an emotional crisis as intense as that of the nineties. In the 1870's the country had been swept by a depression of comparable acuteness and duration which, however, did not give rise to all the phenomena that appeared in the 1890's or to very many of them with comparable intensity and impact. It is often said that the 1890's, unlike the 1870's, form a "watershed" in American history. The difference between the emotional and intellectual impact of these two depressions can be measured, I believe, not by the difference in severity, but rather by reference to a number of singular events that in the 1890's converged with the depression to heighten its impact upon the public mind.

First in importance was the Populist movement, the free-silver agitation, the heated campaign of 1896. For the first time in our history a depression had created a protest movement strong enough to capture a major party and raise the specter, however unreal, of drastic social convulsion. Second was the maturation and bureaucratization of American business, the completion of its essential industrial plant, and the development of trusts on a scale sufficient to stir the anxiety that the old order of competitive opportunities was approaching an eclipse. Third, and of immense symbolic importance, was the apparent filling up of the continent and the disappearance of the frontier line. We now know how much land had not yet been taken up and how great were the remaining possibilities for internal expansion both in business and on the land; but to the mind of the 1890's it seemed that the resource that had engaged the energies of the people for three centuries had been used up. The frightening possibility suggested itself that a serious juncture in the nation's history had come. As Frederick Jackson Turner expressed it in his famous paper of 1893: "Now, four centuries from the discovery of America, at the end of one hundred years of life under the Constitution, the frontier has gone, and with its going has closed the first period of American history."

To middle-class citizens who had been brought up to think in terms of the nineteenth-century order, the outlook seemed grim. Farmers in the staple-growing region had gone mad over silver and Bryan; workers were stirring in bloody struggles like the Homestead and Pullman strikes; the supply of new land seemed at an end; the trust threatened the spirit of business enterprise; civic corruption was at a high point in the large cities; great waves of seemingly unassimilable immigrants arrived yearly and settled in hideous slums. To many historically conscious writers, the nation appeared overripe, like an empire ready for collapse through a stroke from outside or through internal upheaval. Acute as the situation was for all those who lived by the symbols of national power—for

149

the governing and thinking classes—it was especially poignant for young people, who would have to make their careers in the dark world that seemed to be emerging.

The symptomatology of the crisis would record several tendencies in popular thought and behavior that had previously existed only in pale and tenuous form. These symptoms were manifest in two quite different moods. The key to one of them was an intensification of protest and humanitarian reform. Populism, utopianism, the rise of the Christian Social gospel, the growing intellectual interest in socialism, the social settlement movement that appealed so strongly to the college generation of the nineties, the quickening of protest and social criticism in the realistic novel—all these are expressions of this mood. The other mood was one of national self-assertion, aggression, expansion. The motif of the first was social sympathy; of the second, national power. During the 1890's far more patriotic groups were founded than in any other decade of our history; the naval theories of Captain Mahan were gaining in influence; naval construction was booming; there was an immense quickening of the American cult of Napoleon and a vogue of the virile and martial writings of Rudyard Kipling; young Theodore Roosevelt became the exemplar of the vigorous, masterful, out-of-doors man; the revival of European imperialism stirred speculation over what America's place would be in the world of renewed colonial rivalries, and in some stirred a demand to get into the imperial race to avoid the risk of being overwhelmed by other powers. But most significant was the rising tide of jingoism, a matter of constant comment among observers of American life during the decade.

Jingoism, of course, was not new in American history. But during the 1870's and 1880's the American public had been notably quiescent about foreign relations. There had been expansionist statesmen, but they had been blocked by popular apathy, and our statecraft had been restrained.[1] Grant had failed dismally in his attempt to acquire Santo Domingo; our policy toward troubled Hawaii had been cautious; in 1877 an offer of two Haitian naval harbors had been spurned. In responding to Haiti, Secretary of State Frelinghuysen had remarked that "the policy of this Government . . . has tended toward avoidance of possessions disconnected from the main continent."[2] Henry Cabot Lodge, in his life of George Washington published in 1889, observed that foreign relations then filled "but a slight place in American politics, and excite generally only a languid interest."[3] Within a few years this comment would have seemed absurd. In 1895, Russell A. Alger reported to Lodge, after reading one of Lodge's own articles to a Cincinnati audience, that he was convinced by the response that foreign policy, "more than anything else, touches the public pulse of today."[4] The history of the 1890's is the history of public agitation over expansionist issues and of quarrels with other nations.

[1] See Julius W. Pratt: *America's Colonial Experiment* (New York, 1950), pp. 4–13.

[2] Albert K. Weinberg: *Manifest Destiny* (Baltimore, 1935), p. 252. There is a suggestive similarity to the conditions of the nineties in the circumstances attending the Cuban insurrection of 1868–78. The hostilities were even more bitter and exhausting than those of 1895–8; its latter phases also corresponded with an acute depression in the United States; the case of the *Virginius* offered a pretext for war almost as satisfactory as that of the *Maine*. The public and the press raised a clamor about it. But it did not rise even near to the pitch of overwhelming pressure for war. Several things were supplied in the nineties that were missing in the seventies: among them a psychic crisis that generated an expansionist mood; the techniques of yellow journalism; and an adequate navy that made a war with Spain possible to contemplate. Cf. Samuel Flagg Bemis: *A Diplomatic History of the United States* (New York, 1936), pp. 433–5. In the seventies the country was also too close to the completion of an exhausting internal war of its own.

[3] Samuel Flagg Bemis: op. cit., p. 432.

[4] Walter La Feber: *The New Empire* (Ithaca, 1963), p. 250.

I I

THREE PRIMARY INCIDENTS fired American jingoism between the spring of 1891 and the close of 1895. First came
Secretary of State Blaine's tart and provocative reply to the
Italian minister's protest over the lynching of eleven Italians
in New Orleans. Then there was friction with Chile over a
riot in Valparaíso in which two American sailors were killed
and several injured by a Chilean mob. In 1895 occurred the
more famous Venezuela boundry dispute with Britain. Discussion of these incidents would take us too far afield, but note
that they all had these characteristics in common: in none of
them was national security or the natural interest vitally and
immediately involved; in all three American diplomacy was
extraordinarily and disproportionately aggressive; in all three
the possibility of war was contemplated; and in each case the
response of the American public and press was enthusiasti-
cally nationalist and almost unanimous.

It is hard to read the history of these events without concluding that politicians were persistently using jingoism to
restore their prestige, mend their party fences, and divert the
public mind from grave internal discontents. It hardly seems
an accident that jingoism and populism rose together. Documentary evidence for the political exploitation of foreign
crises is not overwhelmingly abundant, in part because such a
motive is not necessarily conscious and where it is conscious it
is not always confessed or recorded.[5] The persistence of

---

[5] The most notable case in our earlier history was Seward's fantastic proposal during the crisis of 1861 that Lincoln attempt to
reunite the North and South by precipitating a foreign war. A classic
expression of the philosophy of this kind of statecraft was made by
Fisher Ames in 1802, after the Federalists had been routed by the
Jeffersonians. "We need as all nations do," he wrote to Rufus King,
"the compression on the outside of our circle of a formidable neigh-

jingoism in every administration from Harrison's to Theodore Roosevelt's, however, is too suggestive to be ignored. During the nineties the press of each party was fond of accusing the other of exploiting foreign conflict. Blaine was not above twisting the British lion's tail for political purposes; and it is hardly likely that he would have exempted Italy from the same treatment. Harrison, on the eve of the Chile affair, for the acuteness of which he was primarily responsible, was being urged by prominent Republican politicians who had the coming presidential campaign in mind to pursue a more aggressive foreign policy because it would "have the . . . effect of diverting attention from stagnant political discussions."[6] And although some Democratic papers charged that he was planning to run for re-election during hostilities so that he could use the "don't swap horses in the middle of the stream" appeal, many Democrats felt that it was politically necessary for them to back him against Chile so that, as one of their congressmen remarked, the Republicans could not "run away with all the capital there is to be made in an attempt to assert national self-respect."[7]

---

bor, whose presence shall at all times excite stronger fears than demagogues can inspire the people with towards their government." Henry Jones Ford: *The Rise and Growth of American Politics* (New York, 1914), p. 69. One of the signal differences between the 1870's and the 1890's was that there was still a usable domestic enemy in the earlier period. "Our strong ground," wrote Rutherford B. Hayes in 1876, "is a dread of a solid South, rebel rule, etc., etc. . . . It leads people away from 'hard times' which is our deadliest foe." J. F. Rhodes: *History of the United States* (New York, 1906), VII, 220.

[6] Donald M. Dozer: "Benjamin Harrison and the Presidential Campaign of 1892," *American Historical Review*, LIV (October 1948), p. 52; A. T. Volwiler: "Harrison, Blaine, and American Foreign Policy, 1889–1893," American Philosophical Society *Proceedings*, Vol. LXXIX (1938), argues plausibly that the imperial mood dawned during Harrison's administration.

[7] Earl W. Fornell: "Historical Antecedents of the Chilean-American Crisis of 1891–92," unpublished M.A. thesis, Columbia University (1950), p. 138; see especially Chs. 11 and 12, for Harrison's exploitation of the war crisis and the intense public reaction.

Grover Cleveland was a man of exceptional integrity whose stand against pressure for the annexation of Hawaii during 1893–4 does him much credit. But precisely for this act of restraint he was accused by Republican jingoes like Lodge and by many in his own party of being indifferent to America's position in the world. And if Cleveland was too high-minded a man to exploit a needless foreign crisis, his Secretary of State, Richard Olney, was not. The Venezuela affair, which came at a low point in the prestige of Cleveland's administration, offered Olney a rich chance to prove to critics in both parties that the administration was, after all, capable of vigorous diplomacy. That the crisis might have partisan value was not unthinkable to members of Olney's party. He received a letter from a Texas congressman encouraging him to "go ahead," on the ground that the Venezuela issue was a "winner" in every section of the country. "When you come to diagnose the country's internal ills," his correspondent continued, "the possibilities of 'blood and iron' loom up immediately. Why, Mr. Secretary, just think of how angry the anarchistic, socialistic, and populistic boil appears on our political surface and who knows how deep its roots extend or ramify? One cannon shot across the bow of a British boat in defense of this principle will knock more *pus* out of it than would suffice to inoculate and corrupt our people for the next two centuries."[8]

This pattern had been well established when the Cuban crisis broke out anew in 1895. It was quite in keeping that

---

[8] Alfred Vagts: *Deutschland und die Vereinigten Staaten in der Weltpolitik* (New York, 1935), I, 511; for the domestic roots of administration policy, see Nelson M. Blake: "Background of Cleveland's Venezuela Policy," *American Historical Review*, XLVII (January 1942), 259–77. For a different view, see La Feber: op. cit., pp. 279–83. La Feber considers domestic pressures of minor consequence, and believes that Cleveland and Olney saw important long-range American interests at stake in Venezuela.

Secretary Olney should get a letter during the 1896 campaign from Fitzhugh Lee, the American consul in Havana, advising that the conservative faction of Gold Democrats become identified with the strong policy of mediation or intervention in Cuba. Thus, he argued, "the 'Sound Democrats' would get, with the Executive, the credit of stopping the wholesale atrocities daily practised here, the acquisition of Cuba by purchase, or by fighting a successful war, if war there be. In the latter case, the enthusiasm, the applications for service, the employment of many of the unemployed, might do much towards directing the minds of the people from imaginary ills, the relief of which is erroneously supposed to be reached by 'Free Silver.' "[9]

When President McKinley took office he was well aware that nationalist enthusiasm had reached a pitch that made war very likely. A few months earlier, he had told Senator Lodge that he might be "obliged" to go to war as soon as he entered the presidency, and had expressed a preference that the Cuban crisis be settled one way or another in the time between his election and inauguration. Although he had promised Carl Schurz that there would be "no jingo nonsense under my administration," he proved not to have quite enough strength to resist the current. He did not himself partake of the hysteria that was mounting throughout the country, and he was concerned that the country was unprepared to wage a war, uncertain even whether war could be confined to a contest with Spain. He soon found himself under incredible pressures for positive action, which he resisted as long as most Presidents would have been able to do. His failure was not in yielding too soon to the war fever but in not taking early initiative to rein it in. Sending the *Maine* to Havana proved to be one of his most vital mistakes, since it gave a hostage to the

---

[9] Vagts: op. cit., II, 1266 n. Cf. Ernest R. May: *Imperial Democracy* (New York, 1961) pp. 75–76.

war party. The act was meant in part to curb the enthusiasm of the jingoes at home, but Cleveland had resisted just such a proposal on the grounds that an inflammatory incident was all too likely. No doubt the actual sinking of the *Maine* on February 16 went even beyond anything that Cleveland or McKinley could have anticipated. From that time onward, the chances of avoiding war seemed slim.

Members of McKinley's own party put a great deal of pressure on him to give the people their war rather than endanger the Republican position. Some of them feared, as an infuriated senator put it to the Secretary of State, that Congress would declare war in spite of him. "He'll get run over and the party with him."[1] For McKinley himself the prospect that Congress might act without him was, by March, a very real fear.[2] It was widely argued that if war was inevitable, as presumably it was, it would be better for the President to lead rather than to be pushed; that resistance to war would be ruinous to the party; that going to war would prevent the Democrats from entering the next presidential campaign with "Free Cuba" and "Free Silver" as their battle cries.[3] After Senator Proctor's moving speech in the Senate on March 17 about conditions in Cuba, the Chicago *Times-Herald*, a McKinley paper, declared that intervention in Cuba, peaceful or forcible, was "immediately inevitable. Our own internal political conditions will not permit its postponement. . . . Let President McKinley hesitate to rise to the just expectations of the American people, and who can doubt that 'war for Cuban liberty' will be the crown of thorns that Free Silver Demo-

---

[1] H. Wayne Morgan: *William McKinley and His America* (Syracuse, 1963), p. 370.

[2] Ibid., pp. 369–70.

[3] Vagts: op. cit., II, 1308 n; Samuel Flagg Bemis: *The Latin American Policy of the United States* (New York, 1943), p. 407; Thomas A. Bailey: *A Diplomatic History of the American People* (New York, 1944), pp. 506–8; C. S. Olcott: *The Life of William McKinley* (Boston, 1916), II, 28.

crats and Populists will adopt at the election this fall. . . . The President would be powerless to stay any legislation, however ruinous to every sober, honest interest of the country."[4] "The people want no disgraceful negotiations with Spain," cried the Chicago *Tribune*. "Should the president plunge his administration into that morass, he and his party would be swept out of power in 1900 by a fine burst of popular indignation. An administration which stains the national honor never will be forgiven."[5] Reporting to McKinley on sentiment in Massachusetts, Henry Cabot Lodge wrote in March: "If the war in Cuba drags on through the summer with nothing done, we shall go down in the greatest defeat ever known. . . . I know that it is easily and properly said that to bring on or even to threaten war for political reasons is a crime & I quite agree. But to sacrifice a great party & bring free silver upon the country for a wrong policy is hardly less odious."[6]

In the facing of mounting pressure for war, McKinley was unable to sustain his negotiations with Spain long enough to exhaust the possibilities of a diplomatic solution. By the beginning of April some important demands had been conceded—an end to the *reconcentrado* policy and reparations for the *Maine*. But it is doubtful that a diplomatic solution could have been arrived at, since both the Cuban revolutionaries and the United States were insisting upon full Cuban independence, leaving no face-saving formula for the Spanish government. In the opening days of April, McKinley resolved upon war. On April 10, as he was about to send Congress his war message, word came from his ambassador in Spain, Stewart L. Woodford, that the Spaniards had yielded to the American demand for a prompt armistice, and Woodford also thought, rather optimistically, that even the demand for independence

[4] Walter Millis: *The Martial Spirit* (New York, 1931), p. 124.
[5] Morgan: op. cit., p. 368.
[6] May: op. cit., p. 146.

might still be met. This news McKinley incorporated anticlimactically at the end of the war message, thus passing up his chance for one final statesmanlike act, an appeal for further delay. That such a step could have avoided war, however, is doubtful. Americans seemed to want not merely the freedom of Cuba but a war for the freedom of Cuba. The Spanish government, insofar as it confronted the realities at all, seemed to think that it was preferable to lose the island "honorably," as the consequence of a war, than to back down. McKinley was caught between the aggressive irrationality of his own people and the decadent irrationality of the ancient Latin power.

Historians often say that the war was brought on by sensational newspapers. The press, spurred by the rivalry between Pulitzer and Hearst, aroused sympathy with the Cubans and hatred of Spain and catered to the bellicosity of the public. No one seems to have asked: *Why was the public so fatally receptive to war propaganda?* I believe the answer must be sought in the causes of the jingoism that had raged for seven years before the war actually broke out. The events of the nineties had brought frustration and anxiety to civically conscious Americans. On one hand, as Mark Sullivan has commented, the American during this period was disposed "to see himself as an underdog in economic situations and controversies in his own country";[7] but the civic frustrations of the era created also a restless aggressiveness, a desire to be assured that the power and vitality of the nation were not waning. The capacity for sympathy and the need for power existed side by side. That highly typical American, William Allen White, recalls in his *Autobiography* how during the nineties he was "bound to my idols—Whitman, the great democrat, and Kipling, the imperialist."[8] In varying degrees the democrat and

---

[7] Mark Sullivan: *Our Times* (New York, 1926), p. 137.
[8] William Allen White: *Autobiography* (New York, 1946), p. 195.

the imperialist existed in the hearts of White's countrymen—
the democrat disposed to free Cuba; the imperialist, to vent
his spleen on Spain.

I suspect that the readiness of the public to overreact to the
Cuban situation can be understood in part through the dis-
placement of feelings of sympathy or social protest generated
in domestic affairs; these impulses found a safe and satisfactory discharge in foreign conflict. Spain was portrayed in the
press as waging a heartless and inhuman war; the Cubans were
portrayed as noble victims of Spanish tyranny, their situation
as analogous to that of Americans in 1776.[9] When one exam-
ines the sectional and political elements that were most enthusiastic about policies that led to war, one finds them not primarily among the wealthy eastern big-business Republicans
who gave McKinley his strongest support and read the dignified conservative newspapers, but in the Bryan sections of the
country, in the Democratic party, among western Republicans, and among the readers of the yellow journals.[1] A great

[9] On the role of the press, see J. E. Wisan: *The Cuban Crisis as
Reflected in the New York Press* (New York, 1934); and M. M.
Wilkerson: *Public Opinion and the Spanish-American War* (Baton
Rouge, 1932). On the evolution of human-interest journalism, see
Helen M. Hughes: *News and the Human Interest Story* (Chicago,
1940); and the same author's "Human Interest Stories and Democ-
racy," *Public Opinion Quarterly*, I (April 1937), 73–83.

[1] Wisan (op. cit., p. 445) notes: "It was no mere accident that most
of the leading proponents of intervention in Congress represented
southern and western states where populism and silver were strongest." Cf. pp. 125–6, 283, 301. A resolution of May 20, 1897, in favor of
granting belligerent rights to the Cubans was passed by the Senate,
41–14, with 33 senators not voting. The yeas came from 19 Democrats,
2 Populists, 3 maverick Republicans, and 17 regular Republicans. The
nays came from 12 Republicans and 2 Democrats. The 17 Republican
votes for recognition broke down as follows: 10 west of the Mississippi, 2 South, 3 Midwest, 2 New England. A New York *Journal*
poll of the House in December 1897, on the question of recognizing
Cuban belligerency, showed: for, 40 Republicans, 117 Democrats, and
27 Populists, total 184; against, 165 Republicans, 5 Democrats, and 2
Populists, total 172 (Wisan: p. 359); cf. Julius W. Pratt: *Expansionists
of 1898* (Baltimore, 1936), pp. 224, 234–6, 242–3. It is noteworthy

many businessmen were known to fear the effects of a war on the prosperity that was just returning, and some thought that a war might strengthen the free-silver movement. During the controversy significant charges were hurled back and forth: conservative peace advocates claimed that many jingoists were hoping for a costly war over Cuba that could be made the occasion of a return to free silver; in reply, the inflammatory press often fell into the pattern of Populist rhetoric, declaiming, for example, about "the eminently respectable porcine citizens who—for dollars in the money-grubbing sty, support 'conservative' newspapers and consider the starvation of . . . inoffensive men, women and children, and the murder of 250 American sailors . . . of less importance than a fall of two points in a price of stocks."[2] As Margaret Leech has remarked, peace "had become a symbol of obedience to avarice."[3] In the case of some of the war enthusiasts it is not clear whether they favored action more because they bled for the sufferings of the Cubans or because they hated the materialism and the flaccid pacifism of the *haute bourgeoisie*. Theodore Roosevelt, who was not in the habit of brooding over the wrongs done to the underdog in the United States, expressed some of this when he cried at Mark Hanna: "We will have this war for the freedom of Cuba in spite of the timidity of the commercial interests."[4]

Although imputations of base motives were made by both

---

that dominant sentiment in the labor movement favored recognition of Cuban belligerency from an early date, and that Cleveland's conservative policy was considered to be another instance of the "coldness" toward the underdog that was held to characterize his labor policies. Cf. John C. Appel: "The Relationship of American Labor to United States Imperialism, 1895–1905," unpublished Ph.D. thesis, University of Wisconsin (1950), Ch. 2. Cf. Ernest May: op. cit., pp. 81–2.

[2] Wisan: op. cit., p. 394.

[3] Margaret Leech: *In the Days of McKinley* (New York, 1959), p. 179.

[4] H. F. Pringle: *Theodore Roosevelt* (New York, 1931), p. 179.

sides, it is also significant that the current of sympathy and agitation ran strong where a discontented constituency, chagrined at Bryan's defeat, was most numerous. An opportunity to discharge hatred of "Wall Street interests" that were coolly indifferent to the fate of both Cuban *insurrectos* and staple farmers may have been more important than the more rationalized and abstract linkage between war and free silver.[5] The primary significance of this war in the psychic economy of the 1890's was that it served as an outlet for expressing aggressive impulses while presenting itself, quite truthfully, as an idealistic and humanitaran crusade. It had the advantage of expressing in one issue both the hostilities and the generous moral passions of the public. The American public on the whole showed little interest in such material gains as might accrue from an intervention in Cuba. It never dreamed that the war would lead to the taking of the Philippines, of whose existence it was hardly aware. Starting a war for a high-minded and altruistic purpose and then transmuting it into a war for annexation was unimaginable. That would be, as McKinley put it in a phrase that later came back to haunt him, "criminal aggression."

William James, who deplored the war fever from the beginning, correctly diagnosed the popular mood when he wrote to a friend in France: "The basis of it all is, or rather was, perfectly honest humanitarianism, and an absolutely disinterested desire on the part of our people to set the Cubans free. . . . Congress was entirely mad, supposing that the people

---

[5] To say this is not to say that the war "originated" among southern and western farmers, a point on which I have been misunderstood. (Cf. May: op. cit., pp. 75, 145.) The clamor for intervention and war was clearly nation-wide, urban as well as rural. My proposition is that it was much stronger among those who were otherwise discontented than among those who were well off. The agrarians, being particularly discontented, are merely a test case for one side of this proposition, just as the reluctant big-business interests are for the other.

was in the same condition, as it probably was, in less degree.
. . . War . . . was the only possible discharge. We were winning the most extraordinary diplomatic victories, but they
were of no use. We were ready (as we supposed) for war and
nothing but war must come." Although he reiterated that the
American disclaimer of desire for conquest was "*absolutely
sincere*" he also shrewdly predicted that once the excitement
of military action was aroused, "the ambition and sense of mastery which our nation has will set up new demands," and he
accurately forecast that although we would never annex Cuba
we might take Puerto Rico and the Philippines.[6]

One might add that inhibitions against going to war were
not so strong as they would have been if a major power had
been involved. Spain, hardly a formidable foe in a war whose
main strategic object was in the Caribbean, had been described
by the press as weak, bankrupt, degenerate, and friendless,
and her military incompetence was demonstrated by the
events in Cuba itself. As T.R. put it to Lodge: "I do not think
a war with Spain would be serious enough to cause much
strain on this country." Lodge himself had a shrewder estimation than many timid financiers of the bearing of war on the
currency question. "If we should have a war," he wrote in
March 1898, "we will not hear much of the currency question
in the elections."[7]

III

THERE IS ONE ODD PARADOX in the evolution of sentiment
from a war over freeing Cuba to a peace treaty ratifying the

---

[6] Ralph Barton Perry: *The Thought and Character of William
James* (Boston, 1935), II, 307; William James: *Letters* (Boston, 1935),
II, 73–4.

[7] H. C. Lodge (ed.): *Selections from the Correspondence of
Theodore Roosevelt and Henry Cabot Lodge* (New York, 1925),
I, 243; Morgan: op. cit., p. 369.

acquisition of the Philippines by conquest. The big-business-conservative-Republican-McKinley element, which was overwhelmingly hostile to this romantic and sentimental war, quickly became interested in the imperialism that grew out of it.[8] The popular Populist-Democratic-Bryanite element, which had been so keen for the war, became the stronghold—although by no means resolute or unbroken—of opposition to the fruits of war. This much, however, must be said of both the populace and the business community: if the matter had been left either to public clamor or to business interests, there would have been no American entrance into the Philippines in 1898.

The dynamic element in the movement for imperialism was a small group of politicians, intellectuals, and publicists, including Senator Henry Cabot Lodge, Theodore Roosevelt, John Hay, Senator Albert J. Beveridge, Whitelaw Reid, editor of the New York *Tribune*, Albert Shaw, editor of the *American Review of Reviews*, Walter Hines Page, editor of the *Atlantic Monthly*, and Henry and Brooks Adams.

Most of these men came from what are known as good families. They were well educated, cultivated, patrician in outlook, of Anglo-Saxon stock, and conservative reformers in politics whose personal goals and standards were non-commercial. Although living in a commercial world, they could not accept business standards for their own careers or become absorbed into the business community. Although they lived in a vulgar democracy, they were not democratic by instinct. They could not and did not care to succeed in politics of the corrupt sort that had become so common in America. They had tried their hands at civic reform, had found it futile, and had become bored with it. When they did not, like Henry Adams, turn away from American life in despair, they be-

---

[8] Pratt: *Expansionists of 1898*, Ch. 7, has a classic treatment of the business attitude.

came interested in some large and statesmanlike theater of action, broader than American domestic policy. Although there were men of this sort in the Democratic ranks, like Walter Hines Page, they were most influential within the Republican party, which had become committed to a policy of aggressive commercial diplomacy.[9]

In general, this group of imperialists was inspired by the navalist theories of Mahan and by the practical example of what they on occasion called Mother England. They saw that a new phase of imperialism had opened in the Western world at large, and they were fearful that if the United States did not adopt a policy of expansion and preparation for military and naval struggle, it would be left behind in what they referred to as the struggle for life or the march of the nations. They were much concerned that the United States expand its army and particularly its navy; that it dig an isthmian canal; that it acquire the naval bases and colonies in the Caribbean and the Pacific necessary to protect such a canal; that it annex Hawaii and Samoa. At their most aggressive they also called for the annexation of Canada and the expulsion of European powers from the Western Hemisphere. They were much interested in the Far East as a new theater of political conflict and of possibilities for investment. They were, indeed, more interested than business itself in the Pacific area, particularly in China, as a potential market. As Julius W. Pratt has observed: "The need of American business for colonial markets and fields for investment was discovered not by business men but by historians and other intellectuals, by journalists and politicans."[1]

---

[9] The best account of the little imperialist elite is in Matthew Josephson: *The President Makers* (New York, 1940), Chs. 1–3; See also Pratt: *Expansionists of 1898*, and Vagts: op. cit., Vol. II, passim.

[1] Pratt: *Expansionists of 1898*, p. 22; for a succinct statement of the outlook of Republican expansionists, see Henry Cabot Lodge: "Our Blundering Foreign Policy," *The Forum*, XIX (March 1895), 8–17;

The central figure in this group was Theodore Roosevelt, who more than any other single man was responsible for our entry into the Philippines. Throughout the 1890's Roosevelt had been eager for a war, whether it be with Chile, Spain, or England. A war with Spain, he thought, would get us "a proper navy and a good system of coast defenses," would free Cuba from Spain, would help to free America from European domination, would give "our people . . . something to think of that isn't material gain," and would try "both the army and navy in actual practice." Roosevelt feared that the United States would grow heedless of its defense, take insufficient care to develop its power, and become "an easy prey for any people which still retained those most valuable of all qualities, the soldierly virtues." "All the great masterful races have been fighting races," he argued. There were higher virtues than those of peace and material comfort. "No triumph of peace is quite so great as the supreme triumphs of war."[2] Such was the philosophy of the man who obtained for Commodore Dewey his appointment to the Far Eastern Squadron and alerted him before the actual outbreak of hostilities to be prepared to proceed from Hong Kong to engage the Spanish fleet at Manila. These orders were confirmed by McKinley two months later, shortly after war was actually declared.

Our first step into the Philippines presented itself to us as a "defensive" measure. Dewey's attack on the Spanish fleet in Manila Bay was made on the assumption that the Spanish fleet, if unmolested, might cross the Pacific and bombard the west coast cities of the United States. I do not know whether American officialdom was aware that this fleet was so decrepit that it could hardly have gasped its way across the ocean.

---

for Mahan's position, see A. T. Mahan: *The Interest of America in Sea Power* (New York, 1898).

[2] See Roosevelt: *Works* (New York, 1925), XIV, 182–99; Pringle: op. cit., Ch. 13.

Next, Dewey's fleet in Manila Bay seemed in danger unless its security were underwritten by the dispatch of American troops to Manila. To be sure, having accomplished his mission, Dewey could have removed this "danger" simply by leaving Manila Bay—and McKinley once remarked to H. H. Kohlsaat that "If Old Dewey had just sailed away when he smashed that Spanish fleet, what a lot of trouble he would have saved us!" However, in war one is always disposed to hold whatever gains have been made, and at Dewey's request American troops were dispatched very promptly after the victory and arrived at Manila in July 1898.

Thus our second step into the Philippines was again a "defensive" measure. The third step was the so-called "capture" of Manila, which was actually carried out in co-operation with the Spaniards, who were allowed to make a token resistance, and in exclusion of the Filipino patriots under Aguinaldo. The fourth step was an agreement, incorporated in the protocol suspending hostilities between the United States and Spain, that the United States would occupy the city, bay, and harbor of Manila pending a final settlement in the peace treaty. The fifth step came much later, on December 21, 1898, when McKinley instructed the War Department to extend the military government already in force at Manila to the entire archipelago. This set off a fierce revolt by the Filipino patriots, who felt that they had been led to expect a much different policy from the American government. Two days before the vote was taken in the Senate on the ratification of the peace treaty, the patriots and the American forces fought their first battle and American soldiers were killed, a fact that seems to have had an important influence on public discussion. Once again, administrative action had given a sharp bias to the whole process of political decision. Tyler Dennett goes so far as to say that by authorizing a campaign of conquest while the Senate was still discussing the issue, McKinley "created a situation . . . which had the effect of coercing the Senate."[3] This is a doubtful conclusion,[4] but there is some reason to believe that the hand of the expansionists was strengthened by the feeling that opposition to the administration's policy would be unpatriotic.

By the time our policy toward the Philippines could be affected by public discussion a great deal had already been accomplished by the annexationists. The argument was already weighted toward staying in simply because we were there. As McKinley put it: "It is not a question of keeping the islands of the East, but of leaving them."[5] It is not an easy thing to persuade a people or a government, at a high pitch of war enthusiasm, to abandon a supposed gain already in hand. Moreover, a great social interest hitherto indifferent to the Philippines, the business community, quickly swung around to an expansionist position. Business began to talk about the Philippines as a possible gateway to the markets of eastern Asia, the potentialities of which were thought to be very large.[6] The Protestant clergy, seeing a possible enlargement of missionary opportunities, also threw in its weight. For the first time the group of imperialists and navalists had powerful allies. Its members took heart and, with the help of navy officers, put increasing pressure upon a rather hesitant administration to follow through.

There seemed four possible ways of disposing of the Philip-

---

[3] Tyler Dennett: *Americans in Eastern Asia* (New York, 1922), p. 631.

[4] W. Stull Holt: *Treaties Defeated by the Senate* (Baltimore, 1933), pp. 170–1, concludes that the struggle in the Philippines had no important effects on the debate; see, however, José S. Reyes: *Legislative History of America's Economic Policy toward the Philippines* (New York, 1923), pp. 33–4; cf. Lodge: op. cit., p. 391; and Morgan: op. cit., pp. 421–2.

[5] *Speeches and Addresses of William McKinley from March 1, 1897, to May 30, 1900* (New York, 1900), p. 174.

[6] Pratt: *Expansionists of 1898*, pp. 233, 261–78.

pine problem. The first, returning the islands to Spain, found favor nowhere. The second, selling or otherwise alienating the Philippines to some other power, seemed to invite a general European war; and it would hardly be more justified morally than remaining in possession ourselves. Moreover, we were being encouraged by England to remain in the Philippines, for American possession of those islands was much more palatable to England than possession by any other power. The third possibility, leaving the Philippines to themselves and giving them the independence Aguinaldo's men had been fighting for, was equivalent in the minds of most Americans to leaving them to anarchy or to conquest. It also seemed to be another way of encouraging a scramble among other powers interested in the Far East—flinging, as McKinley put it, "a golden apple of discord among the rival powers."[7] The final possibility was American possession, in the form of a protectorate or otherwise. In the beginning there was much sentiment for merely retaining a naval base and coaling station on the island of Luzon, or perhaps the island of Luzon itself. Second thoughts suggested, however, that such a base would be endangered if the rest of the islands were left open to possible occupation by other nations. The dynamics of the situation suggested an all-or-none policy, and the administration drifted rapidly toward annexation of the entire archipelago. "I didn't want the Philippine Islands," McKinley said in retrospect, "and in the protocol to the treaty I left myself free not to take them; but—in the end there was no alternative."[8] The sincerity of his own doubts about annexation may be measured by the fact that it took him all of five months to decide that we should take not merely a part but the entire archipelago.

---

[7] Morgan: op. cit., p. 403.
[8] Jacob Gould Schurman: *Philippine Affairs* (New York, 1902), pp. 1–2.

I V

PREVIOUSLY the American public had not been either informed about or interested in the Philippines. In the entire eighty-year period from 1818 through May 1898, only thirty-five articles about the islands had appeared in American magazines.[9] At the moment of Dewey's victory, the press, although given over to encouraging the public jubilation, did not show an immediate interest in taking the islands. However, such sentiment grew with remarkable rapidity. As early as July 1898, the *Literary Digest* noted that the leading Republican papers were pro-expansion. A sample of 65 newspapers taken by the magazine *Public Opinion* in August showed that 43 per cent were for permanent retention of the Philippines, 24.6 per cent were opposed, and 32.4 per cent were wavering. In this case, "wavering" usually meant formerly opposed to expansion but apparently changing views. By December 1898, when the vital debate in the Senate was beginning, the New York *Herald* polled 498 newspapers on the subject of expansion and found that 305, or 61.3 per cent, were favorable. New England and the Middle States showed clear margins in favor of expansion, the West an overwhelming margin. The South alone, by a thin margin, was opposed. The state of press opinion does not *measure* public feeling, but probably does indicate the direction in which public opinion was moving.[1]

To President McKinley, a benign and far from aggressive man, public sentiment was of great importance, and he

---

[9] A. A. Greenberg: "Public Opinion and the Acquisition of the Philippine Islands," unpublished M.A. thesis, Yale University (1937), pp. 2, 18. What is most impressive is the absence of any conscious commitment of the public to the imperial idea before the outbreak of war. Referring to the failure of proposals of Hawaiian annexation, T.R. wrote as late as January 13, 1898, that he was "a good deal dis-

studied press opinion assiduously. He was not a man to lead
the American people in a direction in which their sympathies
were not already clearly bent. There was a current joke:
"Why is McKinley's mind like a bed? Because it has to be
made up for him every time he wants to use it." However
unjust to the President, this does characterize his response to
public opinion. He was not by temperament an expansionist,
but if his immediate advisers and the public at large were preponderantly for annexation, he was willing to go along, and
was thoroughly capable of finding good reasons for doing so.
During the fall of 1898 he left Washington for a tour of the
West, and made a great many brief speeches sounding out
public opinion on annexation of the Philippines, on which he
seems to have tentatively been determined in his own mind.
He was warmly received and his references to expansion met
with an enthusiastic response. Evidently his intent was confirmed by this exposure to public opinion and also by advices
concerning the state of the public mind from correspondents
and advisers. When he returned to Washington those who
were opposed to expansion found him unmovable.[2] The
Peace Commission negotiating the treaty in Paris was instructed to ask for all the Philippine Islands, and this provision
was included in the peace treaty signed on December 10,
1898.

The debate over the retention of the Philippines then went
through two phases. During the the first, which lasted from

---

heartened at the queer lack of imperial instinct that our people show."
W. A. Russ, Jr.: *The Hawaiian Republic* (Selinsgrove, Pa., 1961),
p. 219.

[1] For the development of press opinion, see surveys cited in
Literary Digest, XVII (July 1898), 32 ff., (September 10, 1898),
307–8; and, *Public Opinion*, XXV (August 4, 1898), 132–5, (December
29, 1898), 810.

[2] Greenberg: op. cit., pp. 84–6. "None of us," said Secretary of the
Interior Cornelius Bliss, "have been able to move him since he returned from the west"; Morgan: op. cit., p. 408.

December 1898 to the second week in February 1899, the question was argued both in the Senate and in the forums of public opinion.[3] This phase neared its end when, on February 6, the Senate narrowly voted to ratify the peace treaty; it was definitively closed on February 14, when a resolution sponsored by Senator Bacon of Georgia, calling for early Philippine independence, was rejected by the preciously narrow margin of one vote—the vote of the Vice-President, which resolved a 29–29 tie. The second phase of the debate extended throughout 1899 and 1900, when American policy toward the Philippines was a matter of general public discussion and a partisan issue in the presidential campaign of 1900.

Who was for and who against annexation? In large measure it was a party issue. The New York *Herald* poll showed that of 241 Republican papers 84.2 per cent were for expansion, and of 174 Democratic papers 71.3 per cent were against expansion. In some degree it was also a young man's movement. Geographically it extended throughout all sections of the country, and seems to have been predominant everywhere but in the South, although even there it was strong. We do not have a clear index of public opinion for the period, but the practical politicians, whose business it was to gauge public sentiment in the best way they knew, concluded that the preponderant feeling was overwhelmingly for annexation.[4]

The debate over the acquisition of the Philippines was perhaps no more than a ceremonial assertion of the values of both sides. The real decisions were made in the office of Theodore Roosevelt, in the Senate cloakroom, in the sanctums of those naval officers from whom the McKinley administration got its

---

[3] For the debate in the Senate, see *Congressional Record*, 55th Cong., 3rd sess., passim; Reyes: op. cit., Ch. 2; Holt: op cit., Ch. 8; Marion Mills Miller: *Great Debates in American History* (New York, 1913), III, 245–324; Pratt: *Expansionists of 1898*, pp. 345–60.

[4] For impressive evidence on this point, see Greenberg: op. cit., pp. 35, 42–3, 46–7, 49–50, 60, 67–9, 71, 86.

primary information about the Philippines during its period of doubt over annexation, and, by McKinley's own testimony, in the privacy of his chambers late at night. The public was, by and large, faced with a *fait accompli* that, although theoretically reversible, had the initial impetus of its very existence to carry it along. The intensity of the public discussion, at any rate, showed that the conscience of at least some Americans had really been shocked. No type of argument was neglected on either side. Those who wanted to take the Philippines pointed to the potential markets of the East, the White Man's Burden, the struggle for existence, "racial" destiny, American traditions of expansion, the dangers of a general war if the Philippines were left open to a European scramble, the almost parental duty of assuming responsibility for the allegedly childlike Filipinos, the incapacity of the Filipinos for self-government. The anti-imperialists based their essential appeal on political principle. They pointed out that the United States had come into existence pledged to the idea that man should not be governed without his consent. They suggested that the violation of these political traditions (under which the nation had prospered) was not only a gross injustice to others, of which we should feel deeply ashamed, but also a way of tempting Providence and risking degeneration and disintegration as a sort of punishment for the atrophy of one's own principles. They pointed also to the expense of overseas dominions, standing armies, and navalism, and the danger of being embroiled in imperialist wars, and argued that it would be unwise to try to absorb peoples who were racially incapable of self-government.

Many leading anti-imperialists were men of great distinction; their ranks included by far the greater part of the eminent figures of the literary and intellectual world. Most of them were, however, in the unfortunate position of opposing the fruits of a war that they had either favored or failed to oppose. Unlike the expansionists, they did not have complete control of a major party (there were more expansionists among the Democrats than there were anti-expansionists among the Republicans). They were hopelessly heterogeneous: Gold Democrats, Bryan Democrats, New England-conscience Republicans, and a scattering of reformers and intellectuals.[5]

They organized late—the Anti-Imperialist League grew up in the months after November 1898—and their political leadership, however ardent in sentiment, pursued a hesitant and uncertain course. Their most eminent political leaders were chiefly old men, and the anti-imperialist movement seems to have had its strongest appeal among the old, high-principled elements in the country, while the imagination of the young was fired far more by the rhetoric of expansionism.[6] It seems clear that the main chance of this minority was to use its position in the Senate to deny the necessary two-thirds approval to the peace treaty by which the islands would be acquired from Spain. Here the opponents of annexation might

---

[5] On the anti-imperialist movement, see Fred H. Harrington: "The Anti-Imperialist Movement in the United States, 1898–1900," *Mississippi Valley Historical Review*, XXII (September 1935), 211–30. On the intellectual class and anti-imperialism, see the same author's "Literary Aspects of American Anti-Imperialism, 1898–1902," *New England Quarterly*, X (December 1937), 650–67; William Gibson: "Mark Twain and Howells: Anti-Imperialists," *New England Quarterly*, XX (December 1947), 435–70. Christopher Lasch has pointed out that the anti-imperialist argument, North and South, was almost universally based on racist premises; "The Anti-Imperialists, The Philippines, and the Inequality of Man," *Journal of Southern History*, XXIV (August 1958), 319–31.

[6] Harrington points out that the average age of the prominent Republican members of the Anti-Imperialist League was 71.1 years; that of the forty-one vice-presidents of the League, 58.3. By contrast, the average age of fourteen leaders of expansionism in 1898 was 51.2. The American consul in London, William M. Osborne, wrote to McKinley: "If what I hear and what I read is true there is a tremendous party growing up for expansion of territory, *especially by the younger and more active elements in the country*." (Italics added.) Quoted by Greenberg: op. cit., pp. 46–7.

have delayed it long enough to give themselves a chance to reach the public. But William Jennings Bryan, for reasons that are not altogether clear, persuaded enough members of his party to vote for the treaty to lose the case. Bryan hoped to continue the fight, of course, and grant independence later, but over his conduct and his explanations there hangs a heavy sense of inevitable defeat, stemming from his recognition that the voice of the majority demanded the bold and aggressive policy.[7]

V

IN THE ARGUMENTS for annexation two essential moral and psychological themes appeared over and over again. These themes were expressed in the words Duty and Destiny. According to the first, to reject annexation of the Philippines would be to fail of fulfilling a solemn obligation. According to the second, annexation of the Philippines in particular and expansion generally were inevitable and irresistible.

The people had entered the war for what they felt to be purely altruistic and humanitarian reasons—the relief and liberation of the Cubans. The idea that territorial gains should arise out of this pure-hearted war of liberation, and the fact

---

[7] Bryan argued that the treaty should be ratified because "a victory won against the treaty would prove only temporary if the people really favor a colonial policy," and because the opponents of the treaty, if they won, "would be compelled to assume responsibility for the continuance of war conditions and for the risks which always attend negotiations with a hostile nation." A minority, he argued, could not permanently thwart annexation. His policy was to appeal to the voters in the election of 1900; but it is impossible to make a presidential election a clear referendum on foreign policy. Bryan found, during the campaign of 1900, that anti-imperialism was not a strong talking point. Cf. Bryan: *The Second Battle* (Chicago, 1900), pp. 126–8; *Bryan on Imperialism* (Chicago, 1900), p. 16. On the election, see Thomas A. Bailey: "Was the Presidential Election of 1900 a Mandate on Imperialism?" *Mississippi Valley Historical Review*, XXIV (June 1937), 43 ff.

that before long the Americans stood in the same relation to the Filipinos as the Spaniards had stood to the Cubans, was most uncomfortable. This situation raised moral questions that the anti-imperialists did not neglect to express and exploit. The imperialists were accused of breaking our national word, of violating the pledge made by McKinley himself that by our moral code forcible annexation would be "criminal aggression." They were also accused of violating the solemn injunctions of the Founding Fathers, particularly the principles of the Declaration of Independence. The rhetoric of Duty was a reassuring answer to this attempt to stir feelings of guilt.

The quick victories won by American arms strengthened the psychological position of the imperialists. The feeling that one may be guilty of wrongdoing can be heightened when the questionable act is followed by adversity.[8] Conversely, it may be minimized by the successful execution of a venture. Misfortune is construed as Providential punishment; but success, as in the Calvinist scheme, is taken as an outward sign of an inward state of grace. One of the most conspicuous things about the war was the remarkable successes achieved by American arms, of which the most astonishing was Dewey's destruction, without losing a single American life, of the entire Spanish Eastern Fleet in Manila Bay. Victories of this sort could readily be interpreted as Providential signs, tokens of divine approval. It was widely reported in the United States that this was Dewey's own interpretation. "If I were a religious man, and I hope I am," he said, "I should say that the hand of God was in it."[9] This was precisely the sort of reassurance that was needed. "The magnificent fleets of Spain," declared a writer in a Baptist periodical, referring to Spain's

---

[8] Cf. Sigmund Freud: *Civilization and Its Discontents* (London, 1930), pp. 110–11.

[9] Louis A. Coolidge: *An Old-Fashioned Senator: Orville H. Platt* (New York, 1910), p. 302.

senile and decrepit navy, "have gone down as marvelously, I had almost said, as miraculously, as the walls of Jericho went down." The victory, said an editor of the *Christian and Missionary Alliance*, "read almost like the stories of the ancient battles of the Lord in the times of Joshua, David, and Jehosophat."

Furthermore, what might have seemed a sin became transformed into a positive obligation, a duty. The feeling was: *Providence has been so indulgent to us, by giving us so richly of success, that we would be sinful if we did not accept the responsibility it has asked us to assume.* The Protestant clergy, as guardians of the national conscience, did not hesitate to make lavish use of such arguments. "To give to the world the life more abundant both for here and hereafter," reasoned a writer in the *Baptist Missionary Review*, "is the duty of the American people by virtue of the call of God. This call is very plain. The hand of God in history has ever been plain." "If God has brought us to the parting of the ways," insisted a writer in the *Churchman*, "we cannot hold back without rejecting divine leadership."[1] The rhetoric of secular leaders was hardly less inspired. "We will not renounce our part in the mission of our race, trustees under God, of the civilization of the world," said Senator Albert J. Beveridge. "God has not been preparing the English-speaking and Teutonic peoples for a thousand years for nothing but vain and idle self-contemplation and self-admiration. No! He has made us the master organizers of the world to establish system where chaos reigns. He has made us adepts in government that we may administer government among savages and senile peoples."[2]

---

[1] The quotations are from Pratt: *Expansionists of 1898*, pp. 289–90, 294, 305.

[2] Claude G. Bowers: *Beveridge and the Progressive Era* (New York, 1932), p. 121.

The theme of Destiny was a corollary of the theme of Duty. Repeatedly it was declared that expansion was the result of a "cosmic tendency," that "destiny always arrives,'" that it was in the "inexorable logic of events," and so on. The doctrine that expansion was inevitable had of course long been familiar to Americans; we all know how often Manifest Destiny was invoked throughout the nineteenth century. Albert Weinberg has pointed out, however, that this expression took on a new meaning in the nineties. Previously destiny had meant primarily that American expansion, *when we willed it*, could not be resisted *by others* who might wish to stand in our way. During the nineties it came to mean that expansion "could not be resisted by Americans themselves, caught, willing or unwilling," in the coils of fate.[3] A certain reluctance on our part was implied. This was not quite so much what we *wanted* to do; it was what we *had* to do. Our aggression was implicitly defined as compulsory—the product not of our own wills but of objective necessity (or the will of God).

"Duty," said President McKinley, "determines destiny." While Duty meant that we had a moral obligation, Destiny meant that we would certainly fulfill it, that the capacity to fulfill it was inherent in us. Ours had been a continuous history of expansion; it had always succeeded before, therefore it was certain to succeed in the future. Expansion was a national and "racial" inheritance, a deep and irresistible inner necessity. Here was a plausible traditionalist answer to the accusation of a grave breach of tradition.

It is not surprising that the public should have found some truth in this concept of inevitable destiny, for the acts that

---

[3] Weinberg: *Manifest Destiny*, p. 254. Appropriately enough, as Weinberg shows (p. 279), when independence was at last granted to the Philippines, it was portrayed not as an act of "destiny" but as an act of "our own free will."

first involved their country with the fate of the Philippines were willed and carried out by others and were made objects of public discussion and decision only *after* the most important commitments had been made. The public will was not freely exercised upon the question, and for the citizens at large, who were in the presence of forces they could not understand or control, the rhetoric of Destiny may have been a way of softening and ennobling the *fait accompli* with which they were presented. But what of the men whose wills were really effective in the matter? If we examine their case, we find that the manufacturers of inevitability believed deeply in their own product. Indeed, while the extent to which the idea of Destiny was generally accepted is unknown, its wide prevalence among influential politicians, editors, and publicists is beyond argument. When Senator Lodge wrote to Theodore Roosevelt in 1898 that "the whole policy of annexation is growing rapidly under the irresistible pressure of events," when President McKinley remarked in private to his secretary, concerning the taking of Hawaii, "It is manifest destiny," when he declared in his private instructions to the peace commissioners that "the march of events rules and overrules human action"—what was involved was not an attempt to sell an idea to the public but a mode of communication in which the insiders felt thoroughly at home; perhaps a magical mode of thought by which they quieted their own uncertainties. It is easy to say, from the perspective of the twentieth century, that where contemporaries heard the voice of God we think we can discern the carnal larynx of Theodore Roosevelt. But if the insiders themselves imagined that they heard the voice of God, we must be careful of imputing hypocrisy. It is significant that the idea of Destiny was effective even among people who had very grave doubts about the desirability of remaining in the Philippines. Secretary of the Navy John D. Long, who was affectionately regarded by

Theodore Roosevelt as an old fuddy-duddy on this score, confided to a friend in 1898 that he would really have preferred the United States to remain what it had been during the first half of the nineteenth century—"provincial," as he expressed it, and "dominated by the New England idea. But," he added, "I cannot shut my eyes to the march of events—a march which seems to be beyond human control."[4]

It would be false to give the impression that only high moral and metaphysical concepts were employed in the imperialist argument. Talk about entry into the markets of Asia was heard often after Dewey's victory; but even those who talked about material gains showed a conspicuous and symptomatic inability to distinguish between interests, rights, and duties. Charles Denby, former minister to China and a member of McKinley's commission to study the Philippines, contributed to *The Forum* two interesting articles full of this confusion. The central business of diplomacy, confessed Denby, was to advance commerce. Our right to hold the Philippines was the right of conquerors. So far, Mr. Denby was all *Realpolitik*. But, he continued, he favored keeping the islands because he could not conceive any alternative to doing so except seizing territory in China, and he did not want to oppress further "the helpless Government and people of China"! Thus a rather odd scruple crept in; but Mr. Denby quickly explained that this was simply because China's strength and prosperity were in America's interest. "We are after markets," he went on, sliding back into *Realpolitik*, and along with these markets"—sliding back into morality—"will go our beneficent institutions; and humanity will bless us." In a second article Mr. Denby shuttled back to "the cold, hard practical question. . . . Will the possession of these islands benefit us as a nation? If it will not, set them free tomorrow,

---

[4] Greenberg: op. cit., p. 89.

and let their people, if they please, cut each other's throats." And yet, Mr. Denby made it clear, we did come as benefactors, bringing to our cut-throat friends "the choicest gifts— liberty and hope and happiness."[5]

There was, besides the oscillatory rhetoric of Mr. Denby, a "let's be candid" school, whose views were expressed by the Washington *Post:* "All this talk about benevolent assimilation; all this hypocritical pretense of anxiety for the moral, social, and intellectual exaltation of the natives . . . deceives nobody, avails nothing. . . . We all know, down in our hearts, that these islands . . . are important to us only in the ratio of their practical possibilities, and by no other. . . . Why not be honest?"[6]

There were others who found the primary benefit of our new imperial status in the social cohesion and military spirit that would result when the energies of the country were deflected from internal to external conflict. "Marse" Henry Watterson, the well-known editor of the Louisville *Courier-Journal*, told a New York reporter: "From a nation of shopkeepers we become a nation of warriors. We escape the menace and peril of socialism and agrarianism, as England has escaped them, by a policy of colonization and conquest. From a provincial huddle of petty sovereignties held together by a rope of sand we rise to the dignity and prowess of an imperial republic incomparably greater than Rome. It is true that we exchange domestic dangers for foreign dangers; but in every direction we multiply the opportunities of the people. We risk Caesarism, certainly; but even Caesarism is preferable to anarchism. We risk wars; but a man has but one time to die, and either in peace or war, he is not likely to die until his time

---

[5] Charles Denby: "Shall We Keep the Philippines?" *Forum*, XXVI (October 1898), 279–80; "Why the Treaty Should Be Ratified," ibid., XXVI (February 1899), 644, 647.

[6] Quoted in Grayson L. Kirk: *Philippine Independence* (New York, 1936), p. 25.

comes. . . . In short, *anything is better than the pace we were going before these present forces were started into life.* Already the young manhood of the country is a goodly brand snatched from the burning, and given a perspective replete with noble deeds and elevating ideas."[7]

Probably the most remarkable statement of the meaning of the war and the whole imperial adventure for American thinking was written by Walter Hines Page in the *Atlantic Monthly* not long after the battle of Manila. Page thought the American people would face graver problems after the war than they had experienced in the preceding years. "A change in our national policy may change our very character," he said, "and we are now playing with the great forces that may shape the future of the world—almost before we know it." Up to then, the nation had been going about the prosaic business of peace, a commercial nation absorbed in problems of finance and administration. Now it had come face to face with the sort of problems connected with the management of world empires, and its isolation was at an end. "Shall we be content with peaceful industry, or does there yet lurk in us the adventurous spirit of our Anglo-Saxon forefathers? And have we come to a time when, no more great enterprises awaiting us at home, we shall be tempted to seek them abroad?"

His own conviction was clear. The Americans had sprung from "a race that for a thousand years has done the adventurous and outdoor tasks of the world." Stemming from the English, themselves explorers, conquerors, and founders of states, the Americans had always been engaged with great practical enterprises—fighting Indians, clearing forests, building a new government, extending territory, developing wealth, settling the great issues connected with slavery and

---

[7] *Literary Digest*, XVII (July 2, 1898), 214; italics added.

the Civil War. These had been "as great enterprises and as exciting, coming in rapid succession, as any race of men has ever had to engage it." The old outdoor spirit of the Anglo-Saxon had thus had wide scope in recent experience.

"But now a generation has come to manhood that has had no part in any great adventure." The chief tasks of domestic politics, like civil service and the reform of the currency and of municipal government, had not been exciting to the imagination, and our politics had been attractive only to petty brigands and second-rate men. In literature too we had fallen into decline. In fact, the three books which had found the most readers and most affected the masses were books of utopian social programs and fantastic philosophy—*Progress and Poverty, Looking Backward,* and *Coin's Financial School.* The proliferation of movements for petty social reforms, "societies for the prevention of minor vices and for the encouragement of minor virtues," denoted a lack of adventurous opportunities. It was quite possible that a life of quiet had grown irksome, that it was not "natural" to us. "Is it true that with a thousand years of adventure behind us we are unable to endure a life of occupations that do not feed the imagination?" Perhaps we were still the same old colonizing and fighting race of Anglo-Saxons at heart. "Before we knew the meaning of foreign possessions in a world ever growing more jealous, we have found ourselves the captors of islands in both great oceans; and from our home-staying policy of yesterday we are brought face to face with world-wide forces in Asia as well as in Europe, which seem to be working, by the opening of the Orient, for one of the greatest changes in human history. . . . And to nobody has the change come more unexpectedly than to ourselves. Has it come without our knowing the meaning of it?"[8]

---

[8] Walter Hines Page: "The War with Spain, and After," *Atlantic Monthly,* LXXXI (June, 1898), pp. 721–7, esp. pp. 725–7.

VI

Since Julius W. Pratt published his *Expansionists of 1898* in 1936, it has been obvious that any interpretation of America's entry upon the paths of imperialism in the nineties in terms of rational economic motives would not fit the facts, and that a historian who approached the event with preconceptions no more supple than those, say, of Lenin's *Imperialism* would be helpless. This is not to say that markets and investments have no bearing; they do, but there are features of the situation that they do not explain at all. Insofar as the economic factor was important, it can be better studied by looking at the relation between the depression, the public mood, and the political system.

The alternative explanation has been the equally simple idea that the war was a newspapers' war. This notion, once again, has some point, but it certainly does not explain the war itself, much less its expansionist result. The New Deal period, when the political successes of F.D.R. were won in the face of overwhelming newspaper opposition, showed that the press is not powerful enough to impose upon the public mind a totally uncongenial view of public events. It must operate roughly within the framework of public predispositions. Moreover, not all the papers of the nineties were yellow journals. We must inquire into the structure of journalistic power and also into the views of the owners and editors to find out what differentiated the sensational editors and publishers from those of the conservative press.

There is still another qualification that must be placed upon the role of the press: the press itself, whatever it can do with opinion, does not have the power to precipitate opinion into action. That is something that takes place within the *political* process, and we cannot tell that part of the story without examining the state of party rivalries, the origin and goals of the political elites, and indeed the entire political context. We must, then, supplement our story about the role of the newspapers with at least two other factors: the state of the public temper upon which the newspapers worked, and the manner in which party rivalries deflected domestic clashes into foreign aggression. Here a perennial problem of politics under the competitive two-party system became manifest again in the 1890's. When there is, for whatever reason, a strong current of jingoism running in the channels of public sentiment, party competition tends to speed it along. If the party in power is behaving circumspectly, the opposition tends to beat the drums. For example, in 1896, with Cleveland still in office, the Republican platform was much more exigent on the Cuba issue. When McKinley came into office and began to show reluctance to push toward intervention, the Democratic party became a center of interventionist pressure; this pressure was promptly supplemented by a large number of Republicans who, quite aside from their agreement on the issue, were concerned about its effect on the fate of their party.

When we examine the public temper, we find that the depression, together with such other events as the approaching completion of the settlement of the continent, the growth of trusts, and the intensification of internal social conflict, had brought to large numbers of people intense frustrations in their economic lives and their careers. To others they had brought anxiety that a period of stagnation in national wealth and power had set in. The restlessness of the discontented classes had been heightened by the defeat of Bryan in 1896. The anxieties about the nation's position had been increased among statesmen and publicists by the revival of world imperialism, in particular by the feeling that America was threatened by Germany, Russia, and Japan. The expansionist statesmen themselves were drawn largely from a restless upper-middle-class elite that had been fighting an unrewarding battle for conservative reform in domestic politics and looked with some eagerness toward a more spacious field of action.

Men often respond to frustration with acts of aggression, and allay their anxieties by threatening acts against others. It is revealing that the underdog forces in American society showed a considerably higher responsiveness to the idea of war with Spain than the groups that were satisfied with their economic or political positions. Our entry into the Philippines then aroused the interest of conservative groups that had been indifferent to the quixotism of freeing Cuba but were alert to the possibility of capturing new markets. Imperialism appealed to members of both the business and the political elites as an enlargement of the sphere of American power and profits; many of the underdogs also responded to this new note of national self-assertion. Others, however, looked upon our conduct in the Philippines as a betrayal of national principles. Anti-expansionists attempted to stir a sense of guilt and foreboding in the nation at large. But the circumstances of the period 1898–1900—the return of prosperity and the quick spectacular victories in war—made it difficult for them to impress this feeling upon the majority. The rhetoric of Duty and Destiny carried the day. The anti-expansionists had neither the numbers nor the morale of their opponents. The most conspicuous result of their lack of drive and confidence can be seen in the lamentable strategy of Bryan over the ratification of the treaty.

Clearly this attempt to see the war and expansion in the light of social history has led us onto the high and dangerous ground of social psychology and into the arena of conjecture. But simple rationalistic explanations of national behavior will also leave us dissatisfied. What I have attempted here is merely a preliminary sketch of a possible explanatory model. Further inquiry might make it seem more plausible at some points, more questionable at others.

This study has been narrowly focused on a single incident. Other expansionist crises in our own history would show important differences. I have not tried to compare American imperialism with that of other countries, or to decide how far our behavior is unique to our own country or similar to that which has been found elsewhere. In the history of other nations we can find many parallels to the role of the press and political parties in whipping up foreign crises, and to the role of the administration in committing the nation to a foreign policy before it could be made a matter of public discussion. The rhetoric and ideology of expansion also were not singular to us; duty, destiny, racism, and the other shibboleths were widespread.

I cannot refrain from adding to these notes on the methods of historical understanding another note on the tragicomic procedure of history itself. It may be of some value to us to be reminded how some of the more grandiose expectations of the nineties were realized. Cuba, to be sure, which might have been freed in peace, was freed in the war—insofar as the little country of Batista, Machado, and Castro can be considered free. The sensational newspapers that had boomed the war lost money on expensive extras, costly war-news coverage, and declining advertising.[9] I do not know whether those silverites who wanted the war really expected that it would remonetize silver, but if they did they were rewarded with McKinley's renewed triumph and the Gold Standard Act of 1900. As for business, the gigantic markets of the East never materialized, and the precise value of the Philippines in getting at them is arguable. The islands themselves proved to be a mildly profitable colony that came to absorb a little over 1 per

---

[9] Frank Luther Mott: *American Journalism* (New York, 1947), pp. 537–8.

cent of all United States investments abroad. Yet within a generation the United States had committed itself to restoring independence to the Philippines. When this promise was enacted in 1934 many descendants of Aguinaldo's rebels were unenthusiastic about their new economic and strategic position.[1] Finally, the exact estimation that is to be put on our strategic commitment in the Far East, which began with the Philippines, is still a matter of debate. We should, however, make note of the earlier opinion of one of our most brilliant and farsighted statesmen, who declared in 1907 that the Philippines were the Achilles' heel of our strategic position and should be given "nearly complete independence" at the "earliest possible moment."[2] The author of these remarks was Theodore Roosevelt.

---

[1] Pratt: *America's Colonial Experiment*, pp. 243–4, 291–310.
[2] Pringle: *Theodore Roosevelt*, pp. 408–9.

WHAT HAPPENED
TO THE
ANTITRUST MOVEMENT?

This essay, which at first carried the subtitle "Notes on the Evolution of an American Creed," was written for a conference on the political and social environment of American business, made possible by the Ford Foundation and held on the Berkeley campus of the University of California in January 1964. The papers, written for the conference by a half-dozen authors, were published in *The Business Establishment* (New York, 1964), edited by Earl Cheit, who organized the conference. The version which appears here is substantially revised. A portion appeared also in *Commentary*, August 1964.

I

THE antitrust movement is one of the faded passions of American reform. Historians have always been interested in the old romance, but with remarkable unanimity and an uncharacteristic lack of realism, they have neglected to tell us what happened when it was over. The writers of our general history books deal with the antitrust issue when they tell of the rise of the great corporations and the passing of the Sherman Act and then, again, in discussing antitrust sentiment in the Progressive era and the enactment of further regulatory laws. Most of them touch on it briefly once more when they take up the New Deal antitrust revival, Thurman Arnold, and the T.N.E.C. Then, for the most part, they drop the subject; the student or the general reader must study law, economics, or business administration to become aware that the antitrust enterprise has more significance in contemporary society than it had in the days of T.R. or Wilson, or even in the heyday of Thurman Arnold.

Presumably the historians drop the subject of antitrust at or around 1938 not because they imagine that it has lost its role in our society but because after that point it is no longer the subject of much public agitation—in short, because there is no longer an antitrust *movement*. The intensity of public concern is, of course, a poor guide for historians, but here their neglect embodies a certain self-protective wisdom. They ignore antitrust for the same reason the public ignores it: it has become complex, difficult, and boring. In any case, the intricacies, both legal and economic, of regulating monopoly and competition are intricacies of a sort the historian is ill equipped to handle. It is simpler for him to sweep the whole thing under the carpet, and retire, along with the general public, from the baffling maze of technical refinements which the lawyers and economists have created.

Perhaps, at the risk of oversimplifying a little, the source of the problem can be put in this paradox: once the United States had an antitrust movement without antitrust prosecutions; in our time there have been antitrust prosecutions without an antitrust movement. In its day the antitrust movement had such consequences for our political and intellectual life that no historian who writes about the period 1890–1940 can safely ignore it. But the antitrust enterprise, as an institutional reality, now runs its quiet course without much public attention, and we lose sight of it. In failing to take more cognizance of its work, the historians are missing one of the most delicious minor ironies of our reform history and one of the most revealing facets of our institutional life. In the very years when it lost compelling public interest the antitrust enterprise became a force of real consequence in influencing the behavior of business.

For a long time liberal historians held to a kind of mythological history of the antitrust experience which, though it was not entirely false at any point, ended somehow in being entirely misleading. Antitrust, as an ideology and a movement of reform, always contrasted so sharply with its actual achievements in controlling business that it tempted our powers of satire. The conventional history went something like this: In 1890, as a largely meaningless and cynical gesture to appease public sentiment, an ultra-conservative Congress passed the Sherman Antitrust Act. The act was couched in such vague terms as to confirm our doubts that those who passed it expected that it could ever be enforced. Its early history fully warranted such doubts. From the beginning it was rendered a dead letter by administrative neglect and judicial hostility. Though it had little effect on the big business firms that were supposed to be its main object, it was used with greater success against labor unions. By the time Theodore Roosevelt took office, when the Sherman Act was little more than ten years old, it had become all too clearly a charade behind which the consolidation of big business, notably accelerated between 1898 and 1904, went on apace. It was easy and amusing to debunk the reputation of T.R. as a trust-buster when one considered the infrequency and superficiality of his prosecutions, as well as his own doubts about the value of the whole enterprise, and to compare his robust rhetoric with the comic and pathetic image of the Antitrust Division of the Justice Department sallying out against the combined might of the giant corporations with a staff of five lawyers and four stenographers.

190

Subsequent statutory efforts under Wilson to strengthen regulation of monopolistic conduct, whatever one is to say of their value and the intent behind them, had to be recounted by the historians with a full sense of the denouement in mind. And the denouement required us to say that the antitrust effort went down the drain with the attempt to organize industry for the First World War; that the ensuing saturnalia of reaction during the 1920's, another period of business consolidation, undid the Wilsonian reforms—indeed, that the Federal Trade Commission was converted from an agency to control business into an agency controlled by business. Finally the revival of antitrust under F.D.R., the creation of the Temporary National Economic Commission, and the installation of Thurman Arnold's reforms seemed to be largely a movement of desperation, a return to the old antitrust charade, on the part of an administration which had exhausted its capacity to reform and was having indifferent results in its efforts to bring about recovery. The very appointment of Thurman Arnold as head of the Antitrust Division—a man whose books had effectively ridiculed the antitrust laws as a façade behind which the concentration of American industry could go on unimpeded—seemed to underline perfectly the whole comedy of the antitrust enterprise. And here, for the most part, as I have observed, the standard history of antitrust breaks off, perhaps with a few words about the difficulties Arnold confronted, and how his honest efforts were circumvented during the Second World War.

Without attempting to subvert the elements of truth in this version of antitrust history, it seems important to take account of certain additions to the story. First, it seems fair to say that while there was some impatient cynicism present in 1890 when the Sherman Act was passed, there was puzzlement as well, an honest if ineffectual concern with the problems of size and monopoly, and genuine doubts about the proper means of solving them. The general language of the Sherman Act may be looked upon as a broad enabling measure, which at least some men hoped would be followed by statutory and administrative advances. What has customarily been said of the lax enforcement that followed needs little qualification, except to add that the difficulties involved were the difficulties inherent in the subject as well as in the relatively conservative and circumspect attitudes taken by the Progressive Presidents and their advisers. They were living in a society that wanted to reap the benefits of large-scale enterprise, as well as to prevent the evils of monopolization; and on the whole, despite the confident pronouncements they found it desirable to make in political campaigns, men like T.R. and Wilson were aware that they did not know how to arrive at a quick and satisfactory solution to the problem. Whatever else may be said about all the seemingly empty and futile rhetoric about monopoly and bigness in the Progressive era, it did serve to keep alive the salutary American fear of excessive market power.

Something more must also be said about the antitrust revival under Franklin Roosevelt and Thurman Arnold. Viewed in a very flat time perspective, Roosevelt's 1938 message on monopoly capitalism, the T.N.E.C., and Arnold's prosecution may be set down as having originated out of administrative desperation and may be regarded as substantial failures. But in the longer perspective, they mark the true beginning of effective antitrust action, for it was the efforts begun at this time—not to speak of new personnel Roosevelt brought into the federal judiciary—that created the social and legal climate in which something could be done. The 1940's can be seen retrospectively as a watershed in the history of antitrust jurisprudence. Today, anybody who knows anything about the conduct of American business knows that the managers of the large corporations do their business with one eye constantly cast over their shoulders at the Antitrust Division, and that the antitrust enterprise has gone far to make up for its inability to reverse business concentration by considerable successes in affecting business conduct. Antitrust has won its spurs as a useful approach to the problems of large-scale enterprise, and in the Western world as a whole it is gaining acceptance. Its successes in America have aroused some emulation since the Second World War both in Britain and in France, and antitrust enforcement has reached a rudimentary stage in the Common Market.

II

THE HISTORY of antitrust may be divided into three phases. In the first, from about 1890 to 1914—the era of the founding fathers of antitrust—the opening steps were taken, in statutes and in the courts, to define what form the antitrust efforts of the federal government might take and to see how they would work. The great outburst of business consolidation quickened antitrust sentiment, which was strong throughout the Progressive era. Often a common hostility to big business was the one link that bound together a variety of interest groups that diverged on other issues. The Progressive era, which culminated in 1914 with the passing of the Clayton Act and the creation of the Federal Trade Commission, probably marks the high point of anti-big-business sentiment in our history. As a movement, through hardly as an administrative reality, antitrust was in high gear.

The second phase, lasting from the First World War to about 1937, might be called the era of neglect. Efforts at prosecution during the 1920's were almost minimal, and even the New Deal in its opening years suspended the antitrust laws to accommodate the N.R.A. codes. The present phase, which may be dated from 1937, is the phase of revival, opened by the New Deal's reactivation of the Antitrust Division and the T.N.E.C. investigation. The sharp legal and administrative activity of this period has taken place without any corresponding revival of public sentiment against big business, indeed in the face of a growing public acceptance of the large corporation. Antitrust has become almost exclusively the concern of small groups of legal and economic specialists, who carry on their work without widespread public interest or support.

Whereas the first of these three phases was marked by tentative efforts at enforcement with nearly negligible results, and the second by minimal or token enforcement, the comparative vigor of the third may be measured roughly by the number of prosecutions. During all the years from 1891 to 1938, the government instituted an average of 9 cases a year. The peak years of this barren half-century were 1912 and 1913, with 29 and 27 prosecutions repectively. For about thirty years after 1913 the typical load was about 12 cases, often considerably fewer, and the objects chosen for prosecution were not often vital points in American industry. In 1940, with the Roosevelt-Arnold revitalization well on its way, the number of cases jumped to 85—only two less than the number instituted during the entire first *two decades* of the Sherman Act. Thereafter the number of cases, though still fluctuating, stayed at a level considerably higher than that maintained before 1938.[1] In 1962 the Antitrust Division, employing 300 lawyers and working with a budget of $6,600,000, instituted 92 cases. Figures, of course, are crude,

---

[1] On prosecutions to 1940, see Walton Hamilton and Irene Till: *Antitrust in Action*, T.N.E.C. Monograph No. 16 (Washington, 1940), esp. pp. 135–43; see also *United States versus Economic Concentration and Monopoly*, a Staff Report to the Monopoly Subcommittee on Small Business, House of Representatives (Washington, 1940), pp. 276–89.

but a qualitative analysis of the legal victories of the antitrust revival would show that the decisions it has won from the courts, particularly since 1940, have greatly amplified the possibility of enforcement. Despite the collapse of antitrust feeling both in the public at large and among liberal intellectuals, antitrust as a legal-administrative enterprise has been solidly institutionalized in the past quarter-century.

The antitrust movement and its legislation are characteristically American. Perhaps this is attributable to the particularly flagrant form that monopoly took in America during the early years of its development. It may also be said that, except for the Canadians, no other people has taken the principle of economic competition so earnestly as to try to underwrite it by statute, until recently when some European countries began to show interest in the American approach to the subject.[2] The idea of competition as a means of social regulation —as an economic, political, and moral force—has grown stronger roots in the United States than elsewhere, partly because it has had little to compete with in the way of aristocratic, militaristic, or labor-socialist theories. Founded to some degree in the common-law tradition, whose injunctions against restraint of trade proved an inadequate basis for the protection of competition, the antimonopoly tradition also rested intellectually upon classical economic theory and upon the pluralism of American democratic thought.

But in America competition was more than a theory: it was

---

[2] On European developments in antitrust law, see *Antitrust Developments in the European Common Market*, Report of the Subcommittee on Antitrust and Monopoly of the Committee on the Judiciary, U.S. Senate, 88th Cong., 2nd sess. (Washington, 1964), and *Comparative Aspects of Anti-Trust Law in the United States, the United Kingdom, and the European Economic Community*, Supplementary Publication No. 6 of *International and Comparative Law Quarterly* (London, 1963). For a brief and synoptic comparison of antitrust legislation in the United States, Canada, and Britain, see W. Friedmann: *Law in a Changing Society* (London, 1959), Ch. 8.

a way of life and a creed. From its colonial beginnings through most of the nineteenth century, ours was overwhelmingly a nation of farmers and small-town entrepreneurs —ambitious, mobile, optimistic, speculative, anti-authoritarian, egalitarian, and competitive. As time went on, Americans came to take it for granted that property would be widely diffused, that economic and political power would be decentralized. The fury with which they could be mobilized against any institution that even appeared to violate these expectations by posing a threat of monopoly was manifest in the irrational assault on the Bank of the United States during Jackson's presidency. Their most respected thinkers habitually assured them that their social order was God-ordained or natural, and they probably thought it would last forever.

Then, with extraordinary rapidity as historical time is reckoned, that order was overwhelmed by the giant corporation. In the last three decades of the nineteenth century a wholly new economy came into being. An American born in 1828, the year of Jackson's election, came of age in a society in which the old small-enterprise economy, however dynamic and expansive, had kept its fundamental pattern more or less intact. But in his mature years he would have seen that economy fast becoming obsolete, and if he lived as late as 1904, he would have seen industry concentrated to a degree inconceivable not only to his fathers but even to him during most of his adult life. This economic transformation happened so fast that the mind could not easily absorb it. An entire people could hardly be expected to cease overnight to dream the dreams of the small entrepreneur. In 1900 the problem of big business and the threat of monopoly were still so new that it was hard to get one's bearings. Bigness had come with such a rush that its momentum seemed irresistible. No one knew when or how it could be stopped.

It is hardly surprising that the men of the first antitrust

generation made some frightening projections into the future. In 1890, and even in 1914, bigness had not yet been domesticated either as a force in the economic world or as a factor in the American imagination. A nation that had gone so fast from competitive small enterprise to corporate giantism might readily go with equal speed from corporate giantism to a system of monopolistic tyranny. Hence, discussions of big business in the last decades of the nineteenth and the opening decade of the twentieth century are full of dark prognostications, most of them plausible enough at the time, however little they have been realized.

Since it had been widely assumed that competition, being "natural," would be largely self-perpetuating, the classical theory had not reckoned with the possible necessity of underwriting competition by statute. But by the 1880's the old confidence in the self-sustaining character of competition was dead, and there seemed no adequate protection for competition in existing law. As soon as it became clear that the common-law tradition against restraints of trade had ceased to have any force and that state laws on the subject were altogether inadequate to the purpose, the demand for federal action arose. George Gunton thought in 1888 that "the public mind has begun to assume a state of apprehension almost amounting to alarm," and that the social atmosphere was "surcharged with an indefinite but almost inexpressible fear of trusts."[3] Senator Sherman warned his colleagues that "the popular mind is agitated with problems that may disturb the social order," singling out inequities of wealth and the formation of combinations of capital so great that they threatened to produce "a trust for every production and a master to fix the price for every necessity of life." Congress must heed the appeal of the voters, he said, "or be ready for the socialist, the

---

[3] G. W. Stocking and M. W. Watkins: *Monopoly and Free Enterprise* (New York, 1951), p. 257.

communist, and the nihilist. Society is now disturbed by forces never felt before."[4] Historians, like contemporaries, have differed as to how imperative the demand for federal action was. In a careful survey of articulate opinion on the "trust" problem in 1890, Hans B. Thorelli concludes that public demand, though perhaps less than an irresistible tide, was too strong to be ignored by the politicians.

Was the Congress of 1890 cynically offering a sop to public sentiment? The plutocratic character of that Congress lends some credence to this view, as does the observation of Senator Orville Platt, at one point in the debate, that the conduct of the Senate during the previous days was "not in the line of honest preparation of a bill to prohibit and punish trusts" but was merely an effort "to get some bill headed 'A bill to punish trusts' with which to go to the country."[5] These circumstances of its origins have helped to confirm many historians in their suspicion that antitrust was, from beginning to end, only a charade.

But there is also reason to believe, on the contrary, that most congressmen thought of the competitive order in business as being the cornerstone of the whole democratic way of life and that they considered themselves to be making the first tentative step in formulating a policy for the control of trusts, which, if it could be put on sound constitutional footing, might serve as the basis for corrective litigation and perhaps

---

[4] *Congressional Record*, 51st Cong., 1st sess. (March 21, 1890), p. 2460. "Although this body is always conservative," Sherman said hopefully, "yet, whatever may be said of it, it has always been ready to preserve not only popular rights in their broad sense, but the rights of individuals as against associated and corporate wealth and power."

[5] Hans B. Thorelli: *The Federal Antitrust Policy* (Baltimore, 1955), p. 198. There is a mass of information about the antimonopoly aspects of the American tradition in Arthur P. Dudden's unpublished doctoral dissertation, *Antimonopolism, 1865–1890*, University of Michigan (1950). On contemporary views, see also Sanford D. Gordon: "Attitudes towards Trusts prior to the Sherman Act," *Southern Economic Journal*, XXX (October 1963), 156–67.

subsequent statutory changes. Admittedly, they were breaking new ground. Senator Hoar said that Congress was entering a wholly new field of legislation and that "the opinions of
Senators themselves, of able and learned and experienced
lawmakers, were exceedingly crude in this matter."[6]

It is true, of course, that Congress emerged with a statute
written in the most general terms, which for many years was
emasculated by judicial decisions and administrative lethargy.
But it is very likely that, with its broadly worded prohibition
of conspiracies in restraint of trade and of efforts to monopo-
lize, Congress was attempting to lay down a general declaration of policy that would serve as a guide to future action in
much the same flexible way as the Constitution itself had
served the country after 1787. Many congressmen doubtless
believed that the self-enforcing features of the law would be
far more effective than they actually became—that is, that the
triple-damage suits authorized for victims of restraints of
trade would cause businessmen themselves to carry on a good
deal of the policing of the economy. Perhaps the problem
confronting Congress can be reconstructed with greater sympathy if we try to imagine whether a drastically different and
significantly more effective law would have been passed by a
wholly populistic and militantly anti-big-business Congress,
and whether such a law could have been expected to receive a
more successful implementation than the Sherman Act in the
hands of the subsequent administrative officers and judges.

One may say with reasonable assurance that the confusion
of Congress over the economic significance of antitrust mir-
rored a more general confusion in American society. The
goals of antitrust were of three kinds. The first were economic; the classical model of competition confirmed the belief
that the maximum of economic efficiency would be produced

---

[6] *Congressional Record*, 51st Cong., 1st sess. (April 8, 1890), p.
3146.

by competition, and at least some members of Congress must have been under the spell of this intellectually elegant model, insofar as they were able to formulate their economic intentions in abstract terms. The second class of goals was political; the antitrust principle was intended to block private accumulations of power and protect democratic government. The third was social and moral; the competitive process was believed to be a kind of disciplinary machinery for the development of character, and the competitiveness of the people—the fundamental stimulus to national morale—was believed to need protection.

Among the three, the economic goal was the most cluttered with uncertainties, so much so that it seems to be no exaggeration to regard antitrust as being essentially a political rather than an economic enterprise.[7] A fundamental difficulty in economic thought, troubling from the very start, arose over the relative claims of combination and competition. The Sherman Act was framed and debated in the pre-expert era, when economists as a professional group were not directly consulted by the legislators. But even if they had been, they would have given mixed and uncertain advice. The profession was split. A few years earlier the American Economic Association had been founded by men in revolt against the classical tradition and laissez-faire doctrines, although, of course, many economists of the older school were still ensconced in universities and colleges. Economists were familiar with the argument that the competitive order, far from being fixed in a per-

---

[7] Hans B. Thorelli, after examining carefully the congressional debates on the Sherman Act, concludes, p. 227, that "the Sherman Act is not to be viewed exclusively as an expression of economic policy," and that in safeguarding the rights of the common man in business it "embodies what is to be characterized as an eminently 'social' purpose." Thorelli believes that Sherman and many of his contemporaries in Congress saw the legislation as "an important means of achieving freedom from corruption and maintaining freedom of independent thinking in political life."

manent, beneficent, self-sustaining equilibrium, might have a strong tendency toward self-liquidation through the disappearance of weaker competitors. One of the early historicists, E. Benjamin Andrews, argued in 1893 that laissez-faire was no more than a systematized expression of anarchy, and the following year warned:

> Bills have been brought before half the legislatures of the Union to free competition by making trade syndicates absolutely illegal. To my mind there is no question that such legislation will be vain. The age of competition as we have known it is gone forever. As well try to waken the dead.[8]

The more influential voice of Richard Ely was also raised in protest against the ideal of pure competition. He was among those who insisted that size should not be equated with monopoly, and long before Thurman Arnold he held that antitrust legislation was not only futile but actually encouraging to monopoly, because it caused business leaders to replace "soft" combinations by "hard" combinations in the form of mergers.[9]

No consensus was to be had on the proper line of governmental action on trusts or on the kind of law Congress should pass. Nearly all economists believed that attempts simply to prohibit combinations by law would be futile. There was a growing disposition to consider that both competition and combination needed some measure of control and that neither could be eliminated by law. In this sense, as William Letwin has pointed out, the counsel that was available from the economists, however much attended to or ignored, shared the ambiguity that the legislators themselves could feel as lawyers:

> The economists thought that both competition and combination should play their parts in the economy. The lawyers saw

---

[8] Thorelli: op. cit., pp. 112 n, 316.
[9] Ibid., pp. 314–15.

that the common law permitted combination in some instances and prohibited it in others. Congressmen seized on this hidden agreement, and set out to construct a statute which by the use of common-law principles would eliminate excesses but allow "healthy" competition and combination to flourish side by side.[1]

If one gives due regard to the uncertainties of the matter and to the improbability that any attempt at a quick solution would be effective, one may arrive at a more charitable judgment of the Congress of 1890. Its members were probably trying to lay down general guidelines by means of which their successors might evolve a policy that would give society the advantages of both competition and combination. As Senator Sherman said, "All that we, as lawmakers, can do is to declare general principles."[2] These principles could hardly have been enunciated in more sweeping language than that used in the Sherman Act. Presumably, many congressmen hoped that the courts would find a way of striking at the notoriously unfair methods of competition that had already been used to build such companies as Standard Oil and the National Cash Register Company, without barring useful consolidations or even such restrictive agreements as were intended to eliminate intolerably rigorous competition.

This original uncertainty about the economic rationale for antitrust continued to haunt well-intentioned Progressives in the years before the First World War. The vagueness and inconsistency so often expressed by intelligent and relatively candid political leaders during this era must be taken as a reflection not on the caliber of the leadership but rather on the intrinsic difficulty of the problem.

---

[1] William Letwin: *Law and Economic Policy in America: The Evolution of the Sherman Antitrust Act* (New York, 1965), p. 85; see, in general, Ch. 3 on the intentions of Congress.

[2] *Congressional Record*, 51st Cong., 1st sess. (March 21, 1890), p. 2460. Sherman was here conceding the difficulty of defining in law the precise difference between legal and illegal combinations, and expressing a preference for leaving such decisions to the courts in particular cases.

Theodore Roosevelt represents, on this count, a maximum of shrewdness combined with a minimum of anxiety. With the exception of railroad regulation, Roosevelt was not profoundly interested in the economic issues that agitated the American public during his presidency; indeed, he was quite candid in confessing his reluctance to tackle them head on. When in difficulties, as in 1907, he was disposed to trust to the judgment and the political and financial leadership of the conservatives in the Senate or the economic powers in Wall Street. However, he saw the trust problem as something that must be dealt with on the political level; public concern about it was too urgent to be ignored. He understood how important it was to assure the public that the government of the United States had the will and the power to assert its authority over large corporations. Accordingly, his antitrust prosecutions, although few, were in some cases appropriately spectacular. When he assessed the significance of the Northern Securities case, he did not say that it would open the way to a general assault on bigness, but rather that it was important for showing that "the most powerful men in this country were held to accountability before the law." His fundamental solution for the problem—that bigness must be accepted as a part of the modern industrial and social order, and that its behavior should be subjected to administrative control under full publicity—comes somewhat closer than the views of most of his political contemporaries to anticipating the future course of antitrust procedure.

Roosevelt was accompanied, or perhaps followed, by a school of liberal publicists—among them Charles R. Van Hise, Herbert Croly, and Walter Lippmann—who accepted his conviction that the Sherman Act philosophy was the product of what he called a "sincere rural Toryism" long since outgrown. Lippmann, in one of the most penetrating attacks on the antitrust philosophy, characterized it as the philosophy of "a nation of villagers." This school of Progressives saw the Western world as entering upon a new era of organization and specialization for which the old competitive philosophy was hopelessly retrograde. Some of them, notably Croly and Van Hise, also saw small-scale business as inadequate to the task of competing in the world's markets, which they believed to be a necessity of the American situation. In retrospect, they appear more sophisticated and prophetic than those who put great stock in the Sherman Act as a force for actual dissolution. They foresaw the decline of antitrust as a movement, and in some instances recognized that if the Sherman Act persisted it would be as a basis for occasional *ad hoc* regulatory suits rather than as an instrument for dismantling the corporate economy.

Woodrow Wilson spoke more feelingly for the "rural Toryism" and the village democracy which seem to have been at the center of popular antitrust feeling; but by the same token he illustrated more clearly than Roosevelt their intellectual difficulties. Speaking in the campaign of 1912, which afforded a full-dress display of the differences between the two schools of thought on trusts, he asserted that he too was not against size as such. He was all for bigness as an inevitable and natural growth, whenever it was the outcome of superior efficiency. But he was against "the trusts," which had grown out of illicit competition. He was never very successful, however, in explaining why a business that had become large through legitimate methods might not become just as menacing to competition as one that had grown large through illicit competition. His statement "I am for big business and I am against the trusts" seems hardly more than an unsatisfactory attempt to evade the argument that there is a self-liquidating threat inherent in competition.[3]

---

[3] For Woodrow Wilson's position on monopoly, see his *The New Freedom* (New York, 1913), pp. 163–222. William Diamond, in *The Economic Thought of Woodrow Wilson* (Baltimore, 1943), makes it

III

THE POLITICAL and social arguments against monopoly
were pressed with greater clarity than the economic argument
and with hardly less fervor. Antitrust must be understood as
the political judgment of a nation whose leaders had always
shown a keen awareness of the economic foundations of politics. In this respect, the Sherman Act was simply another manifestation of an enduring American suspicion of concentrated
power. From the pre-Revolutionary tracts through the Declaration of Independence and *The Federalist* to the writings of
the states' rights advocates, and beyond the Civil War into
the era of the antimonopoly writers and the Populists, there
had been a perennial quest for a way of dividing, diffusing,
and checking power and preventing its exercise by a single
interest or by a consolidated group of interests at a single
center. Hence, the political impulse behind the Sherman Act
was clearer and more articulate than the economic theory.
Men who used the vaguest language when they talked about
"the trusts" and monopolies, who had not thought through
the distinction between size itself and monopolistic practices,
who had found no way of showing how much competition
was necessary for efficiency, who could not in every case say
what competitive acts they thought were fair or unfair, or
who could not state a rational program that reconciled their
acceptance of size with their desire for competition, were rea-

---

clear that in his earlier years. Wilson had been committed to the
evolutionist acceptance of size but became more devoted to the competitive principle as he came before the public eye and as he accepted
the advice of Brandeis. By 1913 he seems to have been persuaded that
dissolution was an essential tactic. "Real dissolution in the case of
the trusts is the only thing we can be satisfied with," he wrote
privately, and he indicated that this was part of a program necessary
"to satisfy the conscience of the country." Ibid., p. 112.

sonably clear about what it was that they were trying to avoid: they wanted to keep concentrated private power from destroying democratic government.

One of the glories of the competitive model had been that it purported to solve the question of market power by denying that such power had any particular location. The decisions of the market were beautifully impersonal, since they were only the averagings of the decisions of thousands of individuals, none of whom enjoyed any decisive power. The market mechanism suggested that power was not really exercised by anyone. With the perfect impersonality of Adam Smith's "invisible hand," the market made decisions that ought not be vested in the hands of any particular man or body of men. Hence, the market mechanism met the desire for the diffusion of power and seemed to be the perfect economic counterpart of American democratic pluralism.

Where power *must* be exercised, it was agreed that it should be located in governmental and not in private hands. But the state governments were inadequate; in sheer mass, business enterprises already overshadowed them. Charles William Eliot pointed out as early as 1888 that the large corporations, considered as units of economic organization, had already begun to tower over the states. A Boston railroad company, for example, employed 18,000 persons and had gross receipts of about $40,000,000 a year, whereas the Commonwealth of Massachusetts employed only 6,000 and had receipts of only $7,000,000.[4] Even individually, some corpora-

---

[4] C. W. Eliot: "The Working of the American Democracy," *American Contributions to Civilization* (New York, 1907), pp. 85-6. Three-quarters of a century later the T.N.E.C. found that, as economic units, only ten states had assets greater than the two largest corporations, and that more than half the states were completely overshadowed in size by private businesses. *Final Report and Recommendations of the Temporary National Economic Committee* (Washington, 1941), pp. 676-7; David Lynch: *The Concentration of Economic Power* (New York, 1946), pp. 112-13.

tions were big enough to dominate state governments, and if they should combine among themselves, they might come to dominate the federal government as well.

The existence of the industrial combinations and the threat that under one auspice or another—perhaps that of the investment bankers—there would come about some day a combination of the combinations that would be stronger than civil government itself, provoked a fear that haunted the minds of the writers of the industrial era, including many whose social views were as conservative as Eliot's. The fundamental fear of private power was well put by William Jennings Bryan, in a speech delivered at the Chicago Conference on Trusts in 1899:

> I do not divide monopolies in private hands into good monopolies and bad monopolies. There is no good monopoly in private hands. There can be no good monopoly in private hands until the Almighty sends us angels to preside over the monopoly. There may be a despot who is better than another despot, but there is no good despotism.[5]

And the general sense that the dire economic and political consequences of monopoly were as one was incorporated in the Democratic platform of 1900:

> Private monopolies are indefensible and intolerable. . . . They are the most efficient means yet devised for appropriating the fruits of industry to the benefit of the few at the expense of the many, and unless their insatiate greed is checked, all wealth will be aggregated in a few hands and the Republic destroyed.[6]

The most articulate expression of the Progressives' case against the political power of monopoly was made by Woodrow Wilson in 1912. It was the burden of his argument, against T.R., that once the existence of large-scale combina-

---

[5] Thorelli: op. cit., p. 336.
[6] Kirk H. Porter and Donald B. Johnson: *National Party Platforms* (Urbana, Ill., 1956), p. 114.

tions is accepted, regulation of them by government becomes impossible, because the political power of business combination will be great enough to nullify all attempts at controlling it. Wilson played artfully on the fears and suspicions of the small entrepreneurs. Even some very powerful men, he said, knew that "there is a power somewhere so organized, so subtle, so watchful, so interlocked, so complete, so pervasive, that they had better not speak above their breath when they speak in condemnation of it. . . . They know that somewhere, by somebody, the development of industry is being controlled."[7] He pictured concentrated capital as being already in control of the government: "The masters of the government of the United States are the combined capitalists and manufacturers of the United States. . . . The government of the United States at present is a foster-child of the special interests."[8]

Of necessity this would continue to be the state of affairs until the combinations not only were unseated by the people but also were dissolved—until "this colossal 'community of interest' " was disentangled. It was a thing that the laws must "pull apart, and gently, but firmly and persistently dissect." Otherwise, under Roosevelt's plan for accepting and regulating monopolies, there would only be a union between monopoly and government: "If the government controlled by the monopolies in its turn controls the monopolies, the partnership is finally consummated." "If monopoly persists, monopoly will always sit at the helm of the government. I do not expect to see monopoly restrain itself. If there are men in this country big enough to own the government of the United States, they are going to own it."[9]

---

[7] Wilson: op. cit., pp. 14, 62.

[8] Ibid., pp. 57–8.

[9] Ibid., pp. 118, 207, 286. For a later statement of this view see the dissenting opinion of Mr. Justice Douglas in *U.S. v. Columbia Steel Co.*, 334 U.S. 495 (1948).

The third objective of antitrust action, hardly less important than the others, was psychological and moral. It sprang from the conviction that competition has a disciplinary value for character, quite aside from its strictly economic uses. America was thought to have been made possible by the particular type of character that was forged by competitive individualism, a type that had flourished in the United States because competitive opportunities had been so widespread that alert men could hardly fail to see them, to grasp and use them, and hence, to be shaped by them. The American male character was believed to have been quickened and given discipline by the sight and pursuit of opportunity. For this process to take place it was important that business be carried on fairly —the sporting vocabulary was never far below the surface— and that newcomers be able to enter the game as entrepreneurs on reasonably open terms.

The significance of this faith that competition could be relied upon to form character can be fully grasped only if we bear in mind the Protestant background of our economic thinking. Economists themselves had not been in the habit of analyzing economic relationships in purely mechanical and secular terms, and what may be said of them on this count can be said with greater force about laymen, when they thought about economic issues. Behind the American way of thinking there lay a long Protestant tradition, which tended to identify economic forces with religious and moral forces and which regarded economic processes from the standpoint of their contribution to the discipline and development of character. The economic order was not merely an apparatus for the production of goods and services; it was a set of rules for forging good conduct. Everyone is familiar, I believe, with the proposition that some of the concepts of classical economics were shaped under the influence of a kind of prudential morality in which savings and abstinence were not merely instruments of economic analysis but moral sanctions. In our time we have heard conservatives frankly condemn government fiscal policy that deviates from the prudential rules suitable to a family budget by appealing to the Puritan tradition. Such critics are the legitimate heirs of the men of the nineteenth and the early twentieth century who saw the protection of competition and its incentives as a safeguard of national morale, as a means for mobilizing and rewarding the industrious and the prudent and for penalizing those whom William Graham Sumner called "the poor and the weak, the negligent, shiftless, inefficient, silly, and imprudent . . . the idle, intemperate, and vicious."[1]

Here again one looks to Woodrow Wilson for the most articulate expression of this emphasis on the economic foundations of character and especially to the masterful speeches in 1912 in which he expressed his concern for "the beginner," "the man with only a little capital," "the man on the make," upon whose genius he thought the country had always been built. "The treasury of America," he argued, "lies in those ambitions, those energies, that cannot be restricted to a special favored class." It rests upon the inventiveness and the energy of "unknown men" and would lose its force if the economic order ceased to stimulate such inventiveness and energy. It was possible, he hinted, that under large-scale organization the country would turn its back on its past, which he evoked in poignant terms:

> . . . the ancient time when America lay in every hamlet, when America was to be seen in every fair valley, when America displayed her great forces on the broad prairies, ran her fine fires of enterprise up over the mountainsides and down into the bowels of the earth, and eager men were everywhere captains of industry, not employees; not looking to a distant city to find out

---

[1] William Graham Sumner: *What Social Classes Owe to Each Other* (New Haven, 1925), p. 21.

what they might do, but looking about among their neighbors, finding credit according to their character, not according to their connections, finding credit in proportion to what was known to be in them and behind them, not in proportion to the securities they held that were approved where they were not known.[2]

The prospect that these "fine fires of enterprise" were about to be quenched suggested that the old kind of character would be destroyed, that the old America was about to die—a reason even more imperative than mere industrial efficiency for seeking out the possibilities of antitrust action.

The inherited belief that small property and opportunity for small business have forged the American character, which might well lose its form without the discipline imposed by a particular variety of entrepreneurial competition, is one that has never died out. Near the end of the Second World War the Small Business Committee of the Senate put this faith clearly when it said that the pursuit of opportunity by the small business owner

> has been a great motive force among our people. It stimulates expression of the fundamental virtues of thrift, industry, intelligence, schooling, home ties, and family pride—in short, those fireside virtues which have counted for so much in developing our strength and character.[3]

The preservation of opportunities for small business, as a member of the S.E.C. put it in 1945, is more important than any economic goal; it is "a goal which transcends economic and political forms and processes as such, and remains fundamentally concerned with the character of the men and women who comprise the nation."[4]

---

[2] Wilson: op. cit., pp. 18–19.
[3] Quoted in John H. Bunzel: *The American Small Businessman* (New York, 1962), p. 84.
[4] Rudolph L. Weissman: *Small Business and Venture Capital* (New York, 1945), p. 164.

IV

THERE ARE two salient differences between the problem of bigness as it was perceived about sixty years ago and the problem as it is perceived now; the first is that it is no longer a new problem, and the second is that the economy has performed in a way hardly dreamed of before the Second World War. In 1965 we are as remote in time from the passage of the Sherman Act as the men of 1865 were from the first term of George Washington. The public has had almost three-quarters of a century of experience in living with big business, and analysts of the big-business problem no longer make the same frightening projections as to its future dangers that could be made with entire plausibility sixty or seventy years ago. At the same time, the public is hardly unaware that the steepest rise in mass standards of living has occurred during the period in which the economy has been dominated by the big corporation. Whatever else may be said against bigness, the conception of monopolistic industry as a kind of gigantic, swelling leech on the body of an increasingly deprived and impoverished society has largely disappeared.

About the change in public attitudes from those prevailing sixty years ago we can make only an educated guess. Today we can check our impressions of the public mind against opinion polls; for the earlier era we have impressions alone. But it is very difficult for anyone who reads widely in the political literature of the period 1890–1914 to believe that public concern today over big business has anything like the sense of urgency that it had then. In 1951 the Institute of Social Research of the University of Michigan published the results of an illuminating survey, *Big Business as the People See It*. Its findings show some residues of the old popular suspicion of bigness, but the noteworthy thing is public acceptance. Americans have always had to balance their love of bigness and efficiency against their fear of power and their regard for individualism and competition. The survey indicates that this ambivalence has been largely resolved in favor of the big business organization.

A quarter of the population, as represented in the Institute's national sample, showed some concern over big business and an awareness that it had an important effect on their lives. But a substantial majority reacted favorably to big business. Asked to give a general characterization of its social effects, the respondents answered as follows:

The good things outweigh the bad things	76%
They seem about equal	2
The bad things outweigh the good things	10
Don't know	5
Confused; evaluation not ascertainable	7
	100%

Plainly, big business was no longer a scare word to the public at large. Eighty-four per cent of those polled reacted without apparent emotion to the question, and only a small minority reacted unfavorably. Questioned on particulars, respondents spoke with especial favor of the productive powers of big business and its ability to give jobs and keep prices down. The most critical responses about big business dealt mainly with its effect on "the little man" and the destruction of competition. Very little concern was expressed about the power of big business over its workers (it is commonly regarded as a good employer) and surprisingly little about its influence on government.

Whereas fifty years before, fear of an indefinitely continued increase in the political power of big business was commonplace, the typical expectation expressed in the poll of 1951 was that the power of big business would decline, and properly so. As in the Progressive era, there was a strong

preference for a balance of power and a conviction that
wherever there must be a clear preponderance of power it
should rest in governmental and not private hands. But the
existing state of business power was not widely considered
to be dangerous. In fact, big-business power was ranked third
among five forces—behind national government and labor
unions and ahead of state governments and smaller business.
Stronger feeling was shown against labor unions than against
big business. There was a fraction of the public that saw
big business as more powerful than labor unions and would
have liked to see the situation reversed; but there was a
fraction almost twice as large that saw the unions as more
powerful and would have preferred to see the situation reversed.[5]

The findings of the Michigan group were not widely at
variance with those of Elmo Roper, who a few years earlier
had collated the responses of the public over a span of fifteen
years to questions about business. Roper found that "the public has mixed feelings about big business. There is pride over
the achievements of big business but some apprehension over
the possible abuses of power inherent in big business." The
public was disposed to want a watchdog set upon the amoral
and greedy elements in business, but only about a fourth of
the respondents were found to believe that the disadvantages
of bigness overshadow whatever advantages there might be.[6]

To what can we attribute this public acceptance of big
business? Not much, I believe, to the efforts that big-business-
men have made to cultivate a favorable "image" for the large
corporation. As the fate of the postwar campaign to sell "free
enterprise" suggests, such efforts can miscarry badly when
they represent nothing more than an attempt to make the

[5] Burton R. Fisher and Stephen B. Withey: *Big Business as the
People See It* (Ann Arbor, 1951), passim.
[6] Elmo Roper: "The Public Looks at Business," *Harvard Business
Review*, XXVII (March 1949), 165–74.

public take seriously the blather with which big business sometimes comforts itself.[7] What has really made bigness palatable more than anything else is the remarkable performance of the economy since the beginning of the Second World War. Something too must be credited to the emergence of countervailing bigness in government and labor, whose effects on public attitudes emerge clearly from the Michigan survey. Moreover, anyone who is aware of the historical circumstances under which hostility to big business flourished must be aware that big business has not lived up to the horrifying billing that it got in the age of the muckrakers. It is not merely that no business treats competitors today as they were treated in the early days of the National Cash Register Company or Standard Oil. What is important is that a whole range of fears that existed in the Progressive era, based largely upon a preoccupation with an unknown future, has vanished. We now live in that future, and although it has fears of its own—nightmarish beyond anything anticipated in the days of Bryan and Wilson—they are of a wholly different origin. Probably the worst of the Populist-Progressive nightmares was the notion—expressed in the Pujo Committee's inquiry, in Brandeis's *Other People's Money*, in Wilson's speeches, and in Jack London's *The Iron Heel*—of the formation, under the auspices of the investment bankers, of a giant syndicate, a combination of the combinations, which would rule the country with a tyrannical grip. The self-financing character of the great corporations, the survival of competition in investment banking, and the failure of investment banking to remain a power of the first order after the crash of 1929 have set this specter to rest.

If no sinister central syndicate had to be feared, it did at least seem reasonable at the turn of the century to anticipate a steadily growing concentration of industry that would even-

---

[7] William H. Whyte, Jr., is eloquent on the failure of one such campaign in *Is Anybody Listening?* (New York, 1952).

tually deprive the country of every advantage of competition. And here, insofar as the antitrust enterprise was directed against size itself or against concentration, it was beaten before it ever got started; American industry was already highly concentrated in 1904, when T.R. was boasting about the lessons of the Northern Securities case. But insofar as the Progressives were worried about what the economists later came to call "workable competition" in industry, they might well have been reassured as time went on. The investigations of such economists as M. A. Adelman, G. Warren Nutter, and George J. Stigler have cast considerable doubt on the idea that either the scope of monopoly or the degree of concentration has, in fact, grown since early in the century. "The extent of concentration," Adelman concluded in an important study, "shows no tendency to grow, and it may possibly be declining. Any tendency either way, if it does exist, must be at the pace of a glacial drift."[8] Measuring monopoly is an undertaking of considerable complexity and the issues are controversial. But it is at least safe to say that no one who has due regard for the difficulties of the problem can any longer raise alarmist cries about the rapid growth of monopoly or concentration without flying in the face of much formidable testimony.

Another cause of concern, very real to many men in the

---

[8] M. A. Adelman: "The Measurement of Industrial Concentration," *Review of Economics and Statistics*, XXXIII (November 1951), 269–96. See also the discussion by Adelman and others: ibid., XXXIV (May 1952), 156 ff.; G. Warren Nutter: *The Extent of Enterprise Monopoly in the United States, 1899–1939* (Chicago, 1951); and George J. Stigler: *Five Lectures on Economic Problems* (London, 1949), pp. 46–65. However, on the identity of the largest firms and the mobility of firms into positions of leadership, see Norman R. Collins and Lee E. Preston: "The Size Structure of the Largest Industrial Firms," *American Economic Review*, LI (December 1961), 986–1003. Fritz Machlup: *The Political Economy of Monopoly* (Baltimore, 1952), pp. 469–528, is instructive on the difficulties of the subject. See also Edward S. Mason: *Economic Concentration and the Monopoly Problem* (New York: Atheneum ed., 1964), pp. 16–43.

Progressive era and rather quaint from today's perspective, had to do with the progress of industry. "Monopoly," warned Wilson in 1912, "always checks development, weighs down natural prosperity, pulls against natural advance." In the past, he said, competitive America had produced or developed the steamboat, the cotton gin, the sewing machine, the reaper, the typewriter, the electric light, and other great inventions, but the day was at hand when monopoly might end all this. "Do you know, have you had occasion to learn, that there is no hospitality for invention nowadays? There is no encouragement for you to set your wits at work. . . . The instinct of monopoly is against novelty, the tendency of monopoly is to keep in use the old thing, made in the old way." Only a restoration of freedom could unleash American inventiveness again: "Who can say what patents now lying, unrealized, in secret drawers and pigeonholes, will come to light, or what new inventions will astonish and bless us, when freedom is restored?"[9] To two generations that since 1912 have been astonished and blessed almost to death by inventions, such rhetoric can no longer be alarming or inspiring; it is merely a curiosity. Today the public needs no persuading that it is the large corporations, with their programs of research, that are technologically progressive. As Galbraith has remarked, the showpieces of American industrial progress are, in the main, those dominated by a handful of large firms, and "the foreign visitor, brought to the United States by the Economic Cooperation Administration, visits the same firms as do attorneys of the Department of Justice in their search for monopoly."[1]

Another typical fear expressed in Progressive writing was that the possibility of individual advancement would be

---

[9] Wilson: op. cit., pp. 265–6, 270.
[1] John Kenneth Galbraith: *American Capitalism* (Boston, 1952), p. 96; cf. Joseph A. Schumpeter: *Capitalism, Socialism, and Democracy* (New York, 1947), pp. 81–2.

frozen out, that the upward social mobility that had refreshed and inspired American development in the past would come to an end, when the business of the country was fully dominated by the large corporation. I know of no very certain information on how the American public regards the prospects for social mobility today, although our concerted scramble for educational position and advantage suggests that the middle-class public, and even much of the working-class public, is rather well aware that mobility still exists; it is also aware of the educational machinery through which it can be pursued. What can be said with greater confidence is that informed observers no longer speak so glibly of the decline of mobility or opportunity.

Indeed, there is strong evidence that the opportunity of middle- or lower-class men to rise to top positions in business has somewhat increased over what it was fifty or sixty years ago,[2] and there is some reason to believe that the increase, or at least the persistence, of occupational opportunity has, in fact, impressed itself on the public mind. In fact, the modern corporation has proved to be a better medium for social mobility and opportunity than the old system of individual and family entrepreneurship, whose openness in this respect was always much exaggerated. Oddly enough, the concentration of capital and the divorce of ownership from the entrepreneurial function may prove in the long run to be more conducive to the lowering of social tensions and to political stability than diffused ownership.[3] The ways of achieving occupational advancement and economic success have

---

[2] For a good review of the relevant findings, see Seymour M. Lipset and Reinhard Bendix: *Social Mobility in Industrial Society* (Berkeley and Los Angeles, 1960), Ch. 3.

[3] For a shrewd and heretical statement on the political and social effects of the large corporation, see M. A. Adelman: "Some Aspects of Corporate Enterprise," in Ralph Freeman (ed.): *Postwar Economic Trends in the United States* (New York, 1960), pp. 289–308.

changed; individual entrepreneurship is a much less sure and satisfactory path as compared with bureaucratic careers. The acquisition of specialized skills has become more important, and with it the seizure and exploitation of educational opportunities.

I do not mean to suggest that the old ideal of self-employment or the old confidence in the entrepreneurial path to success has been entirely abandoned in favor of the bureaucratic career. Although the incidence of self-employment and the number of those who actually live by the competitive ideal have shrunk very considerably in the three-quarters of a century since the Sherman Act, most of this is attributable to the numerical decline of family farmers, who in 1890 still comprised nearly half the population and today comprise about a tenth. The farmers, with their dependence on subsidies and government-administered prices, can hardly be looked upon any more as vigorous exponents of the competitive way of life. But the dream of self-employment that dominated the agrarian-entrepreneurial society of the nineteenth century is still alive. It has been estimated that about 20 to 30 per cent of the American working force has been at some time or other self-employed.[4] The growth of small businesses over the past dozen years or so has roughly kept pace in numbers with the growth of the adult population, and the aspirations of small business have been institutionalized in Senate and House committees as well as in some antitrust activities.

But although small business holds its place as an occupational segment of the economy itself, its role as a sector of society committed to the entrepreneurial ideal has declined. Small business can no longer be idealized for its independence and hardihood or its devotion to competitive principles. It, too, looks to government intervention for sustenance,

---

[4] Lipset and Bendix: op. cit., pp. 102–3.

whether in the form of resale price maintenance, anti-chain-store legislation, or the Small Business Administration. Small business, which used to be, as one writer put it,[5] "a symbol of opportunity, enterprise, innovation, and achievement" and of "an independent way of life," has been driven largely into the marginal areas of economic life, where it often tries to maintain itself by waging its own assaults upon the competitive principle. Various segments of small business, in their pressure for support for the Robinson-Patman Act of 1936 and the Miller-Tydings Amendment of 1937, have shown how quickly they can be rallied against competition, when it impinges upon their own interests. Vigorous advocates of the Sherman and Clayton acts where big business is affected, they turn their backs on competitive virility when it suits their purposes. If there is anything rarer than a small-businessman who will question the merits of competition as a principle, it is one who can understand and abide competition when it really afflicts him as a fact.[6]

Not only can the small-businessman not purport, in the eyes of any well-informed observer, to be a vigorous and consistent exemplar of the competitive ideal; he can no longer be idealized by progressive-minded men from other walks of life, as he could, say, in the era when Woodrow Wilson waxed rhapsodical about the new men out of "unknown homes" who had really made America. In the United States and elsewhere, liberal intellectuals now cock a suspicious eye at him, if not as a potential stronghold of support for fascist movements, at least as the backbone of the reactionary wing of the Republican party. An occasional big-business leader

---

[5] Theodore O. Yntema, in the Foreword to A. D. H. Kaplan: *Small Business: Its Place and Problems* (New York, 1948), p. vii.

[6] For an amusing illustration of this incomprehension of competition, see the testimony before the T.N.E.C., quoted in Lynch: op. cit., pp. 155–6.

may stand out for his enlightenment and urbanity, as compared with the small-businessman, who more often than not proves to be a refractory anti-union employer, a parochial and archaic opponent of liberal ideas, a supporter of vigilante groups and of right-wing cranks.[7] As a figure in our economic society, the small-businessman still plays a part of some considerable importance, but as a partner in the American liberal coalition, he has all but disappeared, and with him has gone much of the pristine anti-bigness feeling of the Progressive tradition.

Still, the conviction that American democracy will survive only if small-business enterprise survives to sustain the American character has not disappeared. It has been inherited from the Progressives of yesterday by the conservatives of today. It appears to be, as we shall see, a conviction that flourishes less among the young than among the old, who are often troubled that they cannot persuade their juniors of its importance. "For the development of self-reliance," say two authors of a manual for small-business operation, "for making men as well as money, small business excels."[8] In 1936, when the Robinson-Patman Act was under consideration, this effort to underwrite the middleman was touted by the chairman of the House Committee on the Judiciary as a potential bulwark of the democratic order: "There are a great many people who feel that if we are to preserve democracy in government, in America, we have got to preserve a democracy in business operation.... We must make some effort to *maintain the yeomanry in business*."[9]

---

[7] On the politics of small business, which, of course, still has a liberal minority wing, see Bunzel: op. cit., Ch. 5.

[8] Pearce C. Kelley and Kenneth Lawyer: *How to Organize and Operate a Small Business* (Englewood Cliffs, N. J., 1949), p. 11.

[9] Quoted in Merle Fainsod, Lincoln Gordon, and Joseph C. Palamountain, Jr.: *Government and the American Economy* (New York, 1959), p. 549; italics added.

During the 1940's and 1950's there was evidence of a widespread uneasy conviction that years of war, depression, and bureaucratic expansion had finally drained away the old regard for entrepreneurship among the young, and that the spirit that animated the old competitive ideal had finally succumbed to the world of the large corporation. The signs and portents are numerous, but a memorable article of 1949 in *Fortune* may be taken as a landmark. Surveying "The Class of '49," *Fortune*'s editors pointed out that it was perhaps the most significant college graduating class in our history. It was one of the largest, most mature (with a high proportion of veterans) and responsible; but its distinguishing feature was its aversion to risk, its passion for security. "The class of '49," the editors reported, "wants to work for somebody else—preferably somebody big. No longer is small business the promised land. As for the idea of going into business for oneself, the idea is so seldom expressed as to seem an anachronism." Only in the Southwest, which seems socially and intellectually to lag behind the rest of the country, was there any sign of significant exceptions to this generalization. The generation which had been impressionable children during the depression and which had come of age in the shadow of the war rendered a firm verdict in favor of security, service, and the good life (measured in modest income expectations) rather than risk, self-assertion, and the big prizes. The emergent young man, the editors reported, "is not afraid of bigness; where his father of the twenties, fearful of anonymity, was repelled by hugeness in an organization, he is attracted."[1]

This was the response of a generation raised in an economy of giant corporations, educated very often in universities with thousands of students, disciplined by army life, and accustomed to the imperatives of organization, mass, and effi-

---

[1] "The Class of '49," *Fortune* (June 1949), pp. 84–7.

ciency. No doubt they often saw in big businesses the promise of laboratories and market research to which the atmosphere of the universities had already accustomed them. Because of its army experiences, the class of 1949 may have been unusually security-minded, but there is no reason to doubt that its acceptance of large organization represented a secular trend. Not long after the *Fortune* piece appeared, the Youth Research Institute Survey put to 4,660 high school and college seniors, recent college graduates, and veterans the question: "Do you feel that you will be able to achieve all of your economic desires by working for someone else?" In reply, 61.1 per cent said yes, 20.4 per cent no, and 18.5 per cent were uncertain.[2] In his essay "The Found Generation," an analysis of the expressed life ideals of the class of 1955, David Riesman found not only a bland acceptance of the large corporation as a place in which to do one's life work but also a depressing complacency about the terms and rewards of the corporate life. The class of 1949 had at least been aware of making a somewhat difficult choice in which their individuality might be at stake. The class of 1955 took the bureaucratic career for granted.[3]

It is this acceptance of the bureaucratic career that, more than anything else, tells us why there is no longer an antitrust movement. It is far more revealing than the law cases or the books on the control of monopoly. It is also a perfect illustration of how the problems of yesterday are not solved but outgrown. Only a few people today are concerned about how to make the large corporations more competitive, but millions are concerned about how they are going to live inside the corporate framework. The existence and the workings of the

[2] William H. Whyte, Jr.: *The Organization Man* (New York, 1957), p. 79 n.

[3] David Riesman: "The Found Generation," in *Abundance for What?* (New York, 1964), pp. 309–323.

corporations are largely accepted, and in the main they are assumed to be fundamentally benign. What is questioned, when anything is questioned, is matters of personal style: What can be salvaged, of either individualism or individuality, in an age in which the big corporation has become a way of life? It is this concern that marks the transition from an age in which *The Curse of Bigness* and *Other People's Money* voiced the prevailing anxieties to one in which everyone reads *The Lonely Crowd* and *The Organization Man*.

Long-prevailing systems of values do not usually go under without a fight, and along with the new acceptance there is a good deal of uneasiness about the corporate life. The young may be losing the concern of their elders with the virile prerogatives of enterprise. Certainly they are now much more disposed to ask of the economic order not whether it is raising a nation of enterprising and hardy men but more matter-of-factly whether it is maintaining an adequate level of employment and producing a sufficient increase in the Gross National Product. But there is also a persistent uneasiness, which has its manifestations both on the left and on the right. The left, if it can be called that, rebels in the name of nonconformity and opts out of the whole bourgeois world in the manner of the beatnik and the hipster. The right (in the manner of Barry Goldwater and his enthusiasts) rebels in the name of the older individualism, which believed that economic life should inculcate discipline and character. Though they would hate to admit it, they are both bedeviled in different ways by the same problem; each of them is trying to make its variety of nonconformism into a mass creed—which is a contradiction in terms. The beats opt out of corporate uniformity in their own uniforms and erect themselves into a stereotype. The right-wingers sing their praises of individualism in dreary, regimented choruses and applaud vigilantes who would kill every vestige of genuine dissent.

In politics, of course, it is the right-wingers who really

count—it is they who have the numbers, the money, the political leverage. They can also invoke the old American pieties and can appeal to the kind of old-fashioned American who believes that federal fiscal policy is just like the family budget. Much of our conservative writing echoes with concern over the decline of the older kind of economic morale, which it identifies with small entrepreneurship. But conservatives understandably fear to make the large corporation the object of their criticism; this smacks too much of subversion. They have a safer and more congenial outlet for their animus against the organization of modern life in the form of denunciations of big government. In this way, the large corporation escapes its proper share of odium. But, historically, it was the giant corporation far more than government policy that eclipsed the old-fashioned economic morality.

Here conservatives and liberals have all but reversed their former positions. In the main it is conservatives who are disgruntled with the style of contemporary economic life, while liberals complete the paradox by springing to its defense and, in particular, to the defense of bigness. As we have seen, there were always a number of Progressive intellectuals who preferred to accept corporate organization and to whom the possibilities of rationalization and order were more appealing than the competitive ideal. Today it is men of such views who seem to have inherited what is left of American liberalism. Of course, big business still holds a place as a negative symbol in the liberal creed, and the liberal creed still gives a certain ritualistic compliance to the anti-big-business sentiment that was once very close to the heart of progressivism. But by and large, as Carl Kaysen has remarked, "today's liberals have abandoned the symbol of competition without much struggle."[4]

Some of the most striking efforts to reconcile us to the

---

[4] Carl Kaysen: "Big Business and the Liberals, Then and Now," *The New Republic* (November 22, 1954), pp. 118–19.

business structure have been written in recent years by liberals who derive from the New Deal tradition. If, in 1953, one read a paean to big business asserting, among other things, that the emotional antagonism to which it was subject was based on "abuses long since corrected"; that the big-business leader is "a man with a strong and practical sense of responsibility to the public, and an awareness of the ethics of present-day business competition"; that "big business has performed economic wonders with one hand tied behind its back"; that it has actually increased competition and multiplied small enterprises; that "size is our greatest single functional asset"; that big business nourishes diversity; that "we are living in what is probably the most highly competitive society men have ever known"; that big-business research has multiplied opportunities for small-business enterprise; that ill-considered antitrust prosecutions have "grave implications for national security"; and that "in Bigness we have the material foundation of a society which can further the highest values known to men, values we describe as spiritual"[5]—one no longer expected to find that one had been reading a speech by a General Motors or A. T. & T. director and was not at all surprised to learn that the author was David E. Lilienthal, once one of the most outspoken democratic idealists of the New Deal bureaucracy and a former disciple of Brandeis.

Lilienthal's innocent rhapsodies to big business may perhaps be taken as the effusions of one who had been reshaped by his experiences in giant public enterprises like the T.V.A. and the A.E.C.[6] But there is also A. A. Berle, Jr., another New Dealer, who held his first job in Brandeis's office and whose

---

[5] David E. Lilienthal: *Big Business: A New Era* (New York, 1953), pp. 5, 7, 27, 33, 36, 47, 190, and passim.

[6] For critiques, see Lee Loevinger: "Antitrust and the New Economics," *Minnesota Law Review*, XXXVII (June 1953), 505–68, and Edward S. Mason: *Economic Concentration and the Monopoly Problem* (Cambridge, Mass., 1957), pp. 371–81.

public career was marked by friendships with Robert La Follette, George Norris, and Franklin D. Roosevelt. In his most recent works Berle has been speculating about the possible development of a corporate conscience and arguing that the contemporary business power system is governed by public consensus. In his *Power Without Property* he urged liberals to reconsider their former, and historically justified, antipathy to big business and to judge it in the light of its achievements in increasing income and distributing property.[7] Finally, there is John Kenneth Galbraith, whose book *American Capitalism* has probably done as much as any other work to reconcile the contemporary liberal mind to the diminished role of competition as a force in modern economic society by offering, as an alternative account of the mechanism by which market power is controlled in the public interest, the principle of countervailing power. Of course, neither Berle nor Galbraith advocates doing away with the antitrust laws—Galbraith, in fact, argues that, in the main, federal antitrust policies have helped to produce countervailing power, where it has not emerged spontaneously[8]—but the net effect of their view of our society is to lower the premium on competition and to turn attention to other economic and social mechanisms that promise to control excessive market power.

To be sure, liberal intellectuals have not ceased to be critical of business civilization or, on occasion, of big business. But a variety of other issues—foreign policy, urban development, civil rights, education, and the like—have become more central, and where these issues are concerned, liberals do not always find themselves in a simple antagonistic confrontation with big business, as they did in the past. Their criticisms of business civilization now rest more on cultural than economic

---

[7] A. A. Berle, Jr.: *Power Without Property* (New York, 1959), pp. 11–16.
[8] Galbraith: *op. cit.*, p. 151.

grounds. The last thing they are interested in is the restoration of competition as the solution to the evils that they see.[9] Even a scandal like the General Electric affair, although it confirms their view of what may be expected from businessmen, no longer excites them very much. In short, that "gale of creative destruction" about which Joseph Schumpeter wrote so eloquently, when he described the progressive character of capitalist technology, has driven both the liberal and the conservative ideologies before it.

V

IT IS EASIER to account for the decline of the antitrust movement as a matter of public sentiment than it is to explain the persistence and growth of the antitrust enterprise as a legal and administrative fact. But the fate of antitrust is an excellent illustration of how a public ideal, vaguely formulated and often hopelessly at odds with stubborn realities, can become embodied in institutions with elaborate, self-preserving rules and procedures, a defensible function, and an equally stubborn capacity for survival. Institutions are commonly less fragile than creeds.

The antitrust revival originated in the closing phases of the New Deal. It was a response to the recession of 1937–8, which itself brought about a crisis in the thinking and the political strategy of the New Dealers. The recession gave to the Brandeis liberals, who had always been present in New Deal councils, a chance to reassert their ideas about competition and their suspicion of big business. In 1934, long before

---

[9] Nor are contemporary radicals. The most full-throated indictment of the ruling element in big business that has been written in our time, C. Wright Mills's *The Power Elite*, does not concern itself even fleetingly with the problem of market power. The Sherman and Clayton acts are not listed in its index.

the cartelization of the N.R.A. was abandoned, the economist Gardiner C. Means, then economic adviser to the Secretary of Agriculture, had prepared a memorandum on administered prices that provided the economic rationale for a new approach to the depression. Early in 1935 this memorandum was published by the Senate.[1] Means contrasted market prices, which were made and remade in the market as the result of interactions between buyers and sellers in the fashion of traditional economic theory, with administered prices, which were set by administrative action and held constant for a considerable period of time. Market prices are flexible and respond readily to a fall in demand; administered prices are rigid. Means considered the disparity between flexible and rigid prices to be an important aggravating force in the depression. Although he did not identify administered prices with monopoly, he focused attention once again on those industries in which market power was sufficiently concentrated to make administered prices possible. Some of his contemporaries seized upon the conception as a rationale for stepping up antitrust activity, and Franklin D. Roosevelt invoked it in his message of 1938, calling for the creation of the T.N.E.C. At the same time, other New Deal theorists, notably Assistant Attorney General Robert Jackson, who was then head of the Antitrust Division of the Department of Justice, and Secretary of the Interior Harold L. Ickes, became convinced that

---

[1] Gardiner C. Means: *Industrial Prices and Their Relative Inflexibility*, Senate Document No. 13, 74th Cong., 1st sess. Parts of this document, along with later papers on the same theme, are reprinted in Means's *The Corporate Revolution in America* (New York, 1962). For a critique and some reflections on later interest in the theory, see Richard Ruggles: "The Nature of Price Flexibility and the Determinants of Relative Price Changes in the Economy," in *Business Concentration and Price Policy* (Princeton, 1955), esp. pp. 443–64, and the conflicting views expressed by economists before the Kefauver Committee: *Administered Prices*, Hearings before the Subcommittee on Antitrust and Monopoly of the Committee on the Judiciary, United States Senate (Washington, 1957).

the organized power of big business was attempting to sabotage reform through a "strike of capital" and that a new assault on business power must be undertaken as a basis for further attempts at recovery. The old argument that business power was a threat to democratic government itself thus entered into Roosevelt's T.N.E.C. message.

The new attack on business power took two forms; the first was the elaborate, if inconclusive, T.N.E.C. investigation, which yielded a mass of factual information, much of it new, but no programmatic proposals in which the investigators themselves had any confidence.[2] The second was the stepping up of antitrust activity under the leadership of Thurman Arnold, the new chief of the Antitrust Division. Congress doubled appropriations for Arnold's division in 1939 and then doubled them again in 1940. Between 1938 and 1943 its staff grew almost fivefold.

In retrospect it is instructive to see what results came from uncertain and, at times, ill-considered beginnings. Today the Jackson-Ickes view of the recession seems quite partisan and fanciful; the T.N.E.C. investigation, for all the information it gathered, was from a pragmatic point of view a fiasco; the value of Means's emphasis on administered prices is highly controversial among economists; and Thurman Arnold's experiment with antitrust enforcement can be judged, at least from one angle of vision, a substantial failure. And yet, as in the case of so many of the gropings of the New Deal, there

---

[2] Early in its *Final Report* (p. 4), the Committee confessed that its members "are not rash enough to believe that they can lay down a program which will solve the great problems that beset the world, but they are convinced that the information which this committee has assembled, when eventually properly analyzed and disseminated, will enable the people of America to know what must be done if human freedom is to be preserved." In short, the Committee did not know what precisely to make of its own data but hoped that in due time the public would. See the penetrating critique by two members, Isador Lubin and Leon Henderson: ibid., pp. 51-2.

was a valuable outcome, which in this case can best be got at by looking at the core of success wrapped up in Thurman Arnold's frustration.

Arnold's story is replete with ironies. He had written of the antitrust enterprise with a devastating note of mockery, and the appointment of a man with such views, especially by an administration that had only recently resorted to the wholesale cartelization of the N.R.A., was looked at askance by antitrust-minded senators as a possible effort to sabotage the Antitrust Division. But Arnold proceeded to recruit and inspire a splendid staff and to rehabilitate the entire antitrust function. His goal was not to attack bigness or efficient mass production or efficient marketing, but rather to discipline the pricing policies of business at the vital points where abuses seemed most important. Antitrust was thus to become an instrument of social and economic policy, aimed to stop firms from setting prices above reasonable levels, to prevent businesses from holding new processes off the market, and to reduce unemployment. All this was to be achieved not so much by isolated cases or by responding to this or that complaint, but rather by systematic action against whole industries—motion pictures, petroleum, radio broadcasting, drugs, housing.

From a short-run point of view, Arnold's regime could be judged a failure. His program for housing was spiked when the Supreme Court made it impossible to act effectively against the labor unions, which constituted a linchpin of restraint of trade in that industry; his plan for the food industry lost its point during the war; his program for transportation was put off by the War Production Board.[3] He could not wholly reform a single industry, much less bring about important general structural changes in the economy. And yet he

---

[3] See Corwin D. Edwards: "Thurman Arnold and the Antitrust Laws," *Political Science Quarterly*, LVII (September 1943), 338–55.

succeeded in demonstrating the usefulness of the antitrust laws. In actually *using* the Sherman Act, thanks to the enlarged staff that Congress had given him, he showed for the first time what it could and could not do. Although it could not alter the fundamental character of the economy or make it less liable to cyclical instability (as Arnold had promised it would in his book *The Bottlenecks of Business*), it could significantly affect the conduct of business within the framework of the existing structure. Arnold's division soon won a number of decisions from the courts—particularly in the Alcoa case of 1945 and the American Tobacco case of the following year—which opened new possibilities for enforcement. It won from Congress a permanent reversal of the former policy of niggardly support. And finally, it put the antitrust enterprise on such a footing that it could flourish under both Democratic and Republican regimes.

The return of the Republicans under Eisenhower did not bring a remission of efforts to use the Sherman Act or a retrenchment of the Antitrust Division. Instead, the Eisenhower administration set up the Attorney General's National Committee to Study the Antitrust Laws, which in 1955 returned a unanimous judgment in favor of antitrust policy and of the current state of case law, under which enforcement had been tightened. Although the Committee did not make any dramatic recommendations for more rigorous enforcement, the effect of its work was to reaffirm the bipartisan character of the antitrust commitment by ratifying the achievements of Democratic administrations in the preceding fifteen years.[4] Nor should we forget that the most spectacular and revealing case involving a criminal price conspiracy—the General Electric case—took place during the Eisenhower administration.

---

[4] *Report of the Attorney General's National Committee to Study the Antitrust Laws* (Washington, 1955). For a critique, see Mason: op. cit., pp. 389–401.

What makes it possible to institutionalize antitrust activities at the higher plateau that has been maintained since 1938 is not a consensus among economists as to its utility in enhancing economic efficiency, but a rough consensus in society at large as to its value in curbing the dangers of excessive market power. As in the beginning, it is based on a political and moral judgment rather than economic measurement or even distinctively economic criteria. "It must be recognized," says Edward S. Mason, "that there is an element of faith in the proposition that maintaining competition substantially improves the efficiency of resource use." The option for a minimal level of competition to be underwritten by public policy, although it can be backed by substantial economic arguments, "rests basically on a political judgment," write Carl Kaysen and Donald F. Turner in their inquiry into trust policy: "In our democratic, egalitarian society, large areas of uncontrolled private power are not tolerated." "We found," write J. B. Dirlam and A. E. Kahn in their book *Fair Competition*, "that the decisions [of courts and commissions] could not be fully understood or fairly appraised by economic standards alone. Hence we concluded that the appropriate question for economists to ask about antitrust policy is not whether this is the most efficient way of structuring or reorganizing the economy, but the inverted one: Does antitrust seriously interfere with the requirements of efficiency?" "The rationale of antitrust," writes A. D. Neale, a British student of the American experience, "is essentially a desire to provide legal checks to restrain economic power and is not a pursuit of efficiency as such." "For most Americans," concludes John Kenneth Galbraith, "free competition, so called, has for long been a political rather than an economic concept."[5]

In any case, the state of antitrust enforcement seems to

<hr />

[5] Edward S. Mason in the Preface to Carl Kaysen and Donald B. Turner: *Antitrust Policy* (Cambridge, Mass., 1960), p. xx; ibid., p. 5;

correspond with a public consensus. Economists and lawyers differ profoundly on how effective the antitrust laws have been and on how effective they could be if they were more amply enforced,[6] but there is hardly a major industry that has not seen a significant lawsuit or two, and in most industries in which intervention might be thought desirable, government action has had more than negligible effects.[7] It is also one of the strengths of antitrust that neither its effectiveness nor its ineffectiveness can be precisely documented; its consequences rest on events of unknown number and significance that have *not* happened—on proposed mergers that may have died in the offices of corporation counsel, on collusive agreements that have never been consummated, on unfair practices contemplated but never carried out. Liberals can support it because they retain their old suspicion of business behavior, and conservatives support it because they still believe in competition and they may hope to gain an additional point of leverage in the battle against inflation. No one seems prepared to suggest that the antitrust enterprise be cut back drastically, much less abandoned, and Congress has consistently supported its enlarged staff. The existing state of enforcement conforms to the state of the public mind, which accepts bigness but continues to distrust business morals. Even business itself accords to the principle of antitrust a certain grudging and irritated acceptance, and largely confines its resistance to the courts. Visitations by the Department of Justice are a nuisance, lawsuits are expensive, and prosecution carries an

J. B. Dirlam and A. E. Kahn: *Fair Competition* (Ithaca, 1954), p. 2; A. D. Neale: *The Antitrust Laws of the U.S.A.* (Cambridge, Eng., 1962), p. 487; Galbraith: op. cit., p. 27.

[6] See, for example, the symposium in Dexter M. Keezer (ed.): "The Effectiveness of the Federal Antitrust Laws," *American Economic Review*, XXXIX (June 1949), 689–724.

[7] See the industry-by-industry survey in Simon N. Whitney: *Antitrust Policies: American Experience in Twenty Industries*, 2 vols. (New York 1958).

odious stigma, but the antitrust procedures can be considered an alternative to more obtrusive regulation such as outright controls on prices. At any rate, big business has never found it necessary or expedient to launch a public campaign against antitrust enforcement; the pieties at stake are too deep to risk touching.

A final element in antitrust enforcement rests on the fact that the government itself is now a major consumer, and the points of exposure of industrial prices to official concern and reaction have been multiplied. One of the reasons for the antitrust revival in 1938 was the irritation of government officials over the prevalence of what seemed to be collusively priced bids. Thurman Arnold's hope that consumers could be mobilized behind the new antitrust enforcement was out of keeping with the historical passivity and disorganization of American consumers. But the presence of the government as a consumer may supply some of the leverage he was looking for.

Antitrust reform is not the first reform in American history whose effectiveness depended less upon a broad movement of militant mass sentiment than upon the activities of a small group of influential and deeply concerned specialists. In ceasing to be largely an ideology and becoming largely a technique, antitrust has taken its place among a great many other elements of our society that have become differentiated, specialized, and bureaucratized. Since no layman can any longer concern himself with the enormous body of relevant case law or with the truly formidable literature of economic analysis and argument that has come to surround the issue, the potentialities of antitrust action have become almost exclusively the concern of a technical elite of lawyers and economists. Indeed, the business of studying, attacking, defending, and evaluating oligopolistic behavior and its regulation has become one of our lively small industries, which gives employment to many gifted professional men. No doubt this is another, if lesser, reason why antitrust has become self-sustaining: it is not our way to liquidate an industry in which so many have a stake.

If all this is taken as the preface to some unduly optimistic conclusion, my intention will have been misunderstood. My concern is not to suggest that the old problem of market power is on the verge of being solved; it is merely to illustrate how expectations and creeds can change, and how a particular reform, after two generations of noisy but seemingly futile agitation, has been quietly and effectively institutionalized. But it is one thing to say that antitrust has at last begun to fulfill a function, and another to forget how modest that function is. Although the full range of evils anticipated seventy-five years ago from concentration and monopoly has not materialized, the traditional American fear of concentrated power seems hardly less pertinent today. The American economy, whether or not its concentration is still significantly increasing, is extremely concentrated as it stands, and its business structure has brought into being a managerial class of immense social and political as well as market power. This class is by no means evil or sinister in its intentions, but its human limitations often seem even more impressive than the range of its powers, and under modern conditions we have a right to ask again whether we can ever create enough checks to restrain it. The economy over which it presides has had remarkable successes in increasing its production of goods and services, and yet the urban mass society in which these are produced is still not freed from widespread poverty and impresses us again and again with the deepness of its malaise, the range of its problems that stand unsolved, even in some cases pitifully untried. Today our greatest domestic danger lies not in our failure to produce enough goods because we do not have enough competition, but in our failure to render certain humane, healing, humanly productive and restorative social services that are not comprehended at all in the ethos of competition. At its best, big business will not perform such services. At its worst, it can sustain a class of men who will prevent them from being performed.

FREE SILVER
AND THE
MIND OF "COIN" HARVEY

In 1963 the John Harvard Library republished William H. Harvey's *Coin's Financial School,* the best-selling free-silver tract of the 1890's. Harvey has always been an elusive figure. He left no papers, and it is unlikely that a full biography will ever be written of this man who did as much as any other in our history to give articulate voice to a folk agitation. This essay, now somewhat revised, first appeared as the Introduction to the John Harvard Library edition; it is the most extended account of Harvey that has been written, and it is here set against the complex background of the silver controversy.

I

WHO today can understand without a strenuous effort of imagination the passions once aroused by the cry for free silver? Despite the pointless and long-sustained policy of silver purchases into which the federal government was forced by silver interests in 1934, the once heated issue of the bimetallic standard has been rendered obsolete by modern devices of monetary management. Yet a whole generation of Americans was embroiled from the 1870's to the 1890's in the argument over silver. To the combatants of that era, silver and gold were not merely precious metals but precious symbols, the very substance of creeds and faiths which continued long afterward to have meaning for men living on the echoes of nineteenth-century orthodoxies. In 1933, when Franklin D. Roosevelt took the United States "off gold," Lewis W. Douglas said, at the end of a long and anxious night: "This is the end of Western civilization." From another point of view, Senator Ashurst of Arizona, pressed by Secretary Morgenthau about his obsession with silver, replied: "My boy, I was brought up from my mother's knee on silver and I can't discuss that with you any more than you can discuss your religion with me."[1]

The free-silver campaign of 1896 was one of the stormy, disruptive campaigns of our history, the first since Jackson's day when a presidential election hung on a financial issue. Sentiment for free coinage of silver was not strong enough to elect Bryan, but it was strong enough to wrest control of the Democratic party away from President Cleveland, to split the Republicans into two irreconcilable factions, and to transform the new Populist party into a single-issue satellite of Bryan and the Democrats. It was menacing enough to unite all the forces of goldbug respectability behind McKinley, and to spur an election effort without precedent in our history. In defeating silver the goldbugs were not merely defeating a reform, they were stemming a crusade.

The student who tries to recapture the emotions of this crusade reads Bryan's "Cross of Gold" speech as the great document of the silver cause. Yet his speech sums up a case already made; it assumes much and explains little to a reader ignorant of the preceding years of monetary argument. One cannot tell from it how the silver men arrived at their sense of

---

[1] Raymond Moley: *After Seven Years* (New York, 1939), pp. 159–60; John M. Blum: *From the Morgenthau Diaries* (Boston, 1959), p. 186.

conviction. If Bryan was immediately understood by his audience, it was because he played upon a set of feelings already formed and inflamed by a vast literature of analysis and agitation; and of all this literature, by far the most effective and memorable work was William Hope Harvey's little book of 155 pages, first printed two years before, in June 1894.

Eighteen ninety-four was a grim year. A depression had begun sharply early in 1893. Its effects were heightened by a stock-market panic in May and by the threatened exhaustion of federal gold reserves. By mid-1894 the economy was in its grip. Farmers were frantic over the collapse of wheat and cotton prices. Bank failures and business bankruptcies mounted to unimagined heights. Thousands of men of substance found themselves ruined, as Henry Adams knew when he lamented that his entire generation had had notice to quit. Mills and factories were closing daily, and soon one man of every five in the labor force was unemployed. Long lines of hungry and desperate men tramped the streets and highways. While Harvey was getting *Coin's Financial School* ready for publication, Coxey's "army" of unemployed was marching in protest on Washington, and in the month the book appeared the violent Pullman strike began, which was soon to be smashed by federal troops sent to Illinois by President Cleveland. By the end of 1894 Cleveland's party was quarreling irreconcilably about his fiscal policies, and the Populist party, which some conservatives looked upon as the vanguard of an anarchistic apocalypse, had made serious inroads on the strength of both major parties in the West and South. No one knew how far the crisis would carry the country from its old ways, or how many institutions were still fated to crumble.

Sufferers from the crisis were crying for a simple solution, and their confusion over its causes only heightened their dogmatism about its cure. The dispute over the government's silver purchases, a central issue since 1890, had fixed everyone's mind on the money question, and the near exhaustion of the Treasury's gold reserves commanded nervous day-by-day attention. Almost everyone was either denouncing the free-silver maniacs of the West and South or scourging the bankers and Shylocks of New York and London. *Coin's Financial School* rode on the wave of an almost unbelievable money mania. A correspondent wrote to Cleveland's secretary in May 1895: "Have been pretty well over the country since we last met, traveling through twenty-four States, more than ten thousand miles, South and West. The people in that section are simply crazy on the money question; they cannot discuss it rationally." A rural editor in Kentucky wrote: "Politics down here has gone mad. Every crank in the country is loose and nothing less than a stone wall will stop them." Kenesaw M. Landis reported from Illinois:

> The God's truth is the Democratic party in Indiana and Illinois is wildly insane on this subject. . . . The farmers are especially unruly. . . . I've got a lot of farmer uncles down in Indiana— good honest and intelligent men as honesty and intelligence go at this day—but utterly wild on the money question. You can't do anything with them—just got to let them go.

A Mississippi congressman wrote to Cleveland's Secretary of War in April 1895: "A little free silver book called 'Coin's Financial School' is being sold on every railroad train by the newsboys and at every cigar store. . . . It is being read by almost everybody."[2]

II

FOR A LONG TIME now only a few specialists have read this

---

[2] James A. Barnes: *John G. Carlisle, Financial Statesman* (New York, 1931), pp. 449, 452, 438.

little tract that was once read by "almost everybody." Although printed in the hundreds of thousands, it is hard to come by, and its yellowing pages crack and crumble as they are turned. No doubt thousands of frail copies were simply read and thumbed to death. But neither Harvey nor his pamphlet can be forgotten. He was the Tom Paine of the free-silver movement, and *Coin's Financial School* was to the silver men of 1896 what *Common Sense* had been to the revolutionaries of 1776. That free silver was a losing cause should not blind us to the importance of *Coin's Financial School* as a basic expression of the American popular imagination.

Bryan remarked of *Coin's Financial School* that it was "the most potent of educational forces at work in behalf of bimetallism. It is safe to say that no book in recent times has produced so great an effect in the treatment of an economic question." No one will ever know how many copies were distributed. Harvey wrote to *The Forum* in 1895 that sales during its first eleven months exceeded 400,000 copies. During the campaign of 1896, the National Silver party bought and distributed 125,000 copies. The most conservative estimate of its sales is 650,000, the most generous is Harvey's of 1,500,-000. His widow's more sober guess of 1,000,000 seems closer to the mark, and is by no means implausible.[3] Priced variously at twenty-five cents, fifty cents, and a dollar, published in varying grades of paper and binding, bought in quantities by interested organizations, and widely hawked about by vendors, *Coin's Financial School* was susceptible of a mass circulation reached often in its day by popular magazines but seldom by books.

---

[3] William Jennings Bryan: *The First Battle* (Chicago, 1896), pp. 153–4, 292; *The Forum*, XIX (July 1895), 573 n.; Frank L. Mott: *Golden Multitudes: The Story of Best Sellers in the United States* (New York, 1947), pp. 170–1. In *Coin's Financial School Up to Date* (Chicago, 1895), p. i, Harvey mentioned sales of 5,000 a day.

The literary form chosen for Harvey's presentation of his ideas was simple but effective. "Coin," a young but preternaturally wise little financier, tries to remedy the sufferings of the depression by attacking the intellectual illusions which have brought it about. He establishes a school in Chicago at the Art Institute, to which he invites the young men of the city for a series of six lectures on the money question. The book reports his lectures, but since he is at times interrupted by friendly or argumentative questions, it takes the form of a monologue broken by occasional dialogues. (Harvey may have been led to this dramatic device by the example of the first book his firm published, Archbishop Walsh's tract on bimetallism, which was presented as an interview with a reporter.) As the lectures go on, the audience supposedly fills with actual persons whom Harvey did not scruple to name; a few are obscure friends of the silver cause, but they are mainly well-known editors, politicians, businessmen, lawyers, and economists. The fictitious Coin thus appears to engage in real encounters, heard attentively by men like Philip D. Armour, Marshall Field, H. H. Kohlsaat, and Senator Shelby Cullom.[4] Gold advocates pose questions which they are confident will trip Coin, but he answers with such a majestic command of fact and theory that they are thrown into confusion. Among those most decisively worsted are the leading Chicago banker, Lyman J. Gage, later to be McKinley's Secretary of the Treasury, and the monetary authority J. Laurence Laughlin, professor of economics at the University of Chicago. The introduction of these contemporaries gave the "school" such an air of reality, despite the patently fictional character of its central figure, that many readers believed that

---

[4] In an hour spent with contemporary directories one can identify most of the persons named in *Coin's Financial School*. However, there was no such person as "young Medill" (p. 99), and it is possible that a few other names were also erroneous.

the lectures had actually been given. Laughlin, who was particularly outraged at having been portrayed as worsted by a tyro in economics, found it desirable, along with Gage, Kohlsaat, and some of the others allegedly in attendance at the "school," who had grown tired of answering letters from readers querying them about what they were supposed to have said, to join in a statement that the whole thing was a fiction.

Though Laughlin believed that an amateur work like Harvey's was "not worthy of serious discussion," he found it necessary to answer Harvey in a pamphlet, *Facts about Money*, and even to debate with him on a public platform. Another of the well-known authors who refuted Harvey was Horace White, the economic journalist of the New York *Evening Post* and the author of a standard work on money and banking, who called his onslaught *Coin's Financial Fool: or The Artful Dodger Exposed. A Complete Reply to Coin's Financial School.* The rage for monetary argument and the extraordinary success of Harvey's little book provoked a host of answers by goldbug opponents—and the literature mounted to a point which would make a major project for a bibliographer.[5] The answers were written with varying degrees of economic sophistication and provided with titles of varying flippancy or solemnity: for example, George E. Roberts's *Coin at School in Finance*, Edward Wisner's *Cash vs. Coin*, Jay Loring's *Coin's Financial School Exposed and*

---

[5] Some of the leading items in this literature were reviewed in Willard Fisher's judicious and valuable essay " 'Coin' and His Critics," *Quarterly Journal of Economics*, X (January 1896), 187–208. Harvey wrote a piece about the critics of his book in which he said that they were "slaves set to lash the author of that book and their master is—money." Christ, he said, had been killed at the behest of the money-changers of Judea, and now he, Harvey, was being persecuted by the same "unconquered and relentless" money power. " 'Coin's Financial School' and Its Censors," *North American Review*, CLXI (July 1895), 72, 74–5.

Closed, Robert F. Rowell's *The Mistakes of Coin,* John A. Frazer and Charles H. Serghel's *Sound Money,* Melville D. Landon's *Money, Gold, Silver, or Bimetallism,* John F. Cargill's *A Freak in Finance,* Stanley Wood's *Answer to "Coin's Financial School,"* W. B. Mitchell's *Dollars or What?,* L. G. Power's *Farmer Hayseed in Town: or, The Closing Days of Coin's Financial School,* Charles Elton Blanchard's *Report of Uncle Sam's Homilies in Finance,* Everett P. Wheeler's *Real Bi-Metallism or True Coin versus False Coin.* Yet not one of these appears to have had even a small portion of the impact of the book it was meant to refute.

These titles evoke the atmosphere of an age of polemics; yet perhaps the most remarkable thing about *Coin's Financial School* is the comparative austerity of its tone. To be sure, it has its flashes of sardonic humor, its strokes of dazzling irrelevancy, and its moments of headlong rhetoric. But on the whole, when one considers Harvey's own mettlesome temperament and remembers the intemperance of a time when the goldbug press frequently described silver senators as "fanatics," "cossacks," "border ruffians," "bandits," disloyalists," "traitors," and "lunatics," *Coin's Financial School* seems the more remarkable for an air, however delusive, of sticking to the task of rational analysis. It has behind it the fierce logic of the one-idea mind, the firm conviction that complex social issues can be unraveled to the last point and pinned down for good, that social problems can really be solved, and solved by simple means. However amateurish and unsure, it is a rather technical discussion of one of the most intricate of subjects, the monetary standard; and one can only be touched at the thought of the effort of mind that it must have called forth in many of its readers, who hoped that by reading it carefully they might *understand* what had happened. Probably more than any other of our politico-social best sellers, it makes a primarily ratiocinative demand on its readers. Compared with our other popular tracts on social issues, its appeal is hard to comprehend—its lacks the great revolutionary rhetoric of Paine's *Common Sense*, the alluring pornographic overtones of the widely read anti-Catholic pamphlet *Awful Disclosures* by Maria Monk, the human appeal of *Uncle Tom's Cabin*, the major prophetic gifts and sustained analysis of *Progress and Poverty*, the novelistic form and universal significance of *Looking Backward*. It stays close to details of the money problem, relying mainly upon effective cartoons for its emotional impact. For Harvey himself it was the product of a rare moment. Nothing that he wrote afterward was to have anything like its argumentative surge or its show of coherence. Nothing that he had done before gave any hint that he would be known to the world as the author of a book.

III

WILLIAM HOPE ("COIN") HARVEY was born in 1851 in the little village of Buffalo, in the western part of Virginia, the fifth child of six born to Robert and Anna Harvey.[6] Robert Trigg Harvey was a Virginian of Scottish and English ancestry, and his wife, who had Virginian ancestors traceable to colonial times, was descended also from French stock that had long since peopled the territory around nearby Gallipolis. Almost nothing is known of William Harvey's childhood except that it was disturbed by conflict between the Unionist majority in his region and secessionist sympathizers, among whom were some members of his father's family. One of young Harvey's sisters was sent to a convent for safety's sake

---

[6] Biographical information, except where otherwise indicated, is taken from Jeannette P. Nichols's excellent sketch "Bryan's Benefactor: Coin Harvey and His World," *Ohio Historical Quarterly*, LXVII (October 1958), 299–325.

during the war and, to the family's distress, became a nun. An older brother was wounded fighting under Lee.

At the war's end, young Harvey began study at the little academy in Buffalo, taught school for a few months at the age of sixteen, and afterward briefly attended Marshall College, then a state normal school offering instruction at the secondary school level. His three months there marked the end of his formal education. He spent a short time reading law, in those days the customary way of preparing for the profession, was admitted to the bar at the age of nineteen, and opened practice in the village of Barboursville, West Virginia, the seat of Cabell County. When the railroad tycoon Collis P. Huntington established a depot for the Chesapeake & Ohio Railroad at the Ohio River town which was named for him, William Hope Harvey made the first of his many adult changes of residence and entered practice in partnership with an older brother in Huntington, West Virginia. The town, which was growing rapidly, was the largest place in which Harvey had lived.

Before long, Harvey's restlessness had him on the move. In 1875, at the age of twenty-four, he moved to Gallipolis, Ohio, a busy spot in the Ohio River valley about forty miles above Huntington, and there met Anna Halliday, whom he married in 1876. The couple soon went to Cleveland, where Harvey tried his hand at law in a major center of commerce and industry and where the first two of their four children were born.[7] After three years in Cleveland, Harvey took his growing family to Chicago, but a little more than a year of Chicago was enough for him, and in 1881 the Harveys, now numbering five, returned to Gallipolis. Harvey now became attorney for several wholesale houses in Ohio. In 1883 a

---

[7] Since Ohio was a center of Greenback agitation during the 1870's, it is quite possible that Harvey first became interested in the money question during these years.

client's affairs took him to the southwest corner of Colorado, where prospectors had not long before discovered rich deposits of silver, and there, at the age of thirty-two, Harvey had his first experience with the white metal that was to give him his place in history. The following year he took his family, along with a force of ten young workers, to Colorado. There he started working claims near Ouray, and the young entrepreneur's still growing family was housed in a large mountainside cabin. In the cold of winter, his wife and children moved to California, while he stayed at the mines, except for Christmas time, living near his work in a room fashioned out of one corner of an engine house. For three years Harvey worked arduously, and at some cost to his health, superintending the production of the Silver Bell, a mine of considerable yield. But he had entered silver mining at one of its worst moments. High costs of operation were driving out small enterprisers and favoring large producers. The mine fields swarmed with displaced workers, wages fell, and the industry was riven with strikes. Worst of all, silver prices, which had gone down disastrously in the 1870's, were still falling sharply as production rose.

Harvey soon abandoned the mines for the real estate business, which he combined with his law practice. This occupied him for six years successively in Pueblo, Denver, and Ogden, Utah. He was remembered in Colorado for having sold an "Elixir of Life," which was curative of a variety of human ills, and as one of the promoters of an exposition hall in Pueblo, the Mineral Palace, which housed a collection of Rocky Mountain minerals. Opened with a grand fete in the summer of 1890, the palace was the most gaudy and the most successful of the various enterprises with which Harvey had been associated. The taste of success did not overcome Harvey's wanderlust, for his moves to Denver and Ogden followed his ventures in Pueblo. In Ogden he bought and improved a house, perhaps with permanent settlement in mind. He also bought for development a one-mile frontage along Great Salt Lake, and appears to have tried to promote a festival patterned after the New Orleans Mardi Gras, in which local tradition reports that he lost a substantial sum.

In any case, Harvey had enough capital left to move his brood back to Chicago again in May 1893 and to set up a specialized publishing business dedicated to free silver. At forty-two he was neither a complete failure nor, in his ambitious terms, a success. His restless search for wealth had led him to take up nine residences in the thirteen years since he had begun the practice of law. He had been in Colorado long enough to feel the anguish and disappointment of the silver miners and to absorb the historical and monetary lore of the free-silver advocates, which was as much an orthodoxy in Colorado as the gold standard was in New York. Untutored in the intricacies of academic economics, he had absorbed in a bitter school of experience the convictions that were to bring into focus the major discontents of his time. "Coin" Harvey was prepared for his sudden leap onto the stage of history.

IV

"Coin" Harvey was a money crank, one of a type the United States has produced in substantial numbers. The early demand for an adequate money supply, the perennial want of an adequate central banking system, the open character of our entrepreneurial economy, the violent upheavals and reversals of individual fortunes—all these things have produced a great many economic dissenters and have given their homemade systems of ideas a wide reception. Each depression has been a prolific breeder of panaceas, panacea mongers, and monetary pamphleteers. The striking thing about the depression of the nineties was how rapidly the cry for free coinage of silver shoved other reform proposals from the center of the stage.

To understand this, one must recall briefly the history of monetary issues since the Civil War. Before the war, the United States had been in law (though not, as we shall see, in fact) on a bimetallic standard. In 1861, wartime demands forced the country to suspend specie redemption of its currency and to issue United States notes, the "greenbacks," which were full legal tender, except for the payment of customs duties and interest on the public debt. The nation was now on an inconvertible paper standard. Its greenbacks circulated at a substantial and growing discount in terms of gold. A period of hectic inflation ensued, and when the war was over, many economic and political leaders urged that the greenbacks be retired and that specie payments be promptly resumed. They met with a good deal of resistance from farmers and many businessmen, particularly in the West, who remembered wartime inflation for the prosperity that accompanied it, who had already suffered from the postwar economic relapse, and who dreaded any further currency contraction. (There were also some high-tariff businessmen, East and West, who favored inflation because they thought it would have a protectionist effect.)

Postwar inflationism, then, first took the form of resistance to the retirement of the greenbacks. Superficially, this movement had a moment of success in 1868, when Congress prohibited the further retirement and cancellation of greenbacks, and another such moment in 1874, when, under the stress of the depression, Congress somewhat increased the number of these bills. Indeed, during the depression that began in 1873, greenback inflationism waxed strong. A new Greenback party arose, whose candidates amassed a million votes in the congressional elections of 1878.

But, so far as the price level itself was concerned, the inflationists had been fighting a losing battle since 1865. The men who directed American policy during these years were following a spartan policy. They believed that the currency would not be sound or stable until the government returned to specie payments—more specifically, until it restored, at full value, the gold dollar that had prevailed before the war. In order for this to be accomplished, it was necessary that the American price level fall in relation to European price levels —which were themselves falling. Otherwise, high American prices would lower exports, increase imports, and cause an outflow of gold. This would have undermined the policy of the Treasury, which was to accumulate a gold reserve adequate for ultimate resumption.

The deflationary policy did not require an actual contraction of the currency—a measure always fraught with political danger. In fact, thanks largely to an increase in bank deposits and bank notes, the supply of money in the hands of the public grew steadily from 1870 to 1875 and again after 1878. The drastic—and to gold-standard strategists satisfactory— fall in the price level came not from an actual fall in the money supply, as Greenback theorists seemed to think, but from a rapid rise in real output that outpaced the growth in the money supply. The American economy was being allowed to grow into its monetary skin. The contribution of those who controlled monetary policy was simply to resist political demands for large new issues of greenbacks. Economic growth did the rest.[8] Meanwhile, the Greenback men

---

[8] On deflation and specie resumption, see James K. Kindahl: "Economic Factors in Specie Resumption in the United States, 1865–70," *Journal of Economic History*, LXIX (February 1961), 30–48. On the Greenback movement, see the comprehensive study by Irwin Unger: *The Greenback Era* (Princeton, 1964) and on the money supply, two essays by J. G. Gurley and E. S. Shaw: "The Growth of Debt and Money in the United States, 1800–1950: A Suggested Interpretation,"

in their opposition to deflation fortified an illusion that the silver movement was to inherit. In focusing on greenbacks as though they were the only hope of expanding the money supply, they tended to ignore the sustained increase in the money supply that was being made available by the activities of the banks, and particularly by a large increase in demand deposits. The entire overemphasis on the monetary factor in the business cycle, and the corresponding neglect of other factors, which colored the views of both sides during the battle of the standards in the 1890's, was thus strengthened during the Greenback period.

At any rate, many men of otherwise conservative views and substantial interests were convinced during this period that the return to gold was being bought at a terrible price. But the deflationists were successful in realizing their aims: the greenbacks soon began to recover their value in relation to gold. In 1875 Congress passed the Resumption Act, providing for a return to specie payments on January 1, 1879. The greenback dollar itself steadily rose in value until it finally achieved parity with gold two weeks before the date set for resumption.

Every informed person understood that when specie payments were resumed they would be made in gold alone. Here it may help to bear in mind a distinction between the legal and the actual state of the monetary standard to avoid a confusion that afflicted Harvey and some of his contemporaries. In the beginning, the United States had been legally committed to bimetallism. But in order to have a successful bimetallic standard in fact, a government must be able so to adjust the value

Review of Economics and Statistics, XLI (August 1959), 250–62, esp. p. 258, and Ch. 4 of Seymour Harris (ed.): *American Economic History* (New York, 1961), esp. pp. 111–14. The major work on the whole subject is Milton Friedman and Anna J. Schwartz: *A Monetary History of the United States, 1867–1960* (Princeton, 1963).

of the two metals as to keep them both in circulation. Bimetallism implies that the government will define its monetary unit —in our case, the dollar—as having a certain weight in both metals, maintain their convertibility at a fixed ratio, freely allow their import and export, and buy or coin them in unlimited quantities when they are brought to the mint. It is easy to see how the mechanism of the bimetallic system can be thrown into disorder. The mint ratio of exchange set by the government must correspond very closely with the world market ratio which reflects demand and supply for both monetary and non-monetary uses of the metals. If one of the two metals tends to be worth more in the market than it is at the mint, it is not likely to be brought to the mint for coinage in material amounts.[9] It will go into industrial use or into hoarding, leaving the other metal as the single circulating medium. Thus, if the mint ratio differs significantly from the market ratio, the two metals will circulate together only for a limited time. (Of course, if a number of governments with a sufficient combined demand can concur in a mint ratio, their joint action will tend to stabilize the value of the metals and make possible their simultaneous circulation.)

When the monetary system was organized under Hamilton's guidance, the mint ratio set by Congress at his suggestion was 15 to 1—that is, 15 ounces of silver would exchange

---

[9] Or at least so respectable economic theory tells us. Unfortunately the actual behavior of men in the market does not always fully correspond with the theoretical expectations. In American experience the countervailing facts were such that substantial amounts of silver were presented for coinage while gold was overvalued, and even considerable amounts of gold while silver was overvalued. See H. Gordon Hayes's monitory note, "Bimetallism Before and After 1834," *American Economic Review*, XXIII (December 1933), 677–9, and the circumspect account in Neil Carothers: *Fractional Money* (New York, 1930), Ch. 7. While the facts of coinage did not adapt themselves very neatly to the requirements of economic theory, the character of the money in actual circulation did so well enough.

for 1 ounce of gold. But the commercial market ratio adhered fairly closely to 15.5 to 1—a figure at which it tended to be stabilized because this was the French mint ratio. Since France valued gold more highly in relation to silver than we did, it became profitable for American money brokers to export gold and import silver; after 1800 gold was in circulation only in minuscule amounts, after 1825 not at all. In effect, the nation was on silver.

In 1834, for reasons which need not detain us here, Congress intentionally pushed the pendulum too far in the opposite direction by setting the mint ratio at 16 to 1, expecting that silver would now be displaced by gold. For about a dozen years afterward the two metals circulated together, but at length silver dollars became a rarity. In 1850 the chairman of the House Committee on Ways and Means remarked: "We have had but a single standard for the last three or four years. That has been and now is gold."[1] The *coup de grâce* was given to silver circulation by the mid-century discoveries of gold in California and Australia, which so lowered the value of gold in relation to silver that the silver in a silver dollar became worth about $1.03. It was now worthwhile to melt or export such dollars (and even fractional silver currency), for their bulk silver content, rather than to use them as money.

While still in law committed to bimetallism, the United States had thus been actually on a kind of alternating standard, resting on silver most of the time from 1792 to 1834, and soon after that year on gold. The disappearance of silver from circulation for a generation caused most men to think of gold

---

[1] J. Laurence Laughlin: *The History of Bimetallism in the United States* (New York, 1885), pp. 78–9; see also pp. 52–74 for the background of the Act of 1834. The best-informed and most perspicuous single work I have found on currency history is Neil Carothers: *Fractional Money*, which of necessity goes beyond the constricted promise of its title.

alone when they thought of the specie standard in the 1870's.

This fact provides the background to the Coinage Act of 1873, which within a few years of its uneventful passage was to become enormously controversial. The Act of 1873 was simply an attempt to codify the coinage practices of the country and to simplify the fractional currency, which was in a chaotic state at the end of the Civil War. But in enumerating the coins that were to be maintained, the framers of the act dropped from the list the long defunct silver dollar. At that moment, the silver in a dollar was still worth $1.03,[2] and silver was not being brought to the mint for coinage in any consequential amount. Although changes were already in motion that would shortly lower the value of silver, only the most foresighted and perspicacious students of money could have foreseen that the value of silver would so soon drop so much. The abandonment of the standard silver dollar, which meant the end of legal bimetallism, was not objected to by any of the representatives of silver states in Congress in 1873 nor by anyone else. But the adoption of the Coinage Act happened to coincide closely with the outbreak of a grave depression and another price collapse, and came just on the eve of a drastic fall in the world price of silver. When the Act of 1873 was followed by the Resumption Act of 1875, it was clear to everyone that in 1879, when specie payments were to be resumed, the United States would be in law as it had earlier been in fact on the gold standard. Now the inflationists, though still stressing the defense of the greenbacks, began to demand the remonetization of silver as a remedy for falling prices. Soon the demand for the free and unlimited coinage of

---

[2] While this was true of the silver dollar, it was not true of fractional silver pieces. In 1853 Congress had discovered that fractional coins could be kept in circulation, thus solving a long acute shortage of fractional money, if their silver content was reduced to a point somewhat below face value.

silver at 16 to 1 replaced the greenback issue as the dominant platform of the cheap-money men.

A glance at international price trends from the early 1870's to the middle 1890's will clarify the continuing force of the demand for monetary inflation and the prevalence of world-wide agricultural discontent. The secular downward movement of prices coincided with the formation and spread of the international gold standard, which was considered by many respectable contemporary analysts to be its primary cause. In 1871 (not in 1873, as Harvey dates it) the new German Empire gave the first of a series of shocks to silver when it resolved to adopt the gold standard, and two years afterward it threw upon the world market substantial supplies of silver realized from melting its old coins. The prospect of absorbing this much silver was too much for the countries of the Latin Union—France, Belgium, Switzerland, Italy, and Greece. In 1873 and 1874 they ceased the free and unlimited coinage of silver, thus removing from the market the primary force that had served to stabilize the value of the white metal. Sweden, Norway, and Holland also followed Germany in adopting the gold standard. These events coincided with the opening of huge new deposits of silver in the American West, which boosted supplies of silver just as demand for its use as money was fast declining in the Western world. At the very time the "Coin" Harveys were sweating to extract more silver from their Silver Bells, the price of the metal was undermined. Standing at $1.32 an ounce in 1872, it fell to $1.11 in 1884 and to 63 cents in 1894.

This fall in the price of silver, though more acute, roughly paralleled the general world price trend from the 1870's the the 1890's. In the United States, the level of prices fell sharply with each depression and rallied only slightly in good times. This price trend was a constant hazard to certain types of new and marginal entrepreneurs, who were dependent on easy credit and especially vulnerable to business shocks; but of course it struck with particular severity those chronic debtors, the farmers. Above all, it was intolerable to those farmers who were producing a large portion of their crops for export into a world market increasingly oversupplied with their products—the growers of wheat and cotton. The swiftness and fatality of the fall in the prices of these two agricultural products outstripped all other. Wheat, which brought $1.37 a bushel in 1870, was down to 56 cents in 1894; raw cotton in the same years went from 23 cents a pound to 7 cents. It is easy to see why Coin, hoping to demonstrate the community of interest of farmers and silver, should have chosen to exhibit a table comparing the price histories of just three products: silver, cotton, and wheat. It is a defensible oversimplification to say that the inflationary movement in politics rested mainly upon the common concern of these three segments of the economy, each confronted with a disastrous oversupply of its product in the world market.

V

WHEN THE FREE-SILVER MEN won control of the inflationary forces, they inherited from the Greenbackers a formidable body of agitational literature and political folklore. The Greenback movement had succeeded in focusing the dissenting mind on monetary policy as the primary solution of the nation's ills; and in its opposition to bond issues and gold accumulation as the basis for currency contraction, it had already convinced many people that they were being victimized by a bondholders' conspiracy and that to issue bonds for sale in foreign markets reduced them to " 'hewers of wood and drawers of water' to foreigners." To convert this heritage of agitation to its own uses, the silver movement had to over-come the prejudice held by fiat-money men against all forms of specie, including silver.[3]

But as against the Greenbackers, the silver men had some advantages. The first was intellectual: fiat money seemed un-limited and arbitrary, but hard silver money was tied to a metal of limited supply, of long historic sanction among the money systems of the world, and supported by great econo-mists and statesmen. Legal bimetallism had been traditional in the United States as well as in many other parts of the world; silver could be called, with some oversimplification, "the dol-lar of our daddies," the staple of the currency system from Washington and Jefferson to Jackson. The second advantage was political: the silver-producing states had a formidable bloc in Congress; silver had a good following in both major parties—in sharp contrast with the Greenback party, which even at its height in 1878 did not elect a single senator. The silver states, backed by their allies from the wheat and cotton states, could not easily be ignored. The final advantage was financial: silver-mining interests were able to bring to the sil-ver movement more financial backing than the Greenback movement ever had. As time went on, the paper-money commitment of the Greenback tradition faded into the back-ground, while its more adaptable sentiments about the world, its hostilities to bankers, bondholders, foreigners, and monop-olists, were taken over by the silver spokesmen.

---

[3] In its first national platform, in 1876, the Greenback party men-tioned silver only to protest against the replacement of paper frac-tional currency by silver coins as a policy which "although well calculated to enrich owners of silver mines . . . will still further oppress in taxation an already overburdened people." By 1880 its platform called for "the unlimited coinage of silver as well as gold." In 1884 its platform boasted: "We forced the remonetization of the silver dollar," referring presumably to the Bland-Allison Act. K. H. Porter and D. B. Johnson: *National Party Platforms* (Urbana, Ill., 1956), pp. 52, 57, 68.

In 1878 the silver men had their first legislative success. Discontents aroused during the years of depression since 1873 had led to a great increase in silver agitation in all sections of the country from Pennsylvania to California, and many manufacturers joined with the silver and agrarian inflationists. Late in 1877 the House passed a bill introduced by "Silver Dick" Bland of Missouri calling for free coinage of silver and full legal tender. The margin was overwhelming: 163 to 34. Secretary of the Treasury John Sherman, still preoccupied with the success of his measures for refunding and resumption, saw that some compromises would have to be made with the forces opposed to monetary contraction. Fortified by the knowledge that free coinage would be blocked by the certain veto of President Hayes, he was able to rally Senate opposition around a compromise finally embodied in the Bland-Allison Act of 1878. This measure required the Secretary of the Treasury to buy and to have coined into dollars having full legal tender not less than $2,000,000 nor more than $4,000,000 worth of silver bullion each month. Although he strongly opposed the legal-tender provision, Sherman resigned himself to accepting it: "In a government like ours, it is always good to obey the popular current, and that has been done, I think, by the passage of the silver bill."[4] Happily the passage of this measure coincided with the return of prosperity, but it stemmed neither the general price decline nor the fall in the price of silver. Although conservative Secretaries of the Treasury consistently bought the minimum required amounts of silver, over $378,000,000 was issued under the provisions of the law, chiefly in the form of silver certificates.

The demand for silver purchases only increased with the

---

[4] Jeanette P. Nichols: "John Sherman and the Silver Drive of 1877–78: The Origins of the Gigantic Subsidy," *Ohio Archaeological and Historical Quarterly*, XLVI (April 1937), 164; this article provides the most circumstantial account of this compromise.

agricultural crisis of the late 1880's. In 1889–90 the silver bloc in Congress received powerful reinforcements when six new Western states committed to silver entered the Union. In 1890, to win needed support for its high-tariff program, the Harrison administration made a new concession to the silver men by stepping up the level of silver purchases. The Sherman Silver Purchase Act of 1890 required the Secretary of the Treasury to buy 4,500,000 ounces of silver each month—an amount equal to the approximate output of domestic silver mines—and again to issue legal-tender Treasury notes in payment for it.

The existence of so large an amount of silver certificates was a threat to the gold reserves of the Treasury which had been so carefully built up by Sherman and his predecessors. Under the Sherman Act, the Secretary of the Treasury was required to maintain the two metals "at a parity," which meant that the silver certificates were to be as good as gold. The government was not committed to keep at par with gold all the old greenbacks still remaining in circulation and the silver dollars and the Treasury notes of 1890. Since the Treasury was required to redeem these obligations in gold, they represented a potential demand against its gold supply. The capacity of the Treasury to stand the strain depended on conditions of general prosperity. Prosperity brought about a substantial Treasury surplus, which left a comfortable margin for the luxury of silver purchases. The gold reserve was also momentarily strengthened by years of big European demand for American crops in 1879–81 and in 1891, which brought inflows of gold.

But even before the crisis of 1893, the Harrison administration had begun to undermine the surplus. Tariff revenues, then the main source of government funds, were cut by some provisions of the tariff of 1890, while an extravagant pension act and other enlarged expenditures made big new demands on federal funds. A growing anxiety in the business community about the state of the Treasury's gold stocks sent gold into hoarding. To meet its expenses the Treasury found that it had to pay out greenbacks and Treasury notes, but as these were soon presented for gold redemption they constituted a potential endless drain on gold supplies. When the central banks of Europen countries, themselves afflicted by depression and shaken by the failure of the House of Baring in 1890, began to tighten their gold policies, the situation grew worse.

Many years before, $100,000,000 in gold had been set aside as the reserve deemed necessary for the Treasury to hold to assure successful resumption. In time this figure, considered to be the level of a safe Treasury reserve, came to have a kind of magic significance among right-thinking men in the financial community. As Grover Cleveland put it, the figure was regarded "with a sort of sentimental solicitude." Only six weeks after his inauguration in 1893, the gold reserve fell below this figure, and soon afterward there began a headlong financial panic, marked by a stock-market collapse and a run on banks throughout the country. Cleveland was also aware that India was about to close its mints to silver coinage, which would deal another staggering blow to the price of silver. It was no longer possible to pretend that the United States could afford to redeem its silver issues in gold and stay on the gold standard. Accepting the necessity for a showdown with the silver forces, Cleveland called on June 30 for a special session of Congress to repeal the Sherman Silver Purchase Act.

The prosperity that had made it possible to compromise between silver inflationism and the gold standard was now gone, and in consequence the ensuing congressional debate had all the bitterness that occurs when no real accommodation of interests is possible. The gold men attributed the panic almost entirely to the silver purchase policy and to the failure of business confidence that had been created by uncertainty

261

about future values and by threats to foreign trade and investments. They expatiated on the folly of a commitment to silver
at a time when the metal was constantly falling in value and
when its use as standard money had been abandoned by all the
great trading nations of the West.

Silver men saw the panic in quite different terms: again and
again they charged that it had been deliberately set off by
heartless bankers simply to create conditions of distress under
which they could force the repeal of the Sherman Act.[5] As
for the Sherman Act itself, they held no brief for it, since
what was really needed was the free and unlimited coinage of
silver. But they saw it as the line of defense of the silver
cause—"the last feeble barrier," a Populist senator from
Nebraska called it, "between the patriotic and industrious
masses of our people and that hoard of insolent, aggressive,
and ravenous money-changers and gamblers of Lombard
street and Wall street, who for private gain would . . . turn
the world back into the gloom of the Dark Ages with all its
attendant evil and misery."[6] When they were told that it was
utterly impossible for the United States acting alone to maintain a parity between the two metals and that unlimited coinage was unthinkable at the existing ratio, they tended to fall
back upon assertions of the size and grandeur of the United
States, aspersions upon the states of Europe, and reminders
of the pitiful economic condition of their constituents. In
answer to the argument that free coinage would in effect
mean silver monometallism, they might assert, as Senator

---

[5] Though most of them were ready to admit that the panic had got
out of hand. Cf. "Silver Dick" Bland: "Now the panic has come; and
those who conspired to bring it about have got more than they
bargained for." William V. Byars: *An American Commoner* (Columbia, Mo., 1900), p. 330; cf. the view of Senator Teller of Colorado, in
Elmer Ellis: *Henry Moore Teller* (Caldwell, Idaho, 1941), pp. 222–3.

[6] Senator William V. Allen: *Congressional Record*, 53rd Cong., 1st
sess. (August 24, 1893), pp. 788–9.

Cockrell of Missouri later did, that this would be so much the better: "They can't exhaust the gold reserves too quickly to suit me. We can go to a silver basis without as much as a ripple in our financial system."[7]

Among those prominent in the congressional debates was William Jennings Bryan, who made a long and stirring speech in the House. In the Senate, where action was delayed by an exhausting filibuster, the silver case was argued by some of its ablest exponents, notably Senator Teller of Colorado, who, in the course of describing the miseries that would befall his own state if repeal passed, broke down in tears, slumped to his desk, and buried his face in his hands. Nothing availed: repeal was finally enacted at the end of October 1893, and the silver men had to rest their hopes on an appeal to the public.[8]

It was here that Harvey found his role. All these climactic events must have absorbed his attention during the eighteen months before the appearance of his book. He moved to Chicago precisely at the outbreak of the panic, and was busy setting up the Coin Publishing Company during the months when the silver debate was nearing its climax. His first publication, a book by Archbishop Walsh of Dublin on *Bimetallism and Monometallism*, appeared two months after the congressional decision on repeal. Although he had shown some interest in bimetallism a few years before, no one knows precisely what silver arguments, beyond Walsh's, he had read.[9] But if he had read even a small part of the hundreds of pages

---

[7] Barnes: op. cit., p. 367.

[8] On the fight over repeal, see Allan Nevins: *Grover Cleveland* (New York, 1932), Ch. 29, and Jeannette P. Nichols: "The Politics and Personalities of Silver Repeal in the United States Senate," *American Historical Review*, XLI (October 1935), 26–53.

[9] Harvey's essay "The Free-Silver Argument," *The Forum*, XIX (June 1895), 401–9, recapitulates the main argument of his book, and documents it with collections of statutes and statistics, as well as the Reports of the Monetary Commissions of 1876 and 1878.

of speeches in the *Congressional Record* taken up by the
debate over repeal, he could have found there a basis for all
but the most idiosyncratic of his economic arguments for silver, and he could have found confirmation of all his underlying attitudes and convictions.

VI

No DOUBT the wide currency of these attitudes, which gave
the book its rapport with ordinary readers, had as much to do
with the success of *Coin's Financial School* as its central economic exposition. Before going on to Harvey's notions about
finance, it will be profitable to listen to the tonalities of his
work.

Young Coin himself is a suggestive symbol. Though he
tackles the most intricate of subjects and offers to solve the
most perplexing problems, Coin is not a wise old man but a
figure of youth, almost of childhood. He is drawn by Harvey's cartoonist as dressed in tails and carrying a top hat, but
his pants are knee breeches, his face is boyish, and he is referred to as "the young financier" and "the little lecturer." In
a subsequent book Harvey seemed to push Coin's age back
even further by remarking that Coin was only ten years old at
the time of these lectures. The choice of such a figure as his
spokesman implied that the intricacies of economics, once the
distracting features of selfishness and self-delusion were set
aside, were not too great to be mastered by the acute, simple,
and unspoiled mind of a boy, and hence that the intuitions of
the common man about the money question were sounder
than the complex sophistries of bankers and hireling professors of economics.[1] Harvey took as a congenial Biblical text

---

[1] As Congressman Edward Lane of Illinois said during the House
debates on the repeal of the Sherman Silver Purchase Act, "Mr.

for the volume Matthew 11:25: "I thank thee, O Father, Lord of heaven and earth, because thou hast hid these things from the wise and prudent, and hast revealed them unto babes."

Throughout Harvey's writings the notion recurs that the old are thoroughly corrupted by selfishness and that the hope of civilization lies in setting youth on the straight path. The school conducted by Coin at the Art Institute is established in the first instance for the youth of Chicago, in the hope that they may be led "out of the labyrinth of falsehoods, heresies, and isms that distract the country." It is only after Coin's first lecture succeeds brilliantly with the young that he is requested to open his school to men of all ages, whereupon it is promptly packed with "middle-aged and old men" who hope to confound the youngster with "knotty questions." Now the big businessmen of Chicago get their comeuppance; it is they, and not Coin, who are befuddled. "They had listened critically, expecting to detect errors in his facts or reasoning. There were none. They were amazed. He was logical . . . That it should come from the lips of a boy they were more surprised." "Coin was like a little monitor in the midst of a fleet of wooden ships. His shots went through and silenced all opposition." The mastery of innocent but well-schooled youth over guileful age is complete. The fathers, by their inept conduct of affairs, had brought the country to the edge of disaster. Coin spoke for the hope that lay in the sons.

Harvey portrayed the departure from bimetallism as a kind of violation of natural order, a willful failure to make use of the *two* metals God had put at man's disposal for use as

---

Speaker, my people do not have to consult Chevalier, John Stuart Mill, Ricardo, or any other writer on finance in order to understand their conditions. They know from personal knowledge that they occupy the garden spot of this whole rich country; that their crops for the last decade have been reasonably abundant, yet their pocketbooks are empty." Barnes: op. cit., p. 268.

money, and hence as a kind of disobedience to divine will. "As the two legs are necessary to walk and two eyes to see, so were these two monies necessary to the prosperity of the people." But though both are necessary, they do not have an equal moral or economic significance. Silver, which had historically been the base or component of such small currency units as the ordinary man was likely to see or handle, was held to be the money of the people. Gold was the money of the rich. Silver, which had been abundant, was identified with plenty, gold with niggardliness. The metals were given human characters and fates: poor downtrodden silver was shut out of the mints, while gold, the pampered and petted, was welcomed in. This anthropomorphic treatment of the metals, one of which stood for the downtrodden and neglected masses of farmers and honest working people, was carried out in the cartoons, and found its way into Harvey's language when he spoke of the Act of 1873 as having "deprived silver of its *right* to unrestricted coinage."

Popular animosity in the West and South against the East, and in rural areas against the city, and in folkish tradition against Britain and the monetary power of John Bull and the House of Rothschild, runs through the book and is effectively caught in its cartoons. The United States is seen as having been trapped in "a financial system forced upon us by Europe." This the bankers of the great metropolitan centers accept, but it is destructive almost everywhere else. The mentality of the great centers, preoccupied with personal gain, is narrow and self-deluding. "Cities do not breed statesmen. They breed the specialist. A specialist favors what will tend to promote his business though it may injure the business of others. A statesman must be broad. He must have a comprehensive appreciation of the interests of all the people—especially the poorer classes."

The cartoons, some drawn for the book by H. L. Godall

and others borrowed from silver newspapers, reduce these feelings to simple and striking images: gold smiles cruelly at the corpse of silver, assassinated by the pen; the West and the South, duped by the financial traps of the East, finally unite to overthrow the East; a cow feeding in the West is milked in New York (this was one of the most common of the Populist images); an octopus representing the Rothschilds, centered in England, and labeled "The Great English Devil Fish," grips the entire world in its tenacles; John Bull makes a brutal attack on the female figure of Liberty, while virtuous Silver, helpless in chains, looks on; the British lion is blown out of a cannon by the figure of Uncle Sam; a monstrously rapacious usurer sits clutching his bags of gold.

Yet, for all this, Harvey's language is fairly restrained when he discusses the gold advocates. Harvey made quite a point of the idea that the abuse heaped by the conservative press on silverites was a poor substitute for rational argument, and he preferred to picture Coin as rising nobly above all this. It was, for him, a rare *ad hominem* attack when he described J. Laurence Laughlin as a "professor in a chair of political economy, endowed with the money of bankers, his mental faculties . . . trained with his salary." For the most part, Harvey preferred to picture substantial businessmen as potential friends of silver, willing to listen to reason. The bankers themselves, he said, "as a rule are a patriotic class of men, but they are controlled by a central influence in London and New York."

The stance of rationality and fair play which Harvey struck with most of his contemporaries was possible because silverite hostilities were directed elsewhere—projected backward in time, to the perpetrators of the monstrous Crime of '73, and outward in space, to Britain as the bulwark of the international gold standard and to the House of Rothschild as its financial center. When Harvey discusses the Crime of '73 and the power of Britain, his calm breaks down. The alleged disaster of the demonetization of silver in 1873 was not viewed by Harvey, or by most silverites, as the consequence of a ghastly mistake but as the outcome of a crafty conspiracy. Demonetization, the work of "men having a design to injure business by making money scarce," had accomplished exactly what had been intended: it had created a depression and caused untold suffering. The law of 1873 was passed stealthily, and many of the men who voted for it had no notion of what they were doing. Silver was "demonetized secretly, and since then a powerful money trust has used deception and misrepresentations that have led thousands of honest minds astray." Demonetization

> is commonly known as the crime of 1873. A crime, because it has confiscated millions of dollars worth of property. A crime, because it has made thousands of paupers. A crime, because it has made tens of thousands of tramps. A crime, because it has made thousands of suicides. A crime, because it has brought tears to strong men's eyes, and hunger and pinching want to widows and orphans. A crime, because it is destroying the honest yeomanry of the land, the bulwark of the nation. A crime, because it has brought this once great republic to the verge of ruin, where it is now in imminent danger of tottering to its fall. [Applause.]

The true center of this criminal conspiracy is, of course, London. Almost every step in Coin's argument is interlarded with a renewal of the old hostility to England, and there are times when one feels that one is back in the atmosphere of 1812. Even the foundations of our monetary system, it is argued, dated from "our revolutionary forefathers, who had a hatred of England, and an intimate knowledge of her designs on this country." Harvey had an important tactical reason for wanting to exploit this feeling. The advocates of unilateral free coinage of silver by the United States were carrying on an argument not only with gold-standard advocates but with the international bimetallists, who believed that the use of both metals in monetary standards was desirable but insisted that the United States could not uphold silver unaided without disaster. The argument of the international bimetallists was in fact one of the most formidable arguments of the opponents of unilateral free silver, and a certain frustration in dealing with it no doubt had something to do with the violent rhetoric in which Harvey put his case.

The climactic passage of *Coin's Financial School* occurs in Coin's sixth and last lecture, in which he spells out defiance to English power. Here he urges that the experiment of monetary independence be tried, and that if the argument of the internationalists should prove correct, one should not capitulate to gold but wage war: "If it is true, let us attach England to the United States and blot out her name from among the nations of the earth. [Applause.]" Coin goes on to say that "a war with England would be the most popular ever waged on the face of the earth," and also the most just, since it would be waged against a power that "can dictate the money of the world, and thereby create world-wide misery." But such a war, he continued, would in fact not be necessary if England were defied in American monetary policy. To hope for her concurrence in international action was futile: she was a creditor nation committed to gold. "Wherever property interests and humanity have come in conflict, England has ever been the enemy of human liberty." To shirk the struggle for unilateral bimetallism "means a surrender to England" and involves the risk that internecine war will arise in the United States that will put an end to the republic. If the present policy is continued, he argued, it will end

in England owning us body and soul. She is making a peaceable conquest of the United States. What she failed to do with shot and shell in the eighteenth century, she is doing with the gold standard in the nineteenth century. [Applause.] The conserva-

269

tive monied interest furnished the tory friends of England then, and it furnishes her friends now. [Applause.] The business men of New York City passed strong resolutions against the Declaration of Independence in 1776, and they are passing strong resolutions against an American policy now. [Applause.]

VII

WHILE HARVEY'S was unquestionably the most popular statement of the case for silver, it was far from the best. Indeed it was so much inferior to the speeches of such congressional advocates as Bryan and Teller and to the writings of such American bimetallists as President E. Benjamin Andrews of Brown, President Francis A. Walker of M.I.T., and the silver diplomat and propagandist S. Dana Horton that one is tempted to propound a Gresham's law of popular monetary discussion, by which the weak arguments drive the strong out of circulation. Harvey's case is not developed systematically or logically, and his sense for what is important among the issues is almost touchingly unsure. His greatest failing was his staggering gift for irrelevancy—his readiness to inject into the argument assertions that were either unnecessary to his case or incapable of substantiation. He attached, for example, the highest importance to his assertion that all the gold in the world could be incorporated into a cube of 22 feet; he portrayed Coin's goldbug auditors as being thrown almost into paroxysms by this revelation, although no one was disposed to deny that gold was a scarce commodity. He tempted the ridicule of economists by insisting that it cost $2.00 an ounce to produce silver, when silver had not brought a price of more than about $1.36 an ounce within the memory of living man —thus implying that the metal had been produced for more than a generation out of philanthropy. He made errors of fact, he distorted statutes and quotations, he invented his own confusing terminology ("redemption money"), he forced side issues or non-issues into the center of attention, he made up a monetary history that was largely fictional, and, all in all, he made himself vastly more vulnerable to his critics than his case required.[2]

Indeed, almost everything about Harvey's book can be argued with except its success. The importance of Harvey's pamphlet for the student of history lies in its popularity, which suggests that Harvey's understanding of the case was close to that held by the ordinary silverite of firm convictions and active intelligence but no special training. Harvey was what Gertrude Stein once called another money crank, Ezra Pound—"a village explainer." Like many another movement, free silver had its lowbrow and highbrow culture. Harvey represents the common man thinking, and the essentials of his argument reproduce a very widespread contemporary view. These essentials may be extracted from his cluttered exposition. They consist of four assertions that are primarily historical in character and four that are primarily programmatic and economic. This historical assertions are that the original unit of American currency was the silver dollar, adopted in 1792; that this was the primary element of a successful bimetallic system down to 1873; that in 1873 silver was "secretly" and stealthily demonetized by a Congress so hypnotized or so corrupted by sinister gold interests that it did not know what it was doing; and that the demonetization of silver in 1873 de-

---

[2] The most important contemporary critiques, which go at Harvey's argument point by point, are J. Laurence Laughlin's *Facts about Money* (Chicago, 1895) and Horace White's *Coin's Financial Fool* (New York, 1895). Willard Fisher's article " 'Coin' and His Critics," already cited, made a scrupulous effort to defend Harvey ("an untrained thinker of considerably more than average ability") at a few points where Fisher felt that Harvey's critics had done him injustice, but also marshaled (pp. 190–2) a brief list of Harvey's most extraordinary and gratuitous errors.

prived the country of half the supply of its primary money. The assertions that might be regarded as largely economic are that the depression and misery which the country had endured were simply the consequences of falling prices and the continuing appreciation of gold; that low prices could be remedied by an infusion of new money; that the appropriate source of new money was free and unlimited coinage of silver at 16 to 1; and, finally, that this remedy could be successfully adopted by the United States acting alone and without the cooperation of any foreign country.

Harvey's history of the original American currency system was in fact completely irrelevant to the merits of free coinage of silver as a remedy for the economic conditions of the 1890's. If free silver was good policy in 1894, it mattered not in the least what coinage the Founding Fathers had intended in 1792. After a hundred years of additional experience with currency systems and some advance in economic knowledge, one could hardly expect the currency practices of the founders to have much rational authority for Harvey's contemporaries on either side of the currency issue. But the silver men, like their opponents, cherished their historical lore, and the happy notion that free coinage of silver would restore "the dollar of our daddies" was an important part of it.

Harvey's version of the history of American money could hardly have been more misleading. His elaborate attempt to establish that the original monetary unit was a *silver* dollar, and that gold was "also made money" but that "its value was counted from the silver dollar" is nonsensical, as well as gratuitous. The original monetary unit was simply the dollar, circulated in a variety of pieces of both gold and silver.[3] The dollar was defined as having a certain weight of silver and a

---

[3] The coinage measure of 1792 provided for three gold coins worth $10, $5, and $2.50, for a silver dollar, and for silver half dollars, quarters, dimes, and half dimes, as well as copper pennies and half pennies.

certain weight of gold, bearing to each other the proportions of 15 to 1. The fathers did not in fact cherish any preference for silver over gold. Gold was widely preferred as having a more certain and stable value; but Hamilton, in his report on coinage to Congress in May 1791, recommended a bimetallic unit on the ground that the available quantity of gold was not sufficient to serve as the basis for a money system. If one tries to salvage whatever there may be of fact in Harvey's attempt to claim primacy for silver, it must be simply that gold, being too valuable to serve as common coin, was coined only in units ranging from $2.50 up to the $10 gold eagle, and that the coinage handled by the common man was of silver. ("Gold was considered the money of the rich . . . the poor people seldom handled it, and the very poor people seldom ever saw any of it.")

Harvey's implication that the United States had a smooth-working bimetallic system before the Crime of '73 and that the old American silver dollar had wide circulation in this country was also misleading. In law, as we have seen, bimetallism did exist. In fact, the standard had alternated from silver to gold because Congress failed to set a mint ratio in accord with the world market. This very alternation of standards later persuaded dogmatic gold men to insist—all too glibly—that bimetallism had been proved to be an impossibility. They failed to take into account the fact that it would not have been impossible to arrive at a mint ratio more in harmony with France's if the will to do it had been present in Congress at any time between the days of Hamilton and the Civil War. It is tempting to speculate how much strength international bimetallism might have acquired if Congress had decided soon after 1792 to rectify Hamilton's miscalculation and establish a common ratio with France.

As for the old American silver dollar, Harvey seemed unaware that it had disappeared rapidly from circulation not

273

long after Congress provided for its coinage. This came about because the standard American silver dollar, though lighter in weight than the Spanish silver dollar, was newer, brighter, and less abraded, and thus became more acceptable in certain kinds of foreign trade. Dealers found it profitable to export it in exchange for the Spanish dollars, which were legal tender in the United States, and which became our primary medium of silver circulation. As a consequence of the drainage of the American silver dollar, President Jefferson ordered its coinage discontinued in 1806, and this suspension remained in force for thirty years.

The third of Harvey's historical assertions—that the Coinage Act of 1873 was passed corruptly and in secret at the instance of the gold bankers—was a widespread article of faith among money agitators and had been widely believed for sixteen years. Despite its intrinsic implausibility, gold spokesmen were forced to make elaborate refutations of this charge. No measure could pass Congress in secret, they pointed out, and the Coinage Act had been before Congress almost three years from April 1870 to its passage in February 1873; the chairman of the House Committee of Coinage, Weights and Measures, introducing it to the House, pointed out that it legally established monometallism and declared that it had come to him from a Senate committee that had given it "as careful attention as I have ever known a committee to bestow on any measure"; it was printed thirteen times by order of Congress; it had been debated once in the Senate and twice in the House for a total of 144 columns of the *Congressional Globe;* two Directors of the Mint and other experts had pointed out that the bill demonetized the old silver dollar; Samuel Hooper of Massachusetts, who steered the bill through the House, carefully observed that the gold dollar was being established as the standard of value; several senators referred to the cessation of coinage of the silver dollar; and some of the quotations silver men later invoked to show the stealthy passage of the bill were arrived at by misrepresenting congressional debates.[4]

However, when a delusion like that of the Crime of '73 gets to be so widely believed, it is perhaps quite as important to understand how it came about as to repeat elaborate proofs of its falsity. No doubt economic suffering and social resentments had a great deal to do with the formation and spread of the myth. But there was a soupçon of truth out of which the notion of the Crime of '73 grew: it lies in the fact that even the better-informed men in Congress could hardly have had a very keen sense in 1873 of the full implications of what they were doing when they passed the Coinage Act.

This measure was intended in the first instance to codify the coinage laws and to remedy the chaotic and expensive condition in which our fractional currency had been left at the end of the Civil War. After much talk of the need of such action in the late 1860's, John Jay Knox, the Deputy Comptroller of the Currency, was requested by Secretary of the Treasury George Boutwell to prepare such a bill. It was first presented to Congress in 1870, and was much discussed and amended in the three years before its passage. The question of providing for continued coinage of the standard silver dollar was never an issue, and no attentive congressman need have had difficulty in understanding that its coinage was being dropped. The silver dollar, exported before 1806, not coined from 1806 to 1836, and not circulated from 1836 to 1873, was

---

[4] For standard refutations by gold advocates, see Laughlin: *Facts about Money*, pp. 57–69, and *The History of Bimetallism in the United States*, pp. 95–102; Horace White: *Coin's Financial Fool*, pp. 44–54; David K. Watson: *History of American Coinage* (New York, 1899), pp. 125–37. By far the most knowledgeable and astute account of the origins of the law of 1873 that I have found is Neil Carothers: *Fractional Money*, Ch. 16, and my estimate of the situation follows his.

simply an unfamiliar and half-forgotten coin. No one objected to its discontinuance, not because there was any secret about the matter, but because no one cared. The silver interests, who knew that the weight of silver specified for the defunct silver dollar was actually worth a few cents more than a dollar in the open market, had no reason to demand its continued coinage. When the law of 1873 was introduced, Germany had not yet gone on the gold standard, and even when it was passed the effect of German silver sales in the world market had not yet begun to depress the price of the metal.

Seven months after the passage of the Coinage Act the Panic of 1873 began, and the fall in the price of silver began at about the same time. It was natural for money-oriented reformers to connect the two events. As inflationary demands built up, congressmen who found it politic to take up a pro-silver position now began to explain that in voting for the Coinage Act of 1873 they had not known what they were doing—and if one bears in mind the technical character of the law, it becomes evident that in a certain sense most of them were telling the truth. But, at least for a few of them, to join in the general cry about the Crime of '73 required a certain daring mendacity. For example, Representative William D. Kelley of Pennyslvania, the same man who is quoted above as having assured the House how carefully the bill had been weighed in committee, was one of the few who explicitly pointed out the implications of the Coinage Act for silver. He told the House on January 9, 1872: "It is impossible to retain the double standard." Yet six years later Kelley brazenly joined those who insisted that the Coinage Act of 1873 was a fraud, when he said that, "though the chairman of the committee on coinage, I was ignorant of the fact that it would demonetize the silver dollar, or of its dropping the silver dollar from our system of coins."

276

As for Harvey's contention that the Act of 1873, by de-
monetizing silver, "destroyed one-half of the redemption
money of the United States," his critics were fond of pointing
out that a kind of money that was not in circulation at all
could hardly have been destroyed, and that it could not conceivably have had any consequences for the depression of
1873–79, since the country was then still on the inconvertible
paper standard. They were also fond of pointing out that by
the silver acts of 1878 and 1890 silver dollars had in some
measure been restored to circulation. In fact more silver dollars or silver certificates having legal-tender status had been
put in circulation by 1894 than anyone could have dreamed
of in 1873—without having lifted the general price level or
the price of silver itself.[5]

The history of our money is full of its own subtle mocker-
ies, and there is one ironic aspect of the law of 1873 that must
be noted here: far from having demonetized silver in any
operative sense, it actually came close to remonetizing the
white metal, despite the intention of its framers. While the old
standard silver dollar was dropped from coinage, the law
created—largely to facilitate trade with the silver-standard
countries of the Orient and to compete with the Mexican
dollar—a new silver dollar called the trade dollar. The trade
dollar had a silver content slightly greater than the old standard silver dollar and was not expected to circulate within the
United States. However, the law provided that the trade dollar was not only to be freely coined but also to be legal tender
for payments up to the amount of five dollars within the
country. The legal-tender provision was included to bolster
the foreign standing of this dollar by enhancing its domestic
standing. No one thought this dollar would have any actual

---

[5] By 1894 there were in circulation $326.9 million in silver certifi-
cates, $134.6 million in Treasury notes of 1890, and $52.5 million in
silver dollars. *Historical Statistics of the United States*, p. 648.

domestic circulation, because it was at an even greater pre-mium as silver than the lighter standard dollar that had dis-appeared, and it was not expected to compete for circulation with the then prevailing greenbacks. But the ensuing sudden drop in the value of silver and the rise in that of the green-backs had the effect of causing the trade dollars to circulate in substantial amounts in this country, in addition to being ex-ported to the Orient. Accordingly, the legal-tender character of the trade dollar was removed by Congress in 1876, and when its circulation persisted, its coinage was discontinued in 1878. Its circulation continued until it was finally redeemed by Congress in 1887. But as Charles R. Whittlesey has ob-served, the combined provisions for free coinage and legal tender, while they lasted, had the effect of briefly remonetiz-ing silver and, when one takes account of the greater weight of the trade dollar, of remonetizing it at a ratio of about 16⅓ to 1—a ratio which was by no means unfavorable to silver when one considers what was happening to silver prices. But the inflationary forces, failing to see what they had inadvert-ently gained for their metal by the creation of the trade dol-lar, showed no great interest in blocking the repeal of its legal-tender power. This may be attributed to their failure to understand its potentialities for remonetization. It would have been far easier, politically, to mobilize the growing silver sentiment against this repeal in 1876 than to regain free coin-age of the standard silver dollar. Professor Whittlesey at-tributes this tactical oversight to "economic illiteracy on the part of the silver interests."[6] But on the whole one is im-pressed by the sense that all those involved with currency problems in the 1870's were like men groping in the dark.

---

[6] *Principles and Practices of Money and Banking* (New York, 1954), pp. 206–8. On the trade dollar, see Carothers: op. cit., pp. 233–4, 275–80. In a sense, it is almost anachronistic to speak of the "silver interests" as an organized force in 1876. Sentiment for silver was just

VIII

LET US TURN NOW to the programmatic, as opposed to the historical, side of Harvey's argument. There are two possible ways of looking at the subject. The first is to regard Harvey as though he were a professional economist and to apply to his exposition the same rigorous standards that one would apply to any professional work. In this there is now little point, except by way of establishing the difference between popular agitation and professional analysis. Harvey was an amateur, and his book was at best a caricature of sophisticated bimetallist thought. Of course, it suited contemporary defenders of the gold standard to treat him as though he were a professional, and on this ground they were for the most part unanswerable. He had, after all, presented "Coin" as an expert more authoritative than the experts. J. Laurence Laughlin perhaps spoke with too much personal asperity and failed to reckon with Harvey's honest naïveté when he charged that "the book was intentionally constructed to fit into prevailing

crystallizing, and the dominant inflationary rationale was still that of the Greenbackers.

Paul M. O'Leary has revived the idea of the Crime of '73 in a much modified form. He points out that Henry R. Linderman, a special assistant to John Jay Knox, the Comptroller of the Currency and an active figure in the drafting and redrafting of the Coinage Act of 1873, had become aware by November 1872, three months before the passage of the act, that forces at work in the world were about to cause a depreciation in the value of silver. Linderman, who was a strong gold-standard man, did not bring the relevant facts and their implications to the attention of the congressmen who were about to act on the measure, though he did mention them in a report to the Secretary of the Treasury. At least one person, then—and perhaps two if the Secretary of the Treasury was fully cognizant of the implications of Linderman's report—was aware of the impending decline in the value of silver and possibly aware of the future significance of stopping coinage of the old silver dollar.

However, it remains true that because of the acceptance of the trade dollar, and its subsequent circulation in the United States, the in-

prejudices and consciously deceive," but one must bow to the more dispassionate verdict of another contemporary economist, Willard Fisher, who wrote that it was "of no value to those who have been trained to think about monetary problems," and who found it strange "that so crude a product could have created so great a sensation."[7]

But it is also possible to say that complicated issues like money do on occasion have to be made the object of popular discussion in a democracy, and that they must of necessity be discussed in a simplified way. One may then ask whether, disregarding technicalities, there was any substantive economic merit in the demand for inflation as a remedy for the depression of the nineties, and whether the demand for cheaper money did not also have some moral justification. If the issue is looked at in these broad and indulgent terms, Harvey becomes far more defensible—and in a certain way even prophetic, for in some fields of inquiry yesterday's crank may turn out to be closer than yesterday's accepted spokesman to today's dominant views.

The essence of Harvey's programmatic position is summed up on page 175, where he advocates the remonetization of silver in these words: "You increase the value of all property

---

flationary interests were granted a reprise on the issue between 1873 and 1876, when the trade dollar's coinage was discontinued. This opportunity the inflationary forces failed to seize upon; and one can only conclude that, while the considerations raised by O'Leary do indicate gold-standard malice aforethought, at least by one significant actor on the scene, it is of vital consequence that in a time of confusion and changing policies, the interests of cheap money were ineptly defended. Also it is altogether improbable that the *inception* of the Coinage Act of 1873, which dates back to 1870, could have been induced in any way by the expectation of a change in the value of silver. See Paul M. O'Leary: "The Scene of the Crime of 1873 Revisited: A Note," *Journal of Political Economy*, LXVIII (August 1960), 388–92.

[7] Laughlin: "'Coin's' Food for the Gullible," *The Forum*, XIX (July 1895), 577; Fisher: "'Coin' and His Critics," p. 192.

by adding to the number of money units in the land. You make it possible for the debtor to pay his debts; business to start anew, and revivify all the industries of the country, which must remain paralyzed so long as silver as well as all other property is measured by a gold standard." The imprecision of his way of putting things becomes apparent not only in the unintelligible, though charmingly illustrated, conception of business depressions that follows page 147 but also in the assertion on page 203 that cutting the gold dollar in half would "thereby double the value [presumably he meant prices] of all property in the United States, except debts."[8]

Harvey was, of course, using a rudimentary version of the quantity theory of money. Given stable conditions of demand for money, its value will vary inversely with the quantity available. Hence the general price level varies directly with this quantity. A massive addition to the money supply such as that promised by free coinage of silver would raise the general price level, return inflated debts to a fair level, and reinvigorate the entire economy.

There is a certain danger that we may become so absorbed in the inadequacies of Harvey's case for inflation, and in particular of the quixotic case for free coinage of silver at 16 to 1,

---

[8] Page references are to the John Harvard Library edition.

Such proposals were so commonly regarded by contemporary conservatives as a form of lunatic radicalism that it is worthwhile to notice the element of latent conservatism in this overwhelming emphasis on the monetary factor in depressions. Harvey and his fellow silverites were not trying to develop a fundamental critique of industrial capitalism; they were merely trying to make it work, and they believed that the device that would do so was essentially a simple one. This premise went unnoticed by their conservative critics, but not by the left wing of the Populist party, whose spokesmen objected to free silver on the ground, among others, that it would not go very far to alleviate the basic ills of American society.

It is perhaps important to point out that in 1933, when the gold content of the dollar was cut to 59 per cent of its previous parity, in the hope of bringing about a proportionate rise in prices, the expedient did not work.

that we will ignore the substantial merits of the demand for inflation. Modern economic opinion would treat Harvey's general line of reasoning, especially as applied to the depression of the 1890's which came after a long period of drastic deflation, with much greater respect than dogmatic contemporary professionals. What vitiated Harvey's point of view was his obsession with the bullion basis of the money supply, which in turn reflects his adherence to an old-fashioned view of money, inherited from American agrarian thought. He did not think of money functionally, as a means of payment, but simply as money of account (or, as he would say, a measure of value). He understood "true" money to consist in hard coin. The quantity theory of money, as he employed it (page 188), applied only to "redemption money"—that is, gold or silver. The elaborate apparatus of credit that was growing up in his lifetime he dismissed as irrelevant to the fundamental issue of the monetary standard. The expansion of what he called "credit money" represented no real addition to the money supply—and its overexpansion he could regard only as dangerous (pages 141–3).

Modern statements of the quantity theory of money measure the money supply by taking into account all the means of payment that are available, including demand deposits—that is, bank deposits subject to withdrawal by check. They also consider the velocity of monetary circulation as a dimension that must be taken into account when the supply of money is estimated for any period of time. The concept of velocity, though an old one, was just beginning to be employed in empirical study in Harvey's time; but the fast-growing use of demand deposits was a familiar and measurable fact to his contemporaries. By the 1890's something like 90 per cent of the volume of business transactions was being carried on by check. Harvey could not be persuaded to take any interest in this fact as having a possible bearing on the demand for money, and he dismissed it (pages 145–7) by saying that while "credit money" was convenient in facilitating transactions, it had nothing to do with the measure of values, which was his only concern.

No doubt Harvey's conception of money stemmed from a kind of business experience, then only recently outmoded, that still fashioned the thinking of many farmers and some businessmen. His views reflected the folkish feeling that pieces of money are not really "good" unless they have a roughly equivalent value for nonmonetary purposes, or are directly redeemable in money that has such value. "Some years ago," E. Benjamin Andrews reported in 1894, "I found a man who for a decade owned and carried on the chief store in a flourishing New England village, ignorant how to draw a check. If this in the East, how slight must be the play of banking methods in the West and South."[9] Men out of such village backgrounds naturally thought of the solution to monetary problems entirely in terms of primary money, and were uninterested in the possibilities that lay in devising more flexible instruments of check credit. Perhaps the most severe stricture that can be made against them was that when the nation finally came to the point of trying to devise a mobile credit structure that would make possible a more adequate response to the kind of evil they had protested against, men like Harvey were too firm in their anti-bank prejudices to applaud the effort, and were to be found instead sniping at it as nothing more than a new source of profits and power for usurers.

At any rate, Harvey's notion that the appreciation of gold was the primary source of the hardships of his time throughout the price-depressed Western world was a rough popular version of a view of the matter taken by many more sophisticated contemporaries in the United States and Europe, among

---

[9] *An Honest Dollar* (Hartford, Conn., 1894), pp. 26–7.

them distinguished economists and statesmen. Such respectable contemporaries were profoundly disturbed by business instability and unemployment and by the widespread and growing discontent of the agricultural populations of several nations. They put a heavy burden of blame for depressed prices on the formation of the international gold standard. As they saw it, each new Western nation that clambered aboard the gold-standard bandwagon after 1873 added its own needs to the general scramble for a very limited supply of gold. The metal appreciated and prices dropped. And certainly, if price stability was the thing most urgently desired, the record of the gold standard in these years and afterwards was not inspiring.[1] Bimetallism, moreover, was a respectable proposition in economic theory, and it is easy to be persuaded that things might have been somewhat better had the nations, say, in the 1870's or even the early 1880's, successfully arrived at an agreement to put the Western trading community on a bimetallic basis.

It is impossible for the layman to evaluate the merits of this traditional case against the gold standard. But most economists who are familiar with macro-economic developments have tended in recent years to minimize the effect of the bullion basis of money in the secular price decline, as compared with certain long-range changes that came with industrialism and improvements in transportation. The development of industry brought many long-range cost-reducing improvements. Massive investment in railroads and shipping, improvements in transportation facilities, the opening of the Suez Canal—such changes led to the rapid development of great tracts of virgin land throughout the world and the rapid shrinkage of the world into a single market. The effects of these

---

[1] See, on this count, D. H. Robertson: *Money* (4th ed., Chicago, 1959), pp. 117–19.

changes were felt with special acuteness by the farming populations, which found themselves competing in a crowded international market and victims of a common international
agrarian depression. Studies in the history of the real money
supply, moreover, indicate that changes in banking during
this secular price decline were more and more detaching the
real money supply from the rate of growth of the gold supply. The calculations of J. G. Gurley and E. S. Shaw for the
United States, which take account of demand deposits and
other sources of expansion, show a steady growth in the real
per capita money supply for the decades from 1869 to 1899,
and an annual rate of growth somewhat higher than in the
years before the Civil War.[2] The gold standard may well
have aggravated the price decline but it cannot be assigned
full blame.

To accept these findings, however, is not to deny the merit
of the demand for inflation in the mid-1890's. There was an
excellent case, both economic and moral, for a jolt of control-

---

[2] See the two essays by Gurley and Shaw already cited. There is
an account of the views of economists on the role of monetary factors
in the depression of the 1890's in Rendigs Fels: *American Business
Cycles, 1865–1897* (Chapel Hill, N.C., 1959), Chs. 11 and 12. Charles
Hoffman, in "The Depression of the Nineties," *Journal of Economic
History,* XVI (June 1956), 137–64, concludes that monetary and fiscal
policies were secondary aggravating forces. Lee Benson summarizes
the literature on the transportation revolution and its international
consequences in his essay "The Historical Background of Turner's
Frontier Essay," in *Turner and Beard* (Glencoe, Ill., 1960), pp. 42 ff.;
and A. E. Musson does the same for the literature on "The Great
Depression in Britain, 1873–1896," *Journal of Economic History,* XIX
(June 1959), 199–228. On the limitations of the gold standard in
accounting for the secular price decline, see J. T. Phinney: "Gold
Production and the Price Level," *Quarterly Journal of Economics,*
XLVII (August 1933), 647–79, and E. H. Phelps Brown and S. A.
Ozga: "Economic Growth and the Price Level," *Economic Journal,*
LXV (March 1955), 1–18. Cf. J. M. Keynes: *Treatise on Money*
(London, 1930), II, 164–70, and W. T. Layton and Geoffrey
Crowther: *An Introduction to the Study of Prices* (London, 1938),
Ch. 8.

able inflation that would have stimulated enterprise and readjusted the balance between debtors and creditors. The difficulty was to find a mechanism for such inflation that would have achieved the desired price rise without so dislocating foreign trade and investment and so shaking the confidence of the business community that the anticipated benefits would be undone. Under modern conditions of central banking, the mechanisms are at hand; in the 1890's this was not the case, and so the debate centered on the monetary standard. From the vantage point of a later age there seems to be something genuinely tragic in the clash of the two hypnotic dogmatisms of gold and silver, neither of whose exponents had an adequate comprehension of the problem nor an adequate program for the relief of economic misery.

It is against this background that the true poignancy of Harvey's willfully amateurish attempt to restate the silver case may be seen. There is, of course, a certain innocent amusement to be had from poking fun at cranks. But when cranks acquire the wide popular following that men like Harvey had, it may be the better part of statesmanship to take their agitations, even if not their ideas, seriously. What was being debated in America and Europe during the 1890's was a major social issue which had its moral as well as its technical economic side. And on the moral side, the defenders of the gold standard often seem as dogmatically sealed within their own premises as the most wild-eyed silver men, and usually less generous in their social sympathies. The right-thinking statesmanship of the era, like its right-thinking economics, was so locked in its own orthodoxy that it was incapable of coming to terms in a constructive way with lasting and pervasive social grievances. The social philosophy of J. Laurence Laughlin and the statecraft of Grover Cleveland cannot, in this respect, command our admiration. They accepted as "natural" a stark, long-range price deflation, identified the interests of creditors with true morality, and looked upon any attempt to remedy the appreciation of debt as unnatural and dishonest, as a simple repudiation of sacred obligations—an attempt, as Laughlin put it in his debate with Harvey, "to transfer from the great mass of the community who have been provident, industrious, and successful a portion of their savings and gains into the pockets of those who have been idle, extravagant, or unfortunate."[3] This attitude, as provocative as it was smug, was not calculated to engender humane statesmanship. Allan Nevins, unstinting though he is in his admiration for Grover Cleveland's defense of the gold standard, remarks that the farmers had legitimate grounds for complaint and that "our history presents few spectacles more ironic than that of their Eastern creditors taunting them with dishonesty while insisting upon being repaid in a dollar far more valuable than had been lent."[4] Laughlin himself put the case in a fairer light when he said: "The highest justice is rendered by the state when it extracts from the debtor at the end of a contract the *same purchasing power* which the creditor gave him at the beginning of the contract, no less, no more," and it is quite understandable why Bryan felt that he was only echoing Laughlin when he said in his speech against repeal of the Sherman Silver Purchase Act: "A dollar ap-

---

[3] *Facts about Money*, p. 233; cf. his comments about "the less fortunate, the less successful, the less wise," and "the greater prosperity of the successful [that] is due to the possession of superior industrial power," in " 'Coin's' Food for the Gullible," pp. 574, 576.

[4] Nevins: op. cit., p. 594. Any change in the value of money has the effect of redistributing income among social classes; and changes in the value of money are the consequences, among other things, of the decisions of governments—even if they are only decisions *not* to act. One can readily understand the fury of inflationists, after years of deflationary monetary decisions, at being told that their proposals to raise prices were unwarranted and dishonest efforts to interfere with the course of nature. The gold advocates had taken it upon themselves to define the terms of the controversy in such a way as to make it impossible for them to be wrong.

proaches honesty as its purchasing power approaches stability."[5]

The international bimetallists seem to have been on sound ground insofar as they saw the future solution to deflation in supranational arrangements that would enable the trading powers to maintain stable exchange rates and yet keep some freedom in domestic price policies; whereas the dogmatic gold men, who believed that currency was governed by laws so immutable that money was not susceptible to further management, were looking in the wrong direction. Of course, the overwhelming majority of American silver men were not international bimetallists; like Harvey, they were uncompromising advocates of unilateral action. The difference was vital. The international aspect of the problem was the Achilles' heel

---

[5] Laughlin: *The History of Bimetallism in the United States*, p. 70; Bryan: op. cit., p. 80. The whole question of the price level as one of both policy and morality is circumspectly discussed in Ch. 7 of D. H. Robertson's classic exposition, *Money*. See also the grounds for Keynes's conclusion that "it is worse, in an impoverished world, to provoke unemployment than to disappoint the rentier"; *Essays in Persuasion* (London, 1931), p. 103.

Milton Friedman and Anna J. Schwartz, in *A Monetary History of the United States, 1867–1960*, find that the forces making for economic growth over the course of several business cycles were largely independent of the secular trend in prices. They suggest that, while generally declining or rising prices had little effect on the rate of economic growth, "the period of great monetary uncertainty in the early nineties produced sharp deviations from the longer-term trend." They also suggest that the abandonment of the gold standard "might well have been highly preferable to the generally depressed conditions of the 1890's," but dismiss it only because it was "politically unacceptable." Concerning the severe deflation that arose from the commitment to the gold standard, they observe: "In retrospect, it seems clear that either acceptance of a silver standard at an early stage or an early commitment to gold would have been preferable to the uneasy compromise that was maintained, with the uncertainty about the ultimate outcome and the consequent wide fluctuations to which the currency was subjected." See Ch. 3, esp. pp. 93, 111, 133–4, and in particular the extended footnote on p. 134, in which they suggest reasons why a silver standard might have been preferable to gold before 1897.

of the American silver men—and it is no coincidence that when Harvey comes, near the end of *Coin's Financial School*, to the hopeless problem of maintaining bimetallism in one country, he drops his façade of didactic calm and rational argument and breaks into a tirade against England. The idea that the United States, acting alone, could uphold the value of silver and maintain bimetallism, as opposed to adopting silver monometallism, had long been preposterous; the notion that we could coin unlimited amounts of silver at 16 to 1 at a time when the market ratio had dropped to 32 to 1, and still hold to a bimetallic standard, was understandably regarded by its opponents as a form of economic lunacy. For this reason, the "respectable" bimetallists, in the United States as elsewhere, saw the problem of the monetary standard as an international one. On this count they were regarded by the silver nationalists as abject traitors.

The one reality that the silver nationalists would not face was that the course of events since 1871 had so undermined the international position of silver that nothing short of concerted international action could restore it as a standard money. Few of them were candid enough to admit that, because the value of the two metals had so far parted company in the past twenty years, they had in fact become silver monometallists. Today, when we are no longer enthralled by illusions about the perfection or inevitability of the gold standard, it may still be possible to argue speculatively, as a few candid silver men did in 1894, that it would have been healthier to restore prices through silver monometallism than to accept the drastic and disheartening fall in prices that was still going on. But the switch to a silver standard might have been self-defeating simply because of its blow to the confidence of the business community. And even if one were to dismiss this intangible, the blows to foreign investment and trade would probably have had repercussions serious enough to delay rather than to hasten recovery. The United States was a debtor nation and an importer of capital; and the effects of a silver standard upon its debt service and the investment market might well have constituted a minor disaster. Abstractly, there was nothing wrong with a silver standard, or for that matter a paper standard, but it does not follow that the shift could have been made without causing, as Senator Cockrell so confidently said, "as much as a ripple in our financial system."[6]

One thing that can be said in the light of historical perspective is that the critical moment for a stand for silver through an international agreement had long since passed. Moreover, the American silver movement itself could be charged with having done its own part to weaken the forces working for such an agreement.

Behind this charge lies a long history of international discussion and negotiation, marked by four international monetary conferences in 1867, 1878, 1881, and 1892. It is true that Britain had steadfastly refused to abandon her own gold standard, and her unwillingness to do so had been interpreted, rightly or wrongly, by the other great nations as an insuperable obstacle to satisfactory international action on silver. But,

---

[6] Most historians who have discussed the battle of the standards have written largely as ideologists. Liberal historians have treated the subject as though the sufferings of the farmers and the broad social sympathies of the silver men were an adequate substitute for sound remedial proposals—somewhat in the spirit of Vachel Lindsay's rhetorical poem "Bryan, Bryan, Bryan, Bryan." On the other hand, most conservative historians who have written at length about the merits of the monetary controversy itself have quietly assumed that the orthodoxies of J. Laurence Laughlin are still untouched. They would have us enter uncritically into the spirit of Grover Cleveland's assertion that if the United States went off gold it "could no longer claim a place among nations of the first class." Actually, it is interesting to speculate on what would have happened if the United States had adopted silver monometallism and had made this the occasion of an aggressive effort to dominate the trade of the silver-using Orient and Latin America.

partly because of Britain's growing concern for the stability of silver, a concern arising from her trade with India, which was on a silver standard, British spokesmen would have welcomed action taken by the United States, alone or in concert with other nations, that would have successfully sustained the international use and the price of the white metal. In Britain the gold standard was both a habit and a dogma, but it was not considered to be a proselytizing creed eligible for export.

During the many years when the international bimetallic movement was working for an agreement among the nations on the use of silver, the American silver purchase policy, along with the threat that unlimited coinage might soon follow, had hung like a dark cloud over the international conferences. The more reason the European governments had to expect that American silver purchase policies would give them a dumping ground for their silver and an opportunity to strengthen their gold position, the less likely they were to yield to the arguments of their own bimetallists. American Presidents from Hayes to McKinley, sensitive as they were to the political power of silver, had all been interested in efforts to arrive at an international monetary agreement, but their efforts were constantly undermined not only by the success of the silver interests in Congress in 1878 and 1890 but by the indiscreet interventions of silver congressmen in monetary diplomacy.[7]

Probably the most strategic moment for an international

---

[7] See Jeannette P. Nichols's account of these interventions in "Silver Diplomacy," *Political Science Quarterly*, XLVIII (December 1933), 565–88. Henry B. Russell gives a detailed account of the effects of American silver policies on the international meetings in his *International Monetary Conferences* (New York, 1898); see esp. pp. 192–9, 260, 323–7, 369, 409–10. Concerning the interventions of the silver men and their effects on the prospects of bimetallism, Russell remarks (pp. 324–5): "No doctrine ever stood in such dire need of being delivered from its most officious friends."

agreement was the conference of 1881, when America's gold position was strong and the European powers were suffering a serious gold crisis. A great wave of bimetallist sentiment swept Europe, from which Britain was by no means immune, and British representatives came to the conference quite interested in seeing the *other* nations, perhaps the United States and the Latin Union, open their mints to unlimited coinage. But current American silver purchases under the Bland-Allison Act checked the silver impetus almost as much as the British refusal to go off gold.

Eleven years later, the British, led by Alfred de Rothschild, a director of the Bank of England, came to the conference of 1892 still unwilling to change their own standard, but still concerned about the rupee and solicitous about silver.[8] At this meeting they proposed that the Continental nations, together with the United States, should undertake a common program of silver purchases—in support of which the British offered, as their contribution, to raise the amount of silver acceptable as legal tender in England from £2 to £5. This would have been a small price for Britain to pay to relieve the difficulties of her Eastern commerce by inducing the United States to make a firm commitment to silver purchases. British financiers were indeed trying to make use of the resources of the United States—not by forcing this country onto the gold standard, as the American silverites charged, but by getting it pledged to continue the silver purchases of the Sherman Act.

---

[8] One can only wonder if "Coin" Harvey was aware of the prophetic words of Alfred de Rothschild at this conference, and what he would have made of them: "Gentlemen, I need hardly remind you that the stock of silver in the world is estimated at some thousands of millions, and if this conference were to break up without arriving at any definite result there would be a depreciation in the value of that commodity which it would be frightful to contemplate, and out of which a monetary panic would ensue, the far-reaching effects of which it would be impossible to foretell." Russell: op. cit., p. 385.

The British position was far from disinterested, but it reveals some of the complexities of the economic world that could hardly have been comprehensible to devoted readers of *Coin's Financial School:* "Coin" Harvey, William Jennings Bryan, and Alfred de Rothschild marching arm in arm in a campaign to uphold the American silver purchase policy!

IX

THE REAL WORLD of business and finance was complex, but the mental world of the money agitators was beautifully simple. Among its treasured legends was the idea that the gold standard had been stealthily imposed upon the American people by the British banking powers. The anti-British feeling and the conspiratorial view of monetary history expressed in *Coin's Financial School* were dressed out more elaborately in a propagandistic novel, *A Tale of Two Nations*, which Harvey brought out in September 1894, only three months after the appearance of his masterpiece. This work, possibly the only *roman à clef* ever written about the gold standard, deserves attention in its own right. Written more or less at the same time as *Coin's Financial School*, it makes a fuller statement of some of its sentiments, and it must rank in symptomatic significance with Ignatius Donnelly's *Caesar's Column* as a fantasy in fiction that illuminates the populist mind. Harvey himself never lost faith in this novel's importance, for he reprinted it as late as 1931.[9]

---

[9] By all accounts it was the second most successful of his writings in popularity. Priced at fifty cents, it was bought eagerly by his public; and while we may not accept his own estimation of a circulation of 500,000, the second edition alone appears to have run to at least one fifth of that figure, and there were further editions. The book had the advantage of being advertised in later editions of *Coin's*

A Tale of Two Nations opens in the year 1869, when Baron Rothe (Rothschild), a portly and immensely intelligent banker of an old Jewish house, is discussing his plans with another financier, Sir William T. Cline. The Baron has a daring scheme: if silver can be demonetized in the United States and Europe, gold will double its purchasing power, to the immense advantage of gold owners and holders of debts contracted for payment in gold. Here, he says, is a stroke of policy that will do more for England than a thousand years of conquests by arms. The United States, instead of overshadowing England in world trade, would (in some way not clearly specified) find herself impoverished, her industrial power broken. When his guest demurs that a measure of demonetization amounting to financial suicide would never be enacted by the Congress, Baron Rothe confidently replies that almost no one in Congress knows anything about money, and that a bill framed in sufficiently deceptive terms would go through; its real effects would not be discovered for years. Ruthlessly the Baron outlines his plans: the power of money, skillfully used, would "establish two classes, the rich and the poor. The first to enjoy this world, and the other to live by waiting on the first. We must crush their manhood by making them poor—they then will make good servants and gentle citizens."

The first instrument of this cold-blooded plot is an American senator, John Arnold (John Sherman and Benedict Arnold?), who now visits Baron Rothe in London. Arnold puts up the appearance of noble American statesmanship, but his true character is read by Baron Rothe and by the Baron's beautiful daughter Edith. This dark lady has powers of character diagnosis that are practically occult; she quickly finds

---

Financial School as "the most exciting and interesting novel on American politics ever published." In fact, Harvey appended to such editions the first two chapters of *A Tale of Two Nations* to titillate his readers.

that Arnold is a consummate worshipper of the power of money. Baron Rothe has no difficulty in bribing Arnold to use his influence to work for the demonetization of silver. Three years later the conspiracy brings to Washington the young nephew of the Baron, one Victor Rogasner, a darkly handsome cosmopolitan of sybaritic tendencies, whose mission is to forward the final passage of the demonetization measure. Rogasner is aided by a secretary, by two former Scotland Yard men, whose business it is to work on congressmen, and by a passionate and beautiful Russian Jewess who will do anything necessary to advance the projects or achieve the happiness of the man she loves. Rogasner is full of guile and the spirit of vengeance. "In the highest sense I am a military commander," he muses.

> I am here to destroy the United States—Cornwallis could not have done more. For the wrongs and insults, for the glory of my own country, I will bury the knife deep into the heart of this nation. . . . I will crush their manhood. I will destroy the last vestige of national prosperity among them, and humble that accursed pride with which they refer to their revolutionary ancestors, to the very dust. I will set them fighting among each other, and see them cut each other's throats, and carry devastation into each other's homes, while I look on without loss.

In the corrupt atmosphere of the Grant administration, which Harvey fills in with a few hasty strokes, it becomes quite plausible that still another, unknown, scandal, based on the quest for favorable monetary legislation by the gold interests, could actually have taken place. Rogasner has his moments of doubt and suspense, but before long his strategy carries the day—silver is demonetized, the Crime of '73 is a fact. "The greatest crime ever committed in the world—one that was to cause more suffering than all other crimes committed in a century, had been quietly accomplished." The American congressmen do not yet know what they have done, and it takes them three years to discover it. Later Rogasner is instrumental in bringing about the demonetization of silver in Germany (anachronistically) and France. He then returns to the United States to wage a propaganda battle in favor of the gold standard, because silver advocates are now up in arms. But it proves easy to suborn professors of economics and the greater part of the press. The people are "helpless victims in the power of a soulless gold oligarchy."

The story jumps to 1894, and new characters are introduced. The corrupt Senator Arnold has a ward, Grace Vivian; and Rogasner, now a man of great affluence, in his middle years but still handsome, takes a fancy to her. Grace prefers the attentions of John Melwyn, a noble, handsome, well-proportioned, and eloquent young silverite congressman from Lincoln, Nebraska, who resembles William Jennings Bryan. The contest, nonetheless, seems unequal: Rogasner is rich and Melwyn is poor, and, what is more, Rogasner is wily. American innocence is once more at a disadvantage in confronting European duplicity. "The honest heart and frank directness of the younger man; his simple rearing, uneventful, in a sense, furnished few weapons with which to meet the wily diplomacy and cunning, the broad knowledge and teachings of a life of intrigue, possessed by the polished nephew of Baron Rothe." Worst of all, Senator Arnold cannot bear Melwyn's free-silver views. In this contest between the Englishman and the American for a girl "fair and beautiful enough to typify Columbia," the unscrupulous Senator secretly intercepts Melwyn's letters, in order to give Grace the impression that Melwyn has lost interest in her.

The story moves toward its climax against a background of the stirring events of 1894—the suffering brought by the panic, the fear awakened by the march of Coxey's army on Washington, the bitterness aroused by the Pullman strike. Melwyn's brother turns up as a member of Coxey's army, his father too is ruined, and Melwyn himself is plagued by a mortgage he cannot pay, unaware that the long arm of Rogasner is stiffening the demands of his creditors. Rogasner, hardhearted as ever in the midst of all the distress of the depression years, waits for the day when seventy per cent of the people are in distress—at which point, he believes, the political situation will explode, and the present government of the United States will be either supplanted by a monarchy or completely consumed in a revolution. Meanwhile, as the people worry about a variety of unimportant issues, and are thus distracted from the fundamental money question, "we are shooting from ambush, and are perfectly safe. . . . I shall sink this accursed nation; tear it into threads, and leave it bleeding and disrupted, if for no other purpose than to demonstrate the power of our money."

In an interesting passage, Rogasner pursues a line of thought that sheds light on Harvey's conception of the gold conspirators. For Rogasner proves to be a man who understands full well, with the immemorial wisdom and historic consciousness of the Jew ("it takes one of our race [Jesus] to detect this error in our civilization [usury]"), that lending and hoarding since the times of the Medes and Persians have been the root cause of the breakdown of civilizations. He is even clever enough to outline—in private—a Harveyesque scheme for a "perfect civilization" based on the abolition of debt and usury and the heavy taxation of wealth. Still, knowing the path to perfection as he does, he chooses evil. He is an angel of darkness, a Manichean nightmare.[1]

---

[1] Like the other political characters in the book, Rogasner was probably intended to represent an actual person. It was part of the legend subscribed to by many true believers in the silver cause that a London banker, Ernest Seyd, had come to the United States with $500,000 which he used to bribe congressmen to pass the Coinage Act of 1873. The silver men even purported to have an affidavit from a Denver businessman to show that Seyd had later privately

But his personal defeat awaits him. After an assiduous courtship he at last hungrily proposes to Grace ("The man's eyes blazed with the fire of his race in the old days, the fire that came when David gazed upon Bathsheba, or when the eyes of Jacob first rested on Rachel at the well"). She politely refuses, saying that she would just like to be "good friends." Growing desperate, he now reveals to her for the first time his true identity: he is not an American investment counselor at all, as his conspiratorial activities have required him to pretend; he tells her of his aristocratic family and his wealth and prospects, hoping to appeal to the fortune-hunter or title-hunter that is supposed to lurk in almost every American girl. "I come from one of the oldest and proudest and wealthiest of European families. In fact the oldest and wealthiest in the world. Our millions aid in controlling the affairs of nations. . . . In time I will be a baron."

Rogasner has overplayed his hand; Grace is offended at this attempt to buy her. "You sneer at America and talk of a better civilization of which you say I may be made an orna-

---

confessed to having played such a role. This version of the passage of the Crime of '73 was quite common in silver tracts, and Harvey could hardly have missed it. (The most ample statement I have seen is in Gordon Clark's *Handbook of Money* [n.p., published by the Silver Knight Publishing Company, 1896], pp. 189–206.)

Seyd was in fact a London banker, born in Germany, who had lived in the United States for many years and had been in business in San Francisco. There is no reliable evidence that he was in the United States in 1872, but he was consulted by Representative Samuel C. Hooper about the Coinage Act of 1873, and wrote him a long, technical letter about it, on February 17, 1872, in which he advised, among other things, the *reintroduction* of the long defunct silver dollar at what he regarded a more practicable weight, and a firm commitment to bimetallism. See *Documentary History of the Coinage Act of February 12, 1873* (Washington, U.S. Government Printing Office, n.d. [1894?]), pp. 95–106; cf. Seyd's *Suggestions in Reference to the Metallic Coinage of the United States of America* (London, 1871), and his letter to the Monetary Commission of 1876, Senate Report 703, 44th Cong., 2nd sess. (1876), *Documents Accompanying the Report of the U.S. Monetary Commission*, II, 106–35.

ment. I am proud of being an American woman and I am content with this civilization of which you speak so lightly. It may be barbarous, but I am content." Now Rogasner plays his ace. He goes to Senator Arnold and asks for his intercession. But the Senator, whose one uncorrupted emotion is his affection for his ward, feels that he cannot try to determine her choice of a husband. At home again, Rogasner broods over the possibility of a last resort—blackmailing the Senator with his knowledge of the Senator's corruption. Rogasner's brother, a minor figure in the demonetization conspiracy, chides him for his obsession with Grace: "Are there not women of our own race and faith beautiful enough and with all grace of mind and body to fit them for any man?" But Rogasner is unmoved: "Did not our ancestors, even on Arabian plains, take whatever women of whatever race most pleased their fancy?" Rogasner proceeds to blackmail Senator Arnold, and the threat of exposure reduces the Senator to prostration. Rogasner gloats like the fiend he is—he "was not exactly smiling—he was leering, and he was as happy as Nero was in the death agonies of his mother. The Hebrew was 'harrowing' again." But Grace has overheard his words, and

---

Seyd, who died in 1881, was a Fellow of the Royal Statistical Society and one of the better-known British bimetallists. Most of the silver men who discussed the subject were aware of Seyd's lifelong advocacy of bimetallism, but in their view this by no means ruled out the possibility that his fealty to the British gold power was stronger than his personal convictions. Had they not seen men like Secretary Carlisle converted from solid bimetallists into defenders of the gold standard? Like Rogasner, Seyd could know good and do evil. As Gordon Clark wrote of Seyd: "That very able acquaintance of the Rothschilds—a gentleman of the same Hebrew blood—was no disburser of bribes, in ordinary circumstances, and was a *sincere bimetallist*. But he was also 'the financial adviser of the Bank of England,'" and in this capacity "was forced to postpone his theories when that huge octopus came to see its fat prey in the United States" (pp. 195–6).

The Seyd story became the object of some discussion on the floor of Congress in 1890 and again in 1893. For the latter year, see *Congressional Record*, 53rd Cong., 1st sess., pp. 474–6, 584–9, 1059.

she breaks in on the two men, reproaching her guardian, and upbraiding Rogasner: "You are very shrewd. You are very wise in your way, the commercial way, inbred through generations. The politic, scheming, devious way inbred through generations also. You are as repulsive to me as anything that could exist." As Rogasner arises and approaches her—with who knows what intent—none other than John Melwyn, "the typical American man," breaks in and throws him to the floor.

There is little more to be told. John Melwyn and Grace marry, and Rogasner goes back home to the selfless Jeanne Soutleffsky, "the fair Jewess who had been his agent in so many instances," and who was there to welcome him "like Rebecca solicitous over Ivanhoe." She has patiently endured his pursuit of Grace Vivian, and now "her face was a poem, a great epic poem of the grand old Jewish race." Rogasner needs her: he breaks down and becomes a helpless invalid, and benefits for the rest of his life from her devotion. The book ends on what Harvey's silverite readers must have felt was a chilling note: "On the 29th day of September, 1894, there sailed on the steamer *Paris* from Liverpool a representative of a foreign syndicate to take Rogasner's place."

The mild note of anti-Semitism in Harvey's book will not surprise those who are familiar with the traditional linkage of money crazes and anti-Jewish feeling. In the American silver movement this prejudice was a facet of the far more deeply felt anti-British sentiment; it did not go beyond a kind of rhetorical vulgarity, since no programmatic steps were urged against Jews as such. Like his Populist contemporary Ignatius Donnelly, Harvey had mixed feelings and showed a certain shame about his prejudice which caused him to interlard his anti-Semitic remarks with awkward philo-Semitic amends. In *Coin's Financial School Up to Date* Harvey disavowed prejudice against the Jews—

the brightest race of people that inhabit the earth, and they treat each other with the greatest fairness as a rule. . . . You should not be prejudiced against any race as a race. . . . Among Jews, many became money changers; it seems to be natural with them, probably on account of their excessive shrewdness. They see that it has advantages not possessed by any other business.[2]

Many Jews, it must be said, might have found Harvey's embraces harder to endure than his slurs.

In the end, Harvey could not untangle himself from the Shylock image, which pervades money crankery from the Greenbackers to Father Coughlin and Ezra Pound, and his later writings are dotted with repetitive citations of prohibitions against usury on the part of Christian thinkers. In his *Common Sense, or the Clot on the Brain of the Body Politic*,[3] he borrowed a quotation used in Redpath's *History of the World* which stated that the Jew does not work as most men do, contributes nothing to human industry, but "obtains control of the money market, using the same for the exclusive advantage of himself and his people." In spite of the repeated injunctions of the Christian churches against usury down through the ages, Harvey said, the rulers of the Christian churches "ever had a persistent enemy following them and seeking to loan money—taking pledges, binding borrowers to secrecy and adding to their stock of money till by the 17th century their holdings were enough to choke civilization to a favorable concession." Here he quoted the central passage on usury from Deuteronomy 23: 19–20, in which usury within the tribe is forbidden but what he called the "fatal exception" was made: "Unto a stranger thou mayest lend upon usury."[4] This, he declared, "made money-lenders of the Jews. Regarding the Gentiles as 'strangers,' their enemies, they have sought

---

[2] P. 68. On the similar ambivalence of Ignatius Donnelly, see Martin Ridge: *Ignatius Donnelly* (Chicago, 1962), pp. 263–4, 266 n., 305, 321–3, 336–7, 395–6. C. Vann Woodward has pointed out that the Populists had no monopoly on anti-Semitism in the 1890's. See his

to punish them, to ruin them, with the weapon usury." But there is still hope for the Jews if they will relent and reform:

> A stricken world cries out to them to make public renunciation of usury and to make *restitution* by crowding into the front ranks of reformers against the sin! The Jews come of a noble race, possessing a high order of intelligence, acumen and persistency in a cause; and by recognizing that it is inconsistent with the "brotherhood of man" to wield the Sword of "Usury" against the Gentiles, they will assimilate into the activities of productive civilization, be worthy descendants of their pastoral forefathers, and will become vocationally adapted to the cultivation and rebuilding of their ancient land.

X

DURING HIS CELEBRITY as a silver tractarian Harvey was also briefly active in politics. In 1894 he was busy with the affairs of the populist party of Illinois, which, unlike most other state Populist parties, had a strong labor-socialist wing interested in writing a collectivist plank into the party's program. Harvey's sympathies lay with the more conservative agrarian wing of the party, which repudiated collectivism and put its hopes in monetary reform. When the two factions of the Illinois party finally fell out, he joined with the Prohibitionist leader Howard S. Taylor in curbing the radicals. In 1895 he published *Coin's Financial School Up to Date*, in which Coin returns to expound Harvey's financial ideas in a work marked by a long discussion of greed and ignorance as forces in history, and by attacks on British landholders in the United

---

remarks in *The Burden of Southern History* (Baton Rouge, La., 1960), pp. 154–5.

[3] Monte Ne, Ark., 1920, p. 18.

[4] On the historic interpretation of the prohibition in Deuteronomy, see Benjamin F. Nelson: *The Idea of Usury* (Princeton, 1949).

States. During the same year Harvey engaged in a debate on the silver issue with J. Laurence Laughlin and a series of nine debates with former Congressman Roswell H. Horr. He also tried to organize a kind of political fraternal order, open to members of all existing parties, which he hoped to purify. The organization was to be called the Patriots of America, and its lodges were to have their own ritual, somewhat in the fashion of national fraternal orders; there was to be a kind of women's auxiliary, the Daughters of the Republic. Harvey's book *The Patriots of America* was devoted in large part to a proposed constitution for this order, and pending an election, he offered himself as its First National Patriot. *The Patriots of America* suffered from an excess of incoherence that was to envelop Harvey's later writings, and from a striking note of exaggeration, grandiosity, and suspicion. Good and evil were struggling for control of the world, he held, and things had become so bad that "we must make the last stand of freemen for the civilization of the world." Murders, suicides, crime, insanity, and British and railroad landholdings were all strung together as evidence of the pathological state society had reached: "The United States has been honeycombed by foreign influences and our property is rapidly passing into their hands."[5]

Some features of Harvey's proposed Patriots of America, especially its semi-secrecy, worried Bryan and his supporters, who saw in it a possible source of factionalism. Harvey explained that the organization would "give us the finances for a national campaign" against the money power, and that its secrecy and its required pledge that members must vote in conformity with majority decisions were intended to foil "cunning and unscrupulous" enemies from working within the ranks. "I love you," wrote Harvey to Bryan, "and shall

---

[5] *The Patriots of America* (Chicago, 1895), pp. 12, 28, 39–40.

always have your good in view because I believe you to be one of the first patriots in the country."[6]

During 1896 Harvey worked fervently for Bryan, giving lectures and speeches and distributing silver badges. Harvey (who had originally preferred "Silver Dick" Bland of Missouri) was then a member of the executive committee of the National Silver party, which bought a million copies of Archbishop Walsh's *Bimetallism and Monometallism*, half of them in English and half in a German translation, as well as 125,000 copies of *Coin's Financial School*.[7] After the campaign Harvey spent some months lecturing to raise money for the Democrats. His cordial relations with Bryan continued, and as late as 1913 Bryan was still trying to secure for him a post in the Department of Agriculture under Woodrow Wilson.[8]

The year 1896 was the zenith of the silver cause. In the following year the tide of depression turned. New gold deposits and new methods of extraction hastened a rise in prices that the silver men had thought could come only from the white metal. It soon became apparent that silver was a lost cause, that the ground had been cut from under men whose whole intellectual and political lives had hung upon monetary agitation. Chicago, the scene of his one great success, began to pall for Harvey. In 1899 he published the last book to appear under the aegis of the Coin Publishing Company, *Coin on Money, Trusts and Imperialism*.

Coin, now supposedly a youth of sixteen, returns in this volume for a last effort to stem the tide of reaction. He presents human history as an arena of struggle between two types of people—the humane type, which delights in the

---

[6] Nichols: "Bryan's Benefactor," pp. 321–2.

[7] Bryan, op. cit., p. 292.

[8] Much to the irritation of Secretary of Agriculture David F. Houston, who had always regarded Harvey and his famous book as "huge jokes." D. F. Houston: *Eight Years with Wilson's Cabinet* (New York, 1926), I, 43.

upbuilding of mankind without neglecting self, and the selfish type, which seeks only self-promotion and self-aggrandizement. The first of these forces is now animating the movement for democracy and reform, the second expresses itself in the cry for monarchy and imperialism. Some considerable portion of the book is, of course, given over to Coin's views on money and banking, but it suffers from its lack of concentration on a single theme. It moves on to attack British investors in America and British holders of American land, and then to denounce the British government for permitting moneylenders to shape the laws. Coin then passes on to the trust question, at the time a matter of growing public concern, but Harvey was much less at home with this issue than with money: his main suggestion was that all industrial trusts are nourished by the financial trust, and if the financial trust can be destroyed, the others will disappear with it.

Moving on to imperialism, the great issue of the moment, Coin saw the drive toward imperialism in rather vague moral terms: an evil genius entrenched in the nation's monetary and industrial system naturally sought to extend itself. "A selfish force having despoiled its own people, seeks other people whom it may despoil. Having preyed upon its own people, with an enlarged appetite, it looks about for other peoples to prey upon—which is called *conquest.*" What Coin now began to designate in plain Manichean terms as "the Evil influence" was invoked to explain the development of the Spanish-American War into an imperial enterprise. As an act in behalf of a victimized Cuban people against a dissolute Spanish monarchy, Coin, in common with so many Americans, believed the war to be justified. But privileged classes had seized upon it to take the first step toward installing monarchy in the United States by moving into the Philippines and by keeping the United States in Cuba. Many people, Harvey thought, like expansion because they think it will improve business. In fact, there is ample room within the United States for indefinite expansion, and prosperity can be stimulated by improvements at home. He recommended a canal to connect Lake Michigan with Lake Erie and the development of a system of good roads and irrigation ditches.

The emotional climax of the volume occurs at a point at which Coin links American occupation of the Philippines with the British war against the Boers and indicts President McKinley for showing sympathy for England and following her example. Coin cries:

> I arraign the President *for treason* in waging a war without that war having first been declared by Congress, as required by the Constitution! I arraign him for treason for a *secret alliance* with England against Republics struggling for liberty! I arraign the majority in Congress as the willing puppets of the Evil influence that prompts the President!

This brings the imaginary audience to its feet, cheering and applauding.

One of Harvey's most urgent worries was that expansionism would bring an enlarged standing army of as many as 100,000 men. He believed, as the Founding Fathers had believed, in a citizen soldiery, in state troops. A standing army under national control might well become the instrument of "monarchy," and certainly it would create a mercenary soldiery, dangerous to domestic government and likely to heighten the desire for conquest. Unlike mercenaries, citizen soldiers would refuse to engage in wars of conquest. "Any war that our citizen soldiers will not fight is an unjust war!" The demand for a standing army was only incidental to the struggle that was about to open. "Monarchy is ready to spring at the throat of the Republic!" The privileged few, in their quest for subjugation of the people, have only begun with their demand for a standing army. "If they carry the presidential election in 1900, in four years more, they will disclose openly their desire for a Monarchy! ... The forces of Evil we are combating are organized, and determined of purpose to enslave America!" Harvey left no doubt about what their instrument was: having failed to take over the Democratic party, they had entrenched themselves among the Republicans. Mark Hanna, the symbol of their intentions, had "a bed in the White House ... patterned after the style of the bed the Queen of England sleeps in."[9] The crying need of the hour was to keep the Democratic party pure, to tighten its organization, and to rally for victory.

XI

EVEN BEFORE Bryan's second defeat in 1900 it must have become apparent to Harvey that no victory was to be expected. In March the confident Republicans easily put through the Gold Standard Act, which, while it was largely a formal declaration of a fact already established, seemed to drive the last nail in the coffin of the silver issue. Two months later Harvey was preparing to retreat from Chicago. In May 1900 he appeared in the Ozark Mountain town of Rogers, Arkansas, which he had visited in 1894 and 1896 during his campaigns for silver, and rather abruptly bought a tract of 325 acres in a pleasant and well-watered site then called Silver Springs. In the fall he returned with his family, and announced a plan to open an Ozark summer resort outside Rogers. Soon he had renamed his property Monte Ne (which he imagined meant "mountain of waters" in Spanish) and had formed the Monte Ne investment company in concert with two secretaries he had brought from his Chicago enterprises.

---

[9] *Coin on Money, Trusts, and Imperialism* (Chicago, 1899), pp. 5–6, 9, 31–41, 78, 107, 135, 142–3, 157, 160–1, 171.

The following spring the Hotel Monte Ne was opened, and before long it rang with the tunes of oldtime fiddlers whom Harvey had imported in the hope that a revival of old-fashioned rural entertainment would enliven the resort. Visitors arriving at the resort were ferried across the lake by Venetian gondoliers.

Other enterprises followed. A four-mile railroad spur to Lowell was built in 1902 to bring visitors to this isolated resort area. William Jennings Bryan came to speak at its opening. Excursions were planned with the help of the Frisco Railroad, which brought vacationers from Joplin, Fort Smith, and Springfield. With some local entrepreneurs, Harvey organized the Bank of Monte Ne, capitalized at $25,000, and built a white boxlike structure to house it. He also began to build a huge, rambling hotel consisting of a number of ranges of log cottages, and organized a mercantile company to bring supplies into Monte Ne.

For a few years it must have seemed that Harvey might begin a wholly new career in the resort business with capital saved from the silver days. But ill luck, personal and financial, seemed to dog him. His family had hardly been long in Monte Ne before the homestead acquired with the Silver Springs tract burned down, and Harvey's library, the family piano, silverware, and other household effects brought from Chicago were destroyed. In 1903 his twenty-three old son Halliday, who was studying for the law, was killed in a railroad accident. A campaign Harvey planned to make for Congress in 1904 was quickly abandoned in the face of obstinate local rebuffs. In time the Frisco Railroad grew tired of running unprofitable excursion trains, and it became increasingly difficult to attract visitors to the splendid isolation of Monte Ne. Harvey's own little railroad failed, and his bank, with all depositors paid in full, closed in 1914. Some part of the projected great hotel was finished, and it was operated with modest success for a period of years, but, in the words of a local chronicler,

> after the foundation for the big hotel was well under way, Mr. Harvey ran into a lot of trouble with union labor organizers, and he abandoned the project and left the masonry for future generations to ponder over its origin and intent. That labor row rather soured Mr. Harvey in his outlook on life and affected all his later years at Monte Ne. . . . From this time until his death, Mr. Harvey's life was filled with financial difficulties, legal entanglements over the control of his properties, and the numerous changes in his ambitions.[1]

The handicap arising from Monte Ne's isolation stimulated the last successful effort in Harvey's life, his organization of the Ozark Trails Association to mark and promote 1,500 miles of automobile highways, connecting four towns and five million people in the states of Arkansas, Missouri, Kansas, and Oklahoma. He had seen the railroad fail as a source of transportation for his locality, and it had become evident to any man of vision by 1910, when he first conceived of the Ozark Trails Association, that the automobile was America's coming mode of travel. "My personal interest in the Ozark Trails," Harvey wrote, "is that they all lead to Monte Ne, where we have a delightful resort." For many years after 1913, when he organized the Ozark Trails Association at a meeting held in Monte Ne, Harvey gave his energies to the good-roads movement without expectation of immediate profit. In the hope of bringing what he characteristically called "a vast network of modern auto routes into Arkansas," he spent a great deal of time mapping out and actually marking auto-

---

[1] *Rogers Daily News*, July 1, 1950, a local commemorative issue, which contains news stories, pictures, and reminiscences, is my main source for this last phase of Harvey's life. Some gleanings are also to be found in his periodical *The Palladium*, published at intervals in 1920 and 1925, and in Joseph E. Reeve: *Monetary Reform Movements* (Washington, 1943).

mobile roads, as well as in strenuous efforts to get the backing of businessmen in adjacent cities. For fifteen years Harvey gave unstintingly of his time, receiving in return only the expenses he incurred while actually engaged in travel, road marking, and promotional activities. What was left of his hotel business apparently suffered from the diversion of his energies, but this identification with a thriving cause once again seems to have mobilized the promotional enthusiasm that had always been so strong in him. "When actively in the harness," wrote one of his co-workers in the good-roads movement, "he seemed to be immune to physical discomfort or fatigue. He had an indomitable will, a crusading spirit, and a great reserve of physical power. In the midst of an important campaign, his eyes would burn with the intense fervor of a mystic."[2] This work was largely done by 1920, and Harvey was again free to devote his energy to his agitations.

Harvey's crusading spirit had not been detached from social issues. He never gave up the hope that the world might be induced to listen, that the success of *Coin's Financial School* could somehow be repeated. In 1915 he began publishing again, with a book called *The Remedy*, whose title suggests the hopes he still cherished. *The Remedy* expounded his notion that the forces of good could be strengthened in their battle with evil by a system of character building in the schools. It contained a manual for school instruction in character. In 1920, in his *Common Sense, or The Clot on the Brain of the Body Politic*, he resumed his polemics against selfishness and usury, reviewed the history of money and banking in the United States, and waged a polemic against banking profits under the Federal Reserve system. The Federal Reserve system, he argued, "overshadows the Bank of England, and gives to the money-lenders greater advantage than the old United

---

[2] Quoted by Clara B. Kennan: "The Ozark Trails and Arkansas's Pathfinder, Coin Harvey," *Arkansas Historical Quarterly*, VII (Winter 1948), 312–13.

States bank did, that General Jackson killed. The money-lenders' organization of the banking system may now be regarded as perfected." In his indiscriminate opposition to banks, Harvey was opposing the creation of credit instruments intended to alleviate the very ills that had originally provoked him into becoming a crusader. In this work the paranoid and apocalyptic note sounds stronger than before. Harvey becomes increasingly concerned not merely with Christian prohibitions against usury but with the terrible and sometimes mysterious fate that overcame early opponents of usurious exploitation. Repeatedly he compares the situation of the United States with that of Rome during the persecutions of the Christians:

> The usurers, the money-power in New York City, Chicago, and the large money-lending cities put out the propaganda based on falsehood and misrepresentation as to what the reformers are teaching—as they did in Rome—till the public mind is poisoned and prejudiced and a fair trial is impossible. By suppressing free speech, free press, peaceable assembly, imprisoning and exiling, *the truth is not heard!*

He had become more and more obsessed with the violence and torture inflicted by the Roman Empire, and warned that it was likely to be repeated. ("The blood of the martyred Christians appeals to the people of the world in this second Crisis!") He saw the persecution of the early Christians as a political event, a response primarily to their protest against usury, and he cited Tacitus to warn of the fate that such protest could expect: "Some were nailed on crosses, others sewn up in the skins of wild beasts and exposed to the fury of dogs; others, again smeared over with combustible materials, were used as torches to illuminate the darkness of the night."[3] It is a melancholy thought that this old man, spending his last

---

[3] The theme of martyrdom, and his own identification with Christ, is apparent as early as 1895 in " 'Coin's Financial School' and Its Censors," already cited.

years in the quiet of an Ozark village, should have had to be tormented by such nightmares.

In 1924, aroused by the postwar depression and a new collapse in American agriculture, Harvey brought out, through his Mundus Publishing Company, a little book called *Paul's School of Statesmanship*, in which another fantastic boy, modeled somewhat after Coin, appears in Monte Ne as Coin had appeared in Chicago, and opens another school. This book, which Harvey said "discloses the most important discovery, relating to civilization and the human race, that has been made in all the history of the world," did not have the reception that its importance warranted. In good part, Paul's was a school of character. He promised a government without taxation or bond issues, in a new society, based on gold, of all things, but whose real source of success was the liberal issue of paper currency. The proper understanding of the function of money, Harvey proposed once again, was the key to civilization, but in spite of his promises of a new civilization based upon the solution of the money question, the book showed that Harvey was more than ever persuaded that a total collapse of civilization would result from the rejection of his views. It was followed six years later by a work entitled, with the simple unaffected confidence of a major prophet, *The Book*, in which Harvey restated many of his old ideas, re-used many of his old quotations, rehearsed the historic Christian opposition to usury, warned against dictatorship, reprinted part of *A Tale of Two Nations*, retold the story of the Crime of '73, and called for a new political party.

By now Harvey's faith in the possibility of social reform had grown dimmer. To quote again the local chronicler of his fortunes: "As he grew older and more bitter in his condemnation of existing laws and conditions, he dropped his wealthy friends of these early [business] experiments at Monte Ne and sought the dimes and quarters of the poorer people." In his sixties, Harvey was returning to the agitational frame of mind in which he had come to Chicago, but without the optimism of his earlier days. A civilization incapable of solving the money question was almost certainly headed for disaster. A new vision, announced as early as 1920, began to form in his brain and grew in obsessive strength with the years: he would build in Monte Ne, at the site of his resort, a great Pyramid, in which he would leave copies of his own books and a variety of artifacts representative of the twentieth-century civilization that he was sure would go to ruin. Thus a future civilization "rising from the ashes" would be able to stumble upon the relics of the past, preserved by "Coin" Harvey. As the years went by, his obsession with the Pyramid grew. It would be 40 feet square at the base and rise to 130 feet in height, and at the top, where it would presumably protrude above the dust of the ages, there would be a plaque, reading: "When this can be read go below and find the cause of the death of a former Civilization." Below, the men of the future would find copies of *Paul's School of Statesmanship*, *The Book*, and the Bible, chemically treated to survive time, along with various volumes on the technical and scientific attainments of twentieth-century civilization, and— a thoughtful precaution—a key to the English language so that the works left there would be the more readily decipherable if found by men of a strange tongue.

To raise money to build such a Pyramid, Harvey solicited contributions from the readers of his books. It would be a boon to a later millennium, he pointed out, and "there will be nothing about it that partakes of self or vanity and no one's name will appear on the outside of it." Construction of the Pyramid was actually begun to Harvey's specifications. To make a secure footing for it, he excavated the hills near his home and built what he liked to call the "foyer" of the Pyramid—"an asymmetrical mass of concrete and stone in the form of seats," as a local reporter described it, "but without any semblance of regular order." In surviving pictures it looks like the village of some strange breed of midget Pueblos with disordered minds. At length, its total cost estimated at $100,-000, this project too was abandoned, like Harvey's hotel and his bank and his railroad—but here, at last, he had an unexpected stroke of luck. The "foyer" itself became a kind of curiosity, a substitute for antique ruins, and thousands of visitors were drawn to it, paying admission fees to gaze upon the fragments of Harvey's unrealized dream. They were treated to lectures on financial reform and given the opportunity to buy Harvey's books, old and new, all conveniently displayed.

By the mid-1920's Harvey had given up all business activities and had yielded completely to his messianic dreams. He attempted through his later writings to organize a new national political party, first called the Liberty party and later the Prosperity party. Perhaps he sought advice from "General" Jacob Coxey, who visited him on occasion to discuss old times and bemoan the condition of the world. The Great Depression of the 1930's gave him a last moment of public notice. In 1932 he ran for President and received 800 votes without campaigning. Three years later he reappeared to denounce Roosevelt's policy of silver purchases, which he regarded as absurdly cautious, a "travesty" on silver. In February 1936, forty years after the battle of the standards, Harvey died at the age of eight-four. To the end he never lost the pride and sense of his importance that had made it possible for him, against all the probabilities, to claim the attention of the world. A photograph taken in his later years shows a slender, hawk-nosed man still erect and alert, his face adorned by a dignified white mustache, his brow slightly furrowed, his mien a little apprehensive and harassed, looking very much the part of the small-town businessman or banker. Though he was only of medium size, an acquaintance said, "he stood and walked so straight he gave the impression of being taller than his real height." It was as though by a sheer effort of will he could add a cubit to his stature.

Acknowledgments

I wish to thank Herbert G. Nicholas, my host on the occasion of the Herbert Spencer Lecture, and many friends who have contributed in a variety of ways to the improvement of these essays. It gives me pleasure to acknowledge the encouragement I have had from Alfred A. Knopf for more than twenty years and to appear on his list in the fiftieth anniversary year of his firm. Thanks are due to Phi Beta Kappa for transferring to me the copyright of "The Pseudo-Conservative Revolt"; to John Wiley & Sons for permission to use a revised version of "What Happened to the Antitrust Movement?"; and to the President and Fellows of Harvard College for permission to reprint "Free Silver and the Mind of 'Coin' Harvey."

R. H.

Index

abolitionism, spokesmen for, 9

Acheson, Dean G.: foreign policy criticized, 132

Adams, Brooks, 163

Adams, Henry: in movement for imperialism, 163; turns away from American life, 163

Adelman, M. A., on monopoly, 216

Adorno, Theodore W.: stand on pseudo-conservatism, 43–4, 58

agriculture, American, 1924 collapse of, 312

Alger, Russell A., on foreign policy, 151

American Capitalism, Galbraith, 227

American Economic Association, 200

American Protective Association (1800's), 22

American Review of Reviews, 163

Americans: old-family, 54–6; new-family, 56 ff.; and Americanism, 59–61, 100; and super-patriotism, 61; disappearance of the frontier line, 149; patriotic groups of 1890's, 150; social programs of 1890's, 182

America's Retreat from Victory: The Story of George Catlett Marshall, 26

Andrews, E. Benjamin, on laissez-faire, 201

annexation, *see under* Philippine Islands

Answer to "Coin's Financial School," Wood, 245

Anti-Imperialist League, 173

anti-Semitism, *see under* ethnic groups

antitrust: contemporary significance of, 189–90; decline of, 191, 228; under Thurman Arnold, 191–2, 194, 230, 231–2; revival under Franklin D. Roosevelt, 191–2, 194, 228–9, 235; in the Common Market, 193; history of, 193 ff.; reactivation of Antitrust Division, 194; decisions won since 1940, 195; confusion of Congress over, 199; economic goals, 200 ff.; Congress of 1800, 202; political and social arguments, 205 ff., 233; Democratic platform of 1900, 207; psychological and moral objections, 209; American acceptance of big business, 112 ff., 122 ff.; hostility to big business in history, 215 ff.; anti-chain-store legislation, 220; state of case law, 232; General Electric case, 232; support by liberals of, 234

Armour, Philip D., 243

Arnold, Thurman: antitrust reforms under, 191–2, 194, 230; failure of enforcement, 230–1; recruits staff, 231; program for housing, 231; program for transportation, 231; uses the Sherman Act, 232

Atlantic Monthly, 163, 181

Authoritarian Personality, The, Adorno, 43

i

Index

Protestants (*continued*)
fundamentalist-oriented, 70; Republican, 71; unite with Catholics against communism, 74, 80; moderate, 75; rural Democrats and, 78; favor national Prohibition, 79; protect young against Darwinism, 79; significance of ascetic Protestantism, 79–80; economic thinking affected by, 209
pseudo-conservative: dissatisfaction with American life, 43–4; identity of, 44–5; incoherent about politics, 45; suspicions of, 45–6, 50, 58; capacity as a citizen, 45 ff.; critical of federal government, 46, 50, 58, 100; proposes changes in fundamental law, 47; social-psychological elements of, 49 ff., 82 ff.; economic and political causes of, 49; history of, 50 ff.; ethnic factors, 58, 61–2, 67–8; status anxieties and resentments, 58, 62–3, 66–7, 82 ff.; feeling against the United Nations, 62; intelligible aspects of uprising, 63–5; political style; 64; Goldwater movement, 65, 93–141 *passim;* McCarthyist phase, 69 ff.; leadership fallen to John Birch Society, 70–2; agitators, 99; and disobedience to Supreme Court, 99–100; mentality in action, 115; appeal to toughness, 131; true potential of, 137; *see also* paranoid style in politics; right wing
Public Opinion, 169
Pujo Committee's inquiry, 215
Pulitzer, Joseph, and rivalry with William Randolph Hearst, 158
Pursuit of the Millennium, The, Cohn, 38

racial prejudice: and social mobility, 60; South's position on integration, 76; the Negro "revolution," 80; *see also* ethnic groups
Radical Right, The, 82–5
rationalism, Enlightenment, 10

Real Bi-Metallism or True Coin versus False Coin, Wheeler, 245
Reid, Whitelaw, in movement for imperialism, 163
Remedy, The, Harvey, 310
Report of Uncle Sam's Homilies in Finance, Blanchard, 245
Republicans: inheritance of the party, 55; Anglo-Saxon Protestant, 68; middle- and upper-status, 71; right-wing, 93; moderate, 93, 139, 140; conservatism of recent years, 101; collapse of strength in Congress, 114; ultra-conservative, 139; middle band of, 139; minority position, 139–140; support of William McKinley, 159; split into two factions (1896), 239; *see also* Eisenhower, Dwight D.; pseudo-conservatism; right wing
Republican Senatorial Campaign Committee, 104–5
Resumption Act (1875), 252, 255
Riesman, David, 223
right wing: villains of contemporary right wing, 23 ff.; events since 1939, 24; three basic elements of contemporary thought, 25–6; McCarthyist phase, 26–7, 65, 69 ff., 83 ff.; radical thinking, 48, 65 ff., 71–2, 82 ff.; growth in influence of ultra-right, 65; ethnic minorities, 67, 69; infused with fundamentalism, 67, 73 ff.; recent changes in, 67; leadership fallen to John Birch Society, 70–2; evangelical, 72–3, 79; Churches of Christ, 75; sophisticated wing, 76, 102; religious wing, 76; anti-Communist crusade, 81; resurgence, 83; composition of, 86; Goldwater movement, 93–141 *passim;* philosophy of Dwight D. Eisenhower, 95; enterprise of 1964, 114; true potential of, 137; inability to sustain national leaders, 138; battle for public opinion, 139; as a permanent force, 140; use of

A NOTE ON THE TYPE

The text of this book was set on the Linotype in Janson, a recutting made direct from type cast from matrices long thought to have been made by the Dutchman Anton Janson, who was a practicing type founder in Leipzig during the years 1668–87. However, it has been conclusively demonstrated that these types are actually the work of Nicholas Kis (1650–1702), a Hungarian, who most probably learned his trade from the master Dutch type founder Dirk Voskens. The type is an excellent example of the influential and sturdy Dutch types that prevailed in England up to the time William Caslon developed his own incomparable designs from these Dutch faces.

Composed, printed and bound by
THE HADDON CRAFTSMEN, INC., SCRANTON, PA.

Typography and binding design by
WARREN  CHAPPELL